The Electorate, the Campaign, and the Office

The Electorate, the Campaign, and the Office

A Unified Approach to Senate and House Elections

Paul Gronke

Ann Arbor

THE UNIVERSITY OF MICHIGAN PRESS

First paperback edition 2001

Copyright © by the University of Michigan 2000
All rights reserved
Published in the United States of America by
The University of Michigan Press
Printed and bound by CPI Group (UK) Ltd, Croydon, CR0 4YY

2004   2003   2002   2001   5   4   3   2

A CIP catalog record for this book is available from the British Library.

Library of Congress Cataloging-in-Publication Data

Gronke, Paul, 1961–
   The electorate, the campaign, and the office: a unified approach
to Senate and House elections / Paul Gronke.
      p. cm.
   Includes bibliographical references and index.
   ISBN 978-0-472-11131-2 (cloth : alk. paper)
      1. Elections — United States. 2. United States. Congress — Elections.
   3. Campaign funds — United States. I. Title.

JK1967 .G76 2000
324.973′092—dc21   00-031520

ISBN13 978-0-472-11131-2 (cloth)
ISBN13 978-0-472-08824-9 (paper)
ISBN13 978-0-472-02327-1 (electronic)

To Matthew, Benjamin, Katherine, and Samuel,
who don't care about that "typing" thing I do:
take me, I'm yours!

Contents

Figures

Figures

Tables

Acknowledgments

The intellectual background of this work came almost directly out of my year as one of a long line of "data drones" working for the National Elections Studies at the University of Michigan. During those years, I coded the incoming correspondence regarding proposed changes to the survey. The dogged loyalty that scholars had to particular survey items, most often tied to their specific research agendas, was a source of frustration to me then. I am a lot more understanding now! Still, the dichotomy between scholarly training that preached breadth and generalizability and a job that emphasized narrowness and specificity encouraged me think about broader theories of electoral behavior.

Near the end of my time at the NES, these ideas crytallized as I worked closely with Steven Rosenstone, now Dean of the Social Sciences at the University of Minnesota but then one of the co-directors of the National Election Study, and Santa Traugott, then study director of the NES, on the the National Science Foundation proposal for funding the complete Senate Election Study (the 1988 cycle had ended successfully). The writing, rewriting, fact-checking, endless bibliography reviews, and many conversations with Steve and Santa helped me focus on Senate/House comparisons as one route to a general theory. Both Steve and Santa were tremendously helpful during this final period of my graduate career.

Since then, I have been lucky enough to meet many colleagues who have thought about these issues and influenced my research. The most direct influence would be the person I replaced at Duke University and only know as a distant colleague, David Canon. David's book on candidate emergence and his willingness to share ideas and data were invaluable. I also need to thank my colleagues at Duke, the University of Michigan, and around the country. They listened to my rambling thoughts and reacted to my written work. These friends and colleagues include John Aldrich, Mike Alvarez, Bill Bianco, John Brehm, David Canon, Richard Fenno, Jim Garand, Dave King, Phil Paolino, Pat Sellers, Santa and Mike Traugott, Matt Wilson, and Gerald Wright. Sooner or later, the National Science Foundation will assist the Legislative Studies Section of the American Political Science Association to establish a data archive and web server for the exchange of information. I am indebted for the gracious assistance from Tom Brunell, Gary Jacobson, John Krasno, Tom Palfrey, and especially David Canon. I've tried to reciprocate by sharing my own data when the inevitable and seemingly unending requests have flowed in. Ross Baker, Bill Bianco, Paul Herrnson, Charles Stewart, and two anonymous reviewers commented on earlier drafts of this book. Special thanks go out to Steven Rosenstone, Donald Kinder, Vincent Price, and John Kingdon for guidance and to my friends for all their understanding and confidence.

I don't think I could have completed graduate school without the friendship and of my two longtime drinking buddies, John Brehm, my compatriot as a graduate student at the University of Michigan, coworker and Scrabble maven at the National Election Studies, and now a colleague at Duke University, and Alex Grist, wherever you are. They helped me through a difficult period of my life, and I'll be forever grateful.

This book would not have been possible without financial support from the Duke University Arts and Science Research Council, the Gerald R. Ford Dissertation Fellowship, the Horace H. Rackham Dissertation Fellowship, and the continued patience of the faculty of the Department of Political Science and the administration at Duke University.

Chuck Myers, past editor at the University of Michigan Press, was a godsend. I wish him luck at Princeton. The staff at Michigan has been helpful. Brad Gomez provided research assistance near the end of the project. Carrie Liken and John Rattliff assisted me in the tedious task of responding to the copy editor at Michigan.

Some of the data utilized in this research were made available (in part) by the Interuniversity Consortium for Political and Social Research. Neither the collector of the original data nor the consortium bear any responsibility for the analysis or interpretations presented here.

Finally, my academic career would never have continued without the unflagging support, patience, and love given unselfishly by Karin Purdy. Let's make our dreams come true, together.

CHAPTER 1

Introduction

Social scientists who study American politics have been called the last of the grand area specialists. American institutional arrangements are unusual in many ways: federalism, the separation of powers, a bicameral legislature, and a separately elected executive. Party politics also stands apart. The U.S. system is characterized by two parties and frequent alternations in power. Most parliamentary systems are marked by multiple parties and stability in the ruling coalition. The American public hews more closely to its party, at least as reflected in expressions of party identification than do citizens in many mature multiparty democracies, yet party-line voting, both among the mass of the public and in the legislature, is much lower. American political parties are socially diverse, non-programmatic, vote-maximizing entities, as contrasted with many narrowly based, programmatic parties in Europe, Latin America, and emerging democracies. We cannot understand what the American political system is unless we know what it is not. In order to really understand American politics, scholars must cast their net more broadly, comparing American institutional and political arrangements to those of other countries.

There is certainly a lot of truth in this position. American electoral studies would benefit from a comparative perspective. Still, the breadth and diversity of the American political landscape makes this a daunting task. The very things that make American politics distinctive also make it complicated: multiple institutions, multiple governmental units, and 250 million citizens. The first step toward a comparative analysis of American elections is to understand the similarities and differences *within* the nation. This requires a comparative analysis of elections at a number of different levels of our system: from the presidency, the Senate, and the House down to state and local contests.

Thus, it is ironic, for all the ink that has been spilt over U.S. campaigns and elections, that there have been few attempts to compare across levels in a careful fashion.[1] American electoral scholars have pursued their own subspecialties. A lot is known about presidential primaries, learning in presidential

---

1. Notable exceptions include Carsey and Wright 1998, Alvarez 1996, Atkeson and Partin 1995, Soss and Canon 1995 (all Senate/gubernatorial comparisons), and Krasno 1994.

election campaigns, and the way that voters make their final choices. Many have detailed the reasons why congressional candidates choose to run for office, how these candidates react to one another when they raise money, how they spend that money, and the relationship between candidate quality, candidate spending, and electoral outcomes.

I was forced to learn about the idiosyncracies of American elections as part of my licensing to practice political science. But I ended up realizing that the same set of influences appeared in each of the electoral accounts I read. The same variables were used in the models: heterogeneous and homogeneous electorates, candidate quality, campaign spending, information flow, party identification, candidate image, and issues. Systematic changes in the political world, such as realignments, midterm seat losses by incumbent executives, or the length (or lack of) presidential coattails, pop up in voting studies regardless of the particular institution under scrutiny.

When I reviewed the elections literature, I was surprised to find diversity in the face of apparent unity. Not only did this increase the number of articles and books I had to read, but I could think of a host of reasons why elections should be similar across different offices and levels of the election system. Senate elections are more competitive because states are more heterogeneous—this makes it more likely that a senator will annoy one or another set of district interests and makes it easier to build a competitive support coalition. If true, shouldn't this same explanation apply to the U.S. House or even the New York state legislature? Other examples abound. House candidates spend largely in reaction to their opponents; shouldn't Senate, gubernatorial, and state house candidates react in the same way? Voters behave differently because they have so much information about presidential candidates. They should react in a similar fashion during other, particularly high-profile contests.

There are good theoretical reasons why candidate activity, voter learning, and voting behavior should show substantial similarity no matter what the setting or office. House and Senate elections ought to be brought under a single umbrella. I propose such a model here. I propose a simple, but comprehensive, three-stage model of the electoral process. I describe a small set of variables that characterize each stage. Finally, I tease out causal links between these stages to see if this three-stage model can help me better understand the American electoral drama.

The central methodological lesson that motivates this study is the difference between an argument about different *levels* or inputs and different *causal explanations*. Think of a causal explanation as a black box that translates inputs into outputs via some fixed set of rules. Obviously, if I vary the level of some input, the output will change as well, even though the rules of translation remain the same. The distinction between levels and causal explanations are central to the aspirations of this book. I argue that political observers have been misled into thinking that observed differences in outputs—Senate and House candidate quality, campaign spending, and election results—are a consequence of different causal engines. Instead, I show how a single causal engine drives Senate and House elections and only the inputs vary across institutions.

The central methodological argument in this study is an argument for *pooling* House and Senate data. Obviously, I cannot gain much leverage on comparing and discriminating between two electoral institutions unless I have a common metric. Only by pooling can I find out whether district attributes such as heterogeneity of interests, media coverage, and campaign styles operate in a similar manner for both House and Senate elections. As a first cut, collecting comparable data allows me to ask to what degree Senate and House elections *really* are comparable. Are states more heterogeneous? How many congressional districts are similarly complex? Are all House candidates invisible, and how many Senate challengers suffer from the same problem? Do voters know more about all Senate contenders or just some high-profile ones. Perhaps high-profile House candidates are similarly well recognized.

Once I determine the metric and collect the data, I turn to statistical analysis. I treat the House and Senate races during the 1980s and 1990s, the time period examined in this book, as two independent populations. Then, via both graphical displays and univariate and multivariate statistics, I test whether a null hypothesis of no difference between the House and Senate can be rejected. A set of descriptive analyses, reported in chapters 3 and 4, provide impressive visual evidence that the House and Senate not only can be arrayed on single dimensions but that differences are statistically indistinguishable from zero. The null hypothesis of no institutional difference cannot be rejected. Next, in a series of regression models, reported in chapters 5 and 6, I show that some aspects of the campaign (I take a limited cut at the campaign) and most aspects of voter learning and choice display remarkable stability over time and institution.

The spirit of the work is captured well by Ross Baker's title, *House and Senate,* and his first line: "[A] sustained comparison of the House and Senate is something that most people assume to exist" (1995, 9). As he notes, truly comparative studies of the House and Senate are few and far between. Unlike Baker's study, however, which provides a broad overview of the House and Senate through the eyes of the members, this book focuses on congressional elections, asking to what degree House and Senate elections are comparable and in what ways they differ.

Thus, this work can be situated within an ongoing intellectual effort designed to unify electoral theory. If this effort is to succeed, the U.S. Congress is a particularly good place to start. Comparing elections in the U.S. House and Senate has a number of advantages. Both are parts of a larger institution. Calls for bicameral analysis (e.g., Fenno 1982) remind us to pay attention to differences between the House and Senate; they also remind us that the House and Senate are both representative legislative bodies. Analytically, there is sufficient variation across states and congressional districts and candidates and campaigns to allow the testing of a variety of hypotheses, yet there is also small enough variation that the project is not insurmountable.[2] Finally, I have a wealth of data on House and Senate settings, campaigns, and voters—census data aggregated to the state and congressional district levels, campaign spending data, candidate quality measures, and survey data—and a well-developed academic literature. If I cannot work toward a comparative model in a single branch of government, there is not much hope for extending this analysis across other institutional settings. If, however, the observed differences in Senate and House campaigns and elections are a product of similar influences, this sets up a series of signposts on the road toward a broad comparative model of electoral choice.

Why Compare?

Why do I think a comparative model is possible at all? There are good theoretical reasons to expect that voters use a common set of considerations when voting for the House, the Senate, or the presidency. Voting is a repetitive act, engaged in often (in some localities many times a year), occurring in the same setting (the polling booth), and requiring similar kinds of actions (pull a lever, punch a hole, or mark a ballot). It would be surprising if voters used different rules to make this kind of repetitive decision, especially since decision-making theory predicts that it is just this kind of situation that leads to standardized, routinized rules and behaviors. Similar logic can be applied to campaigns. Campaigns for any political office reflect the quality and nature of competition, the level of resources, and the political, social, and demographic nature of the district. From this perspective, if I choose very similar districts, regardless of the office being contested, major features of the campaign and electoral outcomes would be similar.

The logic of this argument is laid out more explicitly in chapter 2, but some elaboration may be helpful here. American voters cast their ballots in a bewildering variety of contests. There are few standing rules about what constitutes an elective office in the United States. My research assistants encountered this problem when coding "prior elective experience" for House and

2. Contrast this to either the presidency, where the setting is huge (the nation) and there is only a single campaign in any given year, or state legislatures, where the variation in settings is tremendous.

Senate candidates. Is the state treasurer a statewide elective office? Harder to code were the many state secretaries of commerce, a North Dakota state auditor, a freeholder from New Jersey, and the comptroller of New York City (all are elective offices, but the last two are not statewide). Do I expect that voters to use similar criteria across all of these offices?

The short answer is no. Voters will not use the same *criteria* in all circumstances since in many races some considerations are simply not relevant. I do expect, however, to find substantially the same *decision-making process* used across electoral contests. The difference between the two is important to understand. If I compare a contest rife with personal accusations of corruption to one in which the candidates focus on raising or lowering the property tax, surely I ought to expect voters in the first race will consider character while voters in the second will consider taxes. At least, that is all I will be able to observe in the final outcome. This does not mean that character is irrelevant to the second group of voters; it is just not a dimension on which they can discriminate between the candidates. Imagine a voter has a set of switches, and most of these switches (personality, party, issues) are turned off in a low-information, low-intensity election. The greater the amount and variety of information flow, the more switches are turned on and the more considerations enter into the vote choice. The switch box is unchanged, but the inputs, and therefore the outputs, can vary substantially.

The Necessity of Institutional Comparisons

The central problem of this study is how best to gain leverage on the switch box and not be misled by the observed outputs. One way is to make explicit comparisons across diverse institutional settings. Unless I move beyond a single institution, I cannot isolate voting behavior that in this case it is a product of state/congressional district from that which is a product of Senate/House. How different are states and congressional districts on those features that affect competitiveness (e.g., size, media market efficiency, and heterogeneity)? How different is the job of a senator and a House member and do voters perceive these differences? Is it the case that constituency service is more influential for House voters whereas policy opinions play a greater role for Senate voters, as Fenno (1983) suggests? Does the relatively greater prominence of senators versus House members that Foote and Weber (1984) notice translate into greater public awareness of Senate incumbents? It is necessary to consider House and Senate elections simultaneously if I hope to answer these questions.

I am not the first to reach this conclusion. Students of Congress often appeal to a laundry list of Senate/House differences in order to explain differences in campaigns and elections. Some stress variations in the political setting in which the campaigns are held, while others highlight institutional features or focus on the campaign environment and candidate quality (what I call intracampaign dynamics). Based on a reading of this literature, the archetypical Senate and House comparison might look like figure 1.1: two distributions of settings, campaigns, or voters with widely separated means and little overlap. This distribution conforms to the following accounts of Senate and House elections:

> Senatorial constituencies (i.e. states) generally have much larger populations that the constituencies served by members of the House. In other words, senators must attempt to please many more people than representatives. (Hibbing and Brandes 1983, 810)

> One of the reasons that senators are more vulnerable is that they may attract better challengers than House member do. States, after all, are generally larger and more heterogeneous, and have better partisan balance than individual congressional districts. (Dodd and Oppenheimer 1989, 2)

> [T]he size and political importance of Senate constituencies [contribute] to the political visibility of individual Senators. (Abramowitz 1988, 384)

Richard Fenno, in his book comparing the Senate and House, writes extensively about the differences between House and Senate candidates: senators receive greater media coverage (1982, 9–11) and their constituencies are "more heterogeneous, more diffuse, and hence less easily or concretely discerned" (20). Scholars are virtually unanimous: states are more heterogeneous and complex, with a wider variety of conflicting political interests.[3]

These differences between states and congressional districts deserve closer scrutiny. There is too much imprecision about the relationship among settings, campaigns and candidates, and the institutional arrangements underlying these comments. Many of these authors do not specify what they mean by *heterogeneous, complex,* or *politically important.* Some social cleavages are more politically potent than others, so why not take this into account when assessing the impact of heterogeneity? I break district diversity into its component parts in order to test whether some kinds of diversity are politically more consequential than others. In addition, there are untested hypotheses underlying these comments that are relatively easy to examine. If "complexity" operates in some fashion to make Senate races more competitive than House races, it

---

3. Additional sources making this point abound (e.g., Pressman 1986, 66; Bernstein 1989, 83-86; Erikson and Wright 1989, 110; Alford and Brady 1989, 164; Parker 1989, 181; Hershey 1984, 167.)

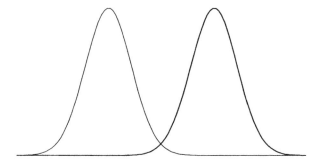

House	Senate
small districts	large districts
homogeneous districts	heterogeneous districts
low spending	high spending
weak challengers	strong challengers
low interest/turnout	high interest/turnout

Fig. 1.1. Ideal type House and Senate differences

should operate in the same fashion *within* each institution. There should be more competitive races in more complex House districts and less competitive Senate contests in less complex states. Similarly, there is no theoretical reason why reactive spending by challengers and incumbents or voter interest and information in response to campaign activity should differ across the House and Senate. I evaluate the comparative impact of district complexity, candidate quality and spending, and voter attention in both the House and Senate.

The second reason why House and Senate deserve closer scrutiny is the kind of evidence—differences in the means—that is being used to support these claims. Focusing solely on averages is seldom a good way to compare things.[4] Differences in means disguise similarities between the House and Senate. The average state is larger and more heterogeneous than an average congressional district. The average Senate challenger is better recognized and spends more money than the average House challenger. Yet this says nothing about how many states are as homogeneous as an average House district or how many House challengers spend as much as the average Senate challenger.[5] The existence of states that look like congressional districts and Senate candidates

---

4. The difference of means test, taught in the first weeks of a statistics course, is based on means *and* standard deviations.

5. Even a superficial glance at demographic measures confirms that states are, on average, much larger and more populous than congressional districts. Does this mean that they are also more heterogeneous? The one study that has compared states and congressional districts finds only minor differences on a summary measure of heterogeneity (Bond, Covington, and Fleisher

that look like House candidates, and vice versa, implies that I should be able to separate out the impact of district diversity, challenger quality, campaign spending, and institutional differences.

In one respect, the distinction I make between political setting and institution is specious. Senate/state and House member/congressional district are inseparable pairs. Differences between states and congressional districts are, in the final analysis, a product of *institutional* arrangements in our Constitution. However, while variations in media markets, population diversity, or candidate quality may be what our Founders had in mind when they designed the U.S. House and Senate, I do not believe this is what neo-institutionalists have in mind when they hear the phrase "institutional differences." Comparisons across institutions helps generalize our theories beyond one institution— I identify the impact of the political setting on the generic event "campaign" without explicit reference to the institutional setting. Comparisons across institutions helps isolate the impact of distributional differences (settings, campaigns, voters), thereby allowing me to discern the true impact of institutional arrangements on electoral outcomes.

The Necessity of Over-time Comparisons

This study compares Senate and House districts and campaigns from 1982 to 1996 and House and Senate voting in 1988 and 1990. Pooling data over time introduces substantial methodological complications. So why do it? Studying events over time increases both the sample size and variation on the independent and dependent variables, thereby reducing the size of standard errors and increasing the precision of statistical estimates. Small samples of *contests* are a particularly acute problem when studying the Senate. There are at most 34 Senate contests in a single year. The working sample size of competitive contests involving incumbents can be reduced to under 25.[6] A similar problem arises in studies of the House, but here the worry is a small number of *competitive contests*. Declining marginals (traditionally defined as any race in which the winner received less than 55 percent of the vote) means that fewer than 10 percent of all House races in any year might be deemed competitive (Jacobson 1997; Alford and Hibbing 1989).

1985). Similarly, Westlye (1991, 1986) found that voter recognition of a significant number of Senate challengers was just as low as for the typical House challenger.

    6. Looking only at incumbent/challenger contests is often necessary in the House because of the small number of open seats. When I compare the Senate and the House, I limit myself to races involving incumbents.

The sample size problems can be partially alleviated by pooling across years. This increases the working sample size of Senate and House races tenfold (or higher if a particular year during the period was especially competitive). The costs of this strategy are fairly obvious: I lose the nuances of any particular year.[7] There is another advantage gained by pooling years, however. In any one year, the greater electoral context—the state of the economy, the popularity of the president, the nature of domestic and world events—is fixed. Pooling over years means that I can be more confident that the results will not be limited to a specific historical context (Kramer 1983).

The Plan of the Book

Chapter 2 briefly reviews previous research on House and Senate elections with an eye to explicit institutional comparisons. I end with an overview of my own approach to the comparison.

In chapters 3 and 4, I explore Senate/House differences on a series of descriptive measures. In chapter 3, I ask whether states and congressional *districts* are really different and in what ways they are comparable. In chapter 4, I undertake a parallel comparison of Senate and House *campaigns and candidates*.

In chapter 5, I test a model of candidate quality and campaign activity, linking campaign dynamics to contextual variation. I try to directly confront a contextual explanation of campaigns with an institutional one. What makes this line of inquiry so compelling is that when the political setting argument is pushed to its limit, as I do in this chapter, what is left over is attributable to "pure" institutional effects. By considering political setting and institutional variations simultaneously, I am able to discern their separate impacts.

In chapter 6, I turn to the voters, incorporating my notions about the political setting into the voter's decision rule. Those characteristics of the political setting which constrain campaigns also constrain voter learning and choice. The research proceeds along two paths: how voters learn about candidates and how voters make choices. I start with a description of the House and Senate electorates. Parallel to the analyses in earlier chapters, I ask whether the House and Senate electorates are significantly different. Are voter interest in and information about Senate elections significantly higher? Are House members or senators more easily recognized and recalled? Do there appear to be different sets of criteria that respondents generate when describing their House members (e.g., casework or delivery of services) versus senators (e.g., more

---

7. Krasno (1994), for example, opts to compare Senate and House elections in a single year. He provides more in-depth analyses of particular races than will be possible in this study, but is hampered by sample size and generalizability problems endemic to a single year study.

policy oriented)? I end this section by exploring some interactions between the campaign environment, the political setting, and campaign learning.

I use the insights gained from my descriptions of the Senate and House electorates, in order to compare voter choice in the House and Senate. The second goal in chapter 6 is to see whether differences in information levels and voting decision rules between the House and Senate electorates can be unpacked into differences in settings (states vs. congressional districts) and campaign environments (candidate quality or campaign spending). In short, do differences between voting for House or Senate disappear once these other variables are taken into account? Since the focus is on potential institutional variation, I concentrate on testing a series of hypotheses about Senate/House differences.

Summary

It is not useful to think about the Senate and House as distinct archetypes. It also doesn't do much good to say that some House elections look like Senate elections and leave it at that. The question is how and why they look alike and how and why they will differ. Institution-specific descriptions of elections help us move toward a general model, but the danger, to use an overworked metaphor, is that we might lose sight of the forest for the trees. This study attempts to bridge the literature on House and Senate elections in order to discover the common elements underlying these electoral contexts.

Does a comparative study destroy the complexity that fascinates observers of American elections? Complexity often confuses as much as it fascinates; a focus on particulars can mask common elements. Social scientists prefer theories that cover a broad range of phenomena. In this spirit, a comparative model of elections will help political scientists identify those political and institutional variables that operate in a wide variety of electoral settings as well as to determine which variations cannot be accounted for. A comparative model of voting and elections will not emerge unless one attends *simultaneously* to the way political institutions, settings, and information structure the actions of parties, candidates, and voters.

This research tests the boundaries of comparative theory. I identify the components of a general approach to campaigns and elections. I compare the political settings of states and congressional districts more comprehensively than has been tried before. I use these measures to account for variations in campaign activity and candidate quality in the House and Senate over a two-decade period. In contrast to previous research, I do not take spending and activity levels as given to explain election margins. Instead, I explain why spending varies so tremendously across states and congressional districts. Finally, I link campaign activity to voters, a link that has been far too hidden in many studies of congressional campaigns.

My intent is less to present a broad-gauge model than to propose a heuristic for understanding elections—a road map, if you will, for a complex and multifaceted process. By identifying patterns within complex informational environments, candidate pairings, and institutional influences, it is possible to specify conditions under which some major categories of variables matter and others do not.

Do the type and magnitude of these differences say anything about how institutions condition electoral outcomes? I show that the barriers to a theory linking House and Senate elections are not insurmountable. The components of such a theory already exist, but they have been masked by insistence in various scholarly camps on one kind of analytical explanation. Many of our electoral theories are implicitly comparative. I show that making these comparisons across institutions is not only possible but rewarding. They amplify the ways in which the House and Senate differ and the ways in which they are converging.

A generic language of elections, rather than talking only about institutional differences, speaks about elections that are hard fought or low key and are held in heterogeneous or homogeneous settings with more or less efficient media markets. A unified theory helps political scientists ask whether politicians and voters behave in similar ways across disparate political settings. It helps us isolate the electoral impact of institutional arrangements. Finally, it helps us organize in a reasonable and intelligible manner a wider array of local, state, and national elections.

In Search of a Unified Model of House and Senate Elections

Diverse and Common Elements in American Elections

The length, expense, and scope of American elections reflect the country's breadth and diversity. The 1996 presidential election, from the first announcement through the general election, took more than 18 months and cost more than $500 million. At the time when I first wrote these sentences, in late 1998, congressional campaign committees were already being formed, fundraising dinners were being held, and polls had been conducted to gauge the state of the electorate—all this almost two years prior to the election of November 2000. In 1998, the average candidate for the U.S. House of Representatives spent almost $600,000 on the campaign, while the average Senate hopeful shelled out $3,500,000.

Individual contests, however, vary tremendously. House campaigns are held in 570,833 square miles in Alaska and in a few square miles in Manhattan. Senate candidates may have to appeal to more than 30 million Californians or less than half a million Wyomians. House members from safe districts may spend little or nothing on their election campaigns, while those in competitive circumstances raise and spend enormous amounts of money. The late William Natcher of Kentucky, who, literally on his deathbed, extended his record for consecutive House votes, spent almost nothing throughout his 40-year House career. In his final campaign, in 1996, he spent only $8,000 (and, as usual, won handily).[1] More typically, Michigan congresswoman Carolyn Cheeks

---

1. Natcher was a fascinating member of Congress, not only because of his distinguished career and almost unbreakable string of consecutive votes but because his electoral history serves as a useful reminder of the limits of quantitative analysis. Studies such as mine simply cannot account very well for congressional careers like Natcher's, who won using a glad-handing, backslapping style that is disappearing in American politics. My work is intended to complement, not replace, scholars who learn about individual candidates, read their literature, and visit their districts.

Kilpatrick racked up less than $175,000 in campaign costs in 1996 while cruising to an 88 percent majority. In contrast, political newcomer Michael Huffington drew on his oil wealth to fund a $5 million attempt to win California's Twenty-Second District seat in 1992. At least Huffington won—this time. He was not so fortunate in 1996, when he spent nearly $30 million dollars in a losing Senate bid. Diane Feinstein's victorious effort was a bargain at only $14 million. The totals amassed in that race set a record, albeit only until the 1998 California race, which was marked by newcomer Dan Issa's unsuccessful $13 million primary bid! And it is not just newcomers who spend freely. Newt Gingrich, Speaker of the House from 1995 through 1998, and during that time one of the best known and most powerful politicians in the country, never had an easy time at home. His 1996 race was one of his least competitive, yet he still racked $5.5 million dollars in campaign expenses. It is this very diversity (and cost) that makes American political campaigns an object of fascination for some and an object of scorn for others (Ashford 1983). It seem improbable that we could capture this diverse spectacle with a few variables and a series of equations.

At the same time, the tides of politics across space and time are remarkably consistent. The American party system has long been characterized by two-party competition with frequent alternation in power. Our current experience with divided control of the executive and the legislative branches is not unusual when looked at over two centuries (Fiorina 1996). Competition between the Democratic and Republican Parties has been the norm for 140 years. Even the fabled one-party South has disappeared: by the mid 1990s, no region experienced one-party dominance. The broad influences on presidential and congressional elections—incumbent popularity, economics, war, and scandals—have been operating in relatively regular fashion since at least 1896 (Kramer 1971). Perhaps de Tocqueville best summed up politics in America 150 years ago: "American society appears animated because men and things are constantly changing; it is monotonous because all these changes are alike" (1969, 614). Homogeneity and commonality of interest are the keys to understanding American politics.

Where does this leave electoral theory? A general theory of elections, one that applies minimally across a variety of electoral settings, should be within reach. Yet, after a review of the major milestones in elections research over five decades, Kinder and Sears concluded that "it is unrealistic and perhaps undesirable to hope for a single, coherent theory of political choice" (1985, 694). I would not want an electoral theory that is so general as to be banal nor so complex as to be incomprehensible. Nor would I want a theory that, in pursuit of generalizability across space and time, does so much damage to the particulars of local and national elections that what it explains is far outweighed by what it misses. Still, complexity often confuses as much as it fascinates; a focus on particulars can mask common elements. Social scientists prefer theories that cover a broad range of phenomena. In this spirit, I propose an electoral model that identifies those political and institutional variables that operate in a wide variety of electoral settings. I specify conditions under which some major categories of variables matter and others do not. Diversity in campaign spending, candidate appeals, voter learning, and voter decision rules could be an outward indication of a common process linking candidates, campaigns, voters, and the electoral setting. In this chapter, I attempt to capture this process in a succinct but powerful way.

I do not propose a single, overarching model of political choice. Kinder and Sears are correct: a unified theory is either unattainable or would be impenetrable. Instead, I suggest a heuristic for understanding elections, a map to a complex and multifaceted process. In the next section, I describe a straightforward, three-stage view of the electoral process. I suggest a small set of variables that can be compared across electoral settings. I propose causal relationships among these variables. Finally, I show how I will use this model to make comparisons across U.S. House and Senate elections. In chapters 3 and 4, I compare the House and Senate from 1982 through 1996. In chapter 5, I compare a set of causal models of candidate quality and campaign spending, using data from the same time period. Finally, I turn to voting (chap. 6), estimating a set of models of voter learning, preferences, and vote choice in 1988 and 1990.

Three Stages of the Electoral Process: A Brief Overview

The electoral process has three stages: the pre-campaign period, the campaign, and the vote. Each stage has an associated set of variables: at stage 1, political settings and institutional arrangements; at stage 2, candidates and campaigns; and at stage 3, voter information and decision rules. I describe these here, showing how they help me understand elections, how they relate to one another, and how I will use these ideas to compare the House and Senate. Figure 2.1 illustrates the relationships between settings, institutional arrangements, candidates, campaigns, and voters.

The political setting and institutional makeup form the stage upon which the electoral drama unfolds. By political setting, I mean those structural features of an election district (such as the size, shape, and communication patterns, or what Fowler and McClure [1989] call "political geography") and constituency (who lives there and what they want from government) that influence candidates. These also may be thought of as district attributes, and practically speaking that is how I will measure them. Theoretically, however, the political

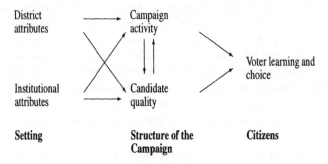

Fig. 2.1. Institutions, political settings, campaigns, and the vote: An exploratory framework

setting can mean much more, including the social and cultural background of an area and the history of social interactions and political competition. This kind of detailed social analysis is beyond the scope of this study and is difficult to comprehend on a national scale.[2]

Institutional arrangements are the ways the institution runs in Washington that have an impact on elections (e.g., term length, size of the parent body, and constitutionally prescribed policy roles). They influence the behavior of political actors but are not controllable by them.[3] Thus, like on a stage, settings and institutions set up boundaries, or constraints, within which campaigners operate.

The setting affects campaigns in two ways. Any feature of the context that might lead to more competitive elections will be associated with higher quality challengers and more active political campaigns. One reason this happens is that competition feeds on itself: when an incumbent is perceived as vulnerable, higher quality challengers emerge and challengers spend more money.

---

2. The past two decades have seen something of a rebirth of "contextual" analysis, however, pioneered by the work of Robert Huckfeldt and John Sprague (1995). These studies examine political behavior on a much reduced scale, usually a single city, but they are able to provide a far richer sense of political setting.

3. Congressional district lines and the makeup of the district are controlled by self-interested political actors, state legislators, and, indirectly, members of Congress (Gronke and Wilson, 1999). Similarly, members of Congress may change the "rules of the game"—institutional attributes—in order to increase their own chances for re-election (Mayhew 1974b). For any particular election, however, it is not inaccurate to place institution and setting outside the boundaries of political control.

When higher quality challengers emerge, incumbents spend reactively and increase their visibility in the district.[4] Some aspects of the setting are associated with more competitive elections. For example, relatively heterogeneous districts contain a more diverse set of political interests. As a result, there are more opportunities for challengers to build competitive coalitions. This is just the kind of circumstance in which higher quality challengers emerge and both challengers and incumbents spend more money relative to their counterparts in more homogeneous, less contentious surroundings (Canon 1990; Jacobson 1997). I test the hypothesis that more diverse districts, more efficient media markets, and more evenly balanced partisan divisions are associated with higher quality challengers and higher levels of campaign activity.

The second way in which the setting affects campaigns is by constraining the kinds of campaign strategies that will be adopted. Campaigns need to be more active (advertise more heavily, schedule more events, and travel more extensively) in larger, more diverse, more evenly balanced districts. Admittedly, there are a wide variety of campaign strategies that might be successful in an identical state or congressional district.[5] Still, this does not mean that *all* strategies might be successful in *all* settings. The makeup of the political district encourages some candidate behaviors and discourages others. This idea is related to what Richard Fenno, in the classic *Home Style,* calls the "fit" between a district and a representative (1978). I merely take this notion a step back to the setting of the election. While there are certainly other forces that influence the strategic decisions of candidates (in particular, national economic and political trends [Jacobson and Kernell 1983]), the district surely plays a role, regardless of whether it is a House or Senate contest.

Candidates also respond to institutions. How can I identify the impact of "institutions"? The facts are clear. Ceteris paribus, higher quality candidates run for the U.S. Senate—Senate incumbents and challengers, Democrat and Republican, all spend more money. These differences have been attributed to the greater attractiveness of the Senate as an institution (senators are more visible, the Senate is a stepping stone to the presidency, and the term is longer) and to differences between congressional districts and states (states are larger, with more even partisan balance and a larger pool of potential candidates). Again, I am left with an unsatisfying mix of accounts. States, campaigns, candidates, and voters are all on our list of suspects. Worded more carefully,

---

4. This also makes it very difficult to sort out cause and effect in campaigns.

5. Westlye (1986, 1991) believes this shows that political settings reveal little about campaign activity. Abramowitz and Segal (1992), in the most comprehensive study of Senate elections, similarly choose to focus on campaigns rather than characteristics of states. Lee and Oppenheimer (1999) and Brunell (1997), on the other hand, in recent studies of Senate representation, argue that context is important.

I reveal to what degree these observed differences in campaigns are a product of special institutional arrangements in the Senate and to what degree they are a function of differences between states and congressional districts. Once variations in settings are controlled for, do institutional differences remain?

Just as political settings and institutions set up boundaries within which candidates act, so candidates and their campaigns influence, though they do not determine, the choice process undertaken by the voter. At their core, campaigns are attempts to provide information that will sway voters to turn out and choose a particular candidate. I should find evidence of active campaigns among voters. Those experiencing active campaigns will be more informed about the candidates—their names, positions, and character flaws. Candidate expertise and prominence should be reflected in positive voter assessments. The first way that candidates and campaigns affect voters, then, can be measured by the quantity and quality of voter information.

Second, more information allows voters to employ more elaborate decision rules. If a voter knows nothing about a candidate besides his or her status as an incumbent or challenger, I would not expect policy or ideological opinions to play much of a role in the vote. In this case, the voter falls back on prior beliefs such as partisanship, general evaluations of the state of the country, or longstanding ties with an incumbent. When, however, the policy stances of both candidates are prominently featured in both campaigns, voters have an opportunity to take policy into account when they choose. Newer information communicated via the campaign trumps long-standing beliefs.[6] The level and quality of information does not *determine* the kind of decision rule that a voter will use. A highly informed voter might opt for party line voting because his or her opinions all run in one direction; a less informed voter might opt for party line voting because he or she knows nothing besides the partisan affiliation of the candidates. However, on average I expect that voters employ a larger set of considerations when information flows are high. Alternatively, I might find greater *variation* in the kinds of rules when there is a lot of information available. At a minimum, the model outlined here predicts that the relationship between voter information and choice and features of candidates and campaigns ought to be similar across institutional settings.

In this section, I have only sketched the outlines of my comparative approach. I have focused more on the logic of the "arrows"—causal links—than the contents of the "boxes." In the rest of this chapter, I flesh out these categories. I provide a more detailed description of the variables used in each stage and explain the causal models estimated in later chapters. These empirical chapters can be understood without reading the rest of this one, but some

---

6. The relationship between established beliefs and exposure to new campaign information is more complex than I describe it here (Zaller 1992).

of the theoretical underpinnings for my argument and my choice of measures will be missed.[7]

A Three-Stage Model of Elections: Theoretical and Empirical Background

Where elections are held matters. Any explanation of the political process needs to start with a description of the political terrain. Individual actions—running for office, selecting a campaign strategy, spending campaign funds, learning about politics, or choosing among competing candidates—take place within an electoral setting. For candidates, this terrain is what Jacobson (1997), among others, calls "context" and Hershey (1984) calls the "environment of political campaigns." In the broadest sense, understanding the context means knowing the ethnic, religious, economic, and political cleavages in a country (e.g., Lipset and Rokkan 1967), the shape and nature of legislative districts, and how votes are translated into seats (Cox 1997). In the United States, a comparison of House and Senate elections starts with congressional districts and states.

Stage One: Politics and the Locality

I was trained in political science as a behavioralist. Thus, when I began this project, my motivation was to compare House and Senate *voting.* I soon realized that a comparison of voting must consider variations in House and Senate *campaigns.* And how could I account for differences in campaigns unless I went even further back, considering House and Senate *districts?* Each stage of the electoral process, in my mind, was intimately linked to the next. Of necessity, I had to start at the first stage of the electoral process—the political setting—in order to understand all the later stages.

Given this intuition, I was surprised to find the impact of political settings relegated to the category of minimal effects. In some studies, district characteristics are ignored. One of the best studies of congressional campaigning, *Campaigning for Congress,* by Goldenberg and Traugott, devotes only four lines in one table to "district characteristics" (1984, 36). The literature on declining marginals (Mayhew 1974b; Fiorina 1977; Cover and Mayhew 1977; summary in Jacobson 1997) and incumbent and challenger spending (Palfrey and Erikson 1993; Green and Krasno 1990, 1988; Jacobson 1997, 1990a, 1985) has

---

7. For many readers, my specification of institutional effects will be unsatisfying. I believe that this is inevitable given the combined demands of theory and data, but interested readers would be wise to attend to the section entitled "Testing for Institutional Differences."

little to say about the impact of the local setting. These scholars have taught us a lot about intracampaign dynamics (and I draw on these studies heavily in my own analysis of campaign spending), but they fail to consider whether variations in campaign spending across districts and states could be a product in part of variations in the political setting (independent of what the challenger or incumbent may be doing). These "minimal effects" findings would seem to be contradicted by a diverse set of research that relates state- or district-level ideology and policy opinions to a variety of performance measures. After all, heterogeneity is only a surrogate for the theoretical construct: diversity of partisan and policy demands among the electorate.[8]

Other comparisons of states and congressional districts have been mainly suggestive in nature. Fenno (1982) speculates extensively on the differences between congressional districts and states:

> States are meaningful historical, cultural, economic, and governmental units in a sense that congressional districts are not. Senate constituencies are more apt to be congruent with media markets. The constituencies [senators] represent tend to be more heterogeneous, more diffuse, and hence less easily or concretely discerned. (11)

These differences are supported in interviews of House members who were later elected to the Senate (Baker 1995). Many of his subjects spoke of a sense of "intimacy" with their congressional districts that was lost in the larger state. Baker describes a state as:

> a circus big top—lots of acts going on at the same time, a jumble of activity, cacophonous and busy. Some congressional districts approximate this theatrical model, but most are places where interests run in a narrower track, where a single racial or ethnic group may be dominant, where a handful of large industries account for most of the payrolls. (101)

Even with all these differences between the House and Senate, both authors recognize an essential fact: some Senate states look a lot like House districts and vice versa.

This empirical observation implies a possible strong version of the political setting argument: similar combinations of constituency characteristics will be associated with similar levels of campaign spending, candidate strategies,

---

8. One way that the electoral context has been brought back into the study of congressional campaigns is through interest in candidate ambition and emergence (e.g., Fowler 1993; Canon 1990; Fowler and McClure 1989).

and ultimately voter informedness and choice *independent* of the institution. As Fenno (1982) argues:

> The effect of constituency size on campaigns can be tested, however, by entertaining the following proposition: Senate campaign styles differ from House campaign styles; but the more a Senate constituency resembles a House constituency, the more will that senator's campaign style resemble a representative's campaign style. (14)

Taking setting seriously, defining its aspects, and measuring it well are essential for understanding both the impact of setting and the effect of institutional differences. *Political setting* and *institutional differences* have been used quite casually in the literature so far. I try to sharpen their definitions in the next two sections.

Defining the Political Setting

The political setting is defined by characteristics of the constituency (who lives in a district and what they want from government), political geography (size, shape, and lines of communication), and partisan balance. I measure the constituency by the diversity of interests in a district, I measure political geography by media market efficiency and population density, and I measure partisan balance by the average vote over the previous four elections. I justify each of these decisions below.

Diversity of Interests

A key constraint on campaigns is the *diversity* of interests in the election district. Candidates and their campaign managers recognize divisions in the district and plan with them in mind. A more diverse district forces the candidate to appeal to multiple interests. This leads to the possibility of alienating one group or another, resulting in more competitive elections (Fenno 1982). Competitive elections are also more likely in districts with deep divisions on ideology and policy. Heterogeneity may also account for split control of a state's Senate seats: heterogeneous states provide more opportunities for building competing coalitions than homogeneous states do (Koetzle 1998; Bullock and Brady 1983).

Empirical tests of the impact of heterogeneity have been inconclusive. Alford and Hibbing (1989) show that state population size is related to the kinds of contacts respondents had with senators. State population is positively related to frequency of media contact relative to other forms of contact. On the other hand, population size has no relationship to a measure of opinion heterogeneity. Krasno (1994) finds no relationship between opinion heterogeneity (variance of partisanship and ideology) and a series of senatorial performance measures. While these studies make great strides in attempting to measure heterogeneity of interests, they are hampered by methodological problems in the survey data.[9] Some studies employ ill-chosen surrogates for political diversity: population size or the number of congressional districts.[10] I will show later that diversity of interests is not related to population size. The most diverse electoral settings are in fact congressional districts. The mixed results relating diversity to competitiveness may be more an indication of bad measures than bad theory.

I move beyond previous studies of the impact of political heterogeneity in two ways. First, I rely on more precise measures of heterogeneity. Rather than employing summary measures of diversity or heterogeneity, I unpack heterogeneity into its constituent elements. I examine those politically charged demographic categories, such as race, class, income, education, and urban/rural, that form long-standing cleavages in national and local politics. There is no good reason, either theoretically or empirically, to lump these divisions into a summary measure (see also Koetzle 1998). Second, I examine not just average levels of heterogeneity but distributions as well. The degree of overlap is central to my claim that I can compare the impact of district diversity in the House and Senate.[11]

Media Market Efficiency

The information environment is a second feature of the political setting that has a bearing on campaign spending and voter decision making (Hinckley 1981, chap. 1; Goldenberg and Traugott 1984, chap. 8). A primary goal of an election campaign is to communicate information to voters in order to inform them, reinforce their preferences, try to change their minds, and encourage

---

9. The studies that used the 1988 National Election Study's Senate Election Study (NES/SES) study to measure state ideology suffer from the small and varying state samples. The NES/SES sample size varied dramatically across states, from a low of 32 (Hawaii) to a high of 89 (Maine). Sample sizes of 75 (the target) are already rather low for making point estimates; the variations in sample size makes these estimates even more unreliable.

10. Hibbing and Brandes (1983) speculate that an electoral district's population is negatively related to incumbent electoral success. Lee and Oppenheimer (1999), Abramowitz (1988), Krasno (1994), and Westlye (1991) all rely on a population-based measure (the latter two use the number of congressional districts in the state) as a predictor of Senate election outcomes.

11. More specific information on data sources, variable operationalization, and recodes are contained in appendix A.

them to vote. Communication can be facilitated or impeded by the efficiency of media markets where "efficiency" includes the ease and cost of reaching potential voters. Free media coverage is more easily available when districts are relatively contiguous with media markets because television, radio, and newspapers are more likely to cover campaigns when a relatively high proportion of their audience are also voters in a particular election (Stewart and Reynolds 1990). Challengers can spend their media dollars more efficiently when media markets and electoral districts overlap. In more efficient media markets, voters are more likely to report that they have seen a candidate on television and are less likely to vote for the incumbent (all else being held equal).[12] Prinz (1991a) found that market efficiency, while generally irrelevant for House incumbents, is an important determinant of House challenger success. One limitation of Prinz's work is that, unlike Stewart (1989b), he is unable to produce continuous measures of market efficiency and advertising costs for the House. He relies on a dichotomy to distinguish efficient and inefficient media markets. Neither compares the House and Senate. If there is greater coverage of campaigns, and if candidates can more efficiently target their campaign dollars, presumably voters in efficient media markets will be exposed to more campaign information.

I compare states and congressional districts on their relative levels of media market efficiency. Overall campaign spending will be higher when markets are inefficient, although candidates could turn to more traditional modes of campaigning such as canvassing, leafletting, and personal appearances when markets are inefficient. To the degree to which market inefficiency does require higher levels of spending, weakly funded challengers should be disadvantaged. Relatedly, I expect that it is easier for challengers to overcome the recognition hurdle if media markets overlap with political districts and media advertising is relatively cheap. For all the reasons listed here, media market efficiency will be positively correlated with challenger recognition and success.

My operationalization of media market efficiency resembles those of Stewart (1989b; Stewart and Reynolds 1990) and Prinz (1991a, 1991b). I share in the weaknesses of both of these studies. First, there are no data available for newspaper and radio market coverage. My theoretical expectations about media market efficiency can only be tested in the context of television markets. Even though both House and Senate candidates are relying more and more on television advertising, the inability to represent all aspects of the mass media is a major drawback. Also, campaigns are not required to break down their spending into various categories, so I am unable to test the relationship

---

12. For results, see Stewart and Reynolds 1990, tables 5 and 8. There are several alternative ways to conceptualize "efficiency." Actual calculations, as well as data sources, are reported in appendix A. See also Prinz 1991a, 1991b; Stewart 1989a; and Stewart and Reynolds 1990.

between market efficiency and spending specifically on television advertisements. Unlike Stewart, I develop media market measures for the House and the Senate rather than just the Senate. If market efficiency affects the mix of contacts that respondents report, this relationship ought to be evident in both institutions. Unlike Prinz, who uses a dichotomous market efficiency measure, my congressional district measures are continuous, thus allowing a more efficient estimate of the impact of market efficiency.

Partisan Balance

The last feature of the local setting that I consider is partisan balance. No matter how advantageous the demographic and media market features of a congressional district or state may be, it is hard for a Democrat to win in a Republican stronghold. Partisan balance plays a central role in explaining campaign competition.[13]

Not surprisingly, many studies conclude that partisan balance plays a large role in the competitiveness of a state or congressional district (Powell 1991; Bond, Covington, and Fleisher 1985; Bianco 1984). States generally have more even partisan balance than congressional districts do, leading in some degree to the greater competitiveness of Senate races (Canon 1990; Erikson and Wright 1989; Abramowitz 1980) and possibly to split Senate delegations (Powell 1991). Like these studies, I operationalize partisan balance simply as the percentage skew in favor of the incumbent or challenger. I expect that partisan skew in favor of the incumbent will be associated with lower levels of challenger quality and lower levels of challenger spending in both the House and the Senate.

Testing for Institutional Differences

Is it reasonable to talk about institutions in a category separate from political setting? After all, it is no happy accident that states and congressional districts look different—this is the result of the Connecticut Compromise. Many of the features we associate with the prototypical senator (visibility, presidential timber) and Senate campaign (hard fought, high expenditures) could also be a natural outgrowth of politics in a large, heterogeneous political setting.

---

13. It is also important to include partisan balance because of probable covariation between partisanship and demographic diversity. Demographics may operate indirectly through partisanship. The redistricting process makes this almost a certainty. Gerrymanders shuffle citizens according to their partisan leanings. They also shuffle according to demographic groupings (Lublin 1997; Gronke and Wilson, 1999).

One way to proceed is to examine what the terms *institution, institutional analysis,* and *new institutionalism* mean to political scientists. Institutional variables are those rules, norms, and standardized operating procedures that govern the way actors (here senators and House members) interact. In the broadest sense, political settings are a consequence of institutional arrangements. Senators are elected from larger, more heterogeneous, and more media efficient political districts precisely because these features distinguish states from congressional districts. However, I believe that calling these institutional differences confuses rather than clarifies the issue. *Institution* does not generally include such things as district size, heterogeneity, or communications patterns.[14]

James Madison and his coauthors, if not the first, were among the earliest institutionalists in American politics. The Founders hoped that institutional arrangements in the Constitution, combined with assumptions about human nature and political action, would have advantageous consequences. Regarding the Senate and House, the framers placed great emphasis on the salutary effects of bicameralism. The two chambers were different in almost every respect: term length, size of the chamber, and constitutionally assigned policy prerogatives.

The frequency of elections and the structure of the electoral districts are supposed to give the House an "immediate dependence and ... intimate sympathy" with the people (Madison et al. 1961, 337).[15] The Senate provides a "restraining, stabilizing counterweight, ... being the source of a more deliberate, more knowledgable, longer-run view of good public policy" (Fenno 1982, 3). The smaller size of the Senate inoculates it against "yield[ing] to the impulse of sudden and violent passions" (Madison et al. 1961, 379). The equal size of each state's delegation is intended to represent states' interests alongside those of citizens (as reflected in the House). The six-year term was designed to foster political and policy stability—senators could focus on public policies that require "... continued attention, and a train of measures" (381).

If Madison and his colleagues were the first institutionalists, they have lots of company today. The major tenets of neoinstitutionalism, however, differ from the institutional features elaborated earlier. This discrepancy between institutional effects, broadly construed, and neoinstitutionalism is a potential source of confusion.

Political institutions are social units that channel political activity through rules, procedures, and norms; they provide a structure within which political

---

14. I have at least two allies in this terminological debate: Alford and Hibbing (1989) make a similar distinction.

15. All quotes in this paragraph are from the New American Library edition of *The Federalist Papers* (Madison et. al. 1961).

actors can supply meaning to their activities. Cooper tells us that institutions are "planned social units that are created and structured to perform certain functions or tasks" (1977, 140). McCubins and Sullivan define institutions as "the rules of the game that constrain individual choices and provide incentives for individual action" (1987, 3). Shepsle describes institutions as "a framework or rules, procedures, and arrangements" (1986, 52). March and Olsen (1989) do not provide an explicit definition, but their focus on rules and standardized patterns of behavior resonates with McCubbins and Sullivan and Shepsle:

> Students of institutions emphasize the part played by political structures in creating and sustaining islands of imperfect and temporary organization in potentially inchoate political worlds. (16)
>
> Institutions have a repertoire of procedures, and they use rules to select among them. (21)
>
> [I]nstitutions constrain and shape politics through the construction and elaboration of meaning. (39)

The common thread in all these definitions is an interest in the constraints operating on decision makers acting within an institutional framework. The new institutionalists generally focus on the dynamics of the institution itself: how rules are applied, how norms develop and the consequences of various structural arrangements.

For many institutionalists, although certainly not all, it is less important how representatives get to Washington than how they behave once they get there. For an electoral scholar, however, the situation is not so clear-cut. An electoral scholar has to simultaneously attend to institutional concerns—chamber size, frequency of election, and policy prerogatives—and the nature of the electoral district—heterogeneity, media market efficiency, and population size.

If *institutional* becomes all-encompassing, then it is impossible to speak about political settings in a generic sense. Institution and setting are completely collinear. I argue that institution and setting are distinct conceptually, even if they are tangled empirically. Current usage of *institution* does not include such things as population diversity, media market efficiency, and partisan balance. Furthermore, it is analytically useful to keep institution and setting separate. Political setting explanations can help build electoral theories that apply across institutions; institutionally bound explanations, by their very nature, point out the limits of a general theory.

Effects attributable to the political setting are those effects that are a direct consequence of the nature of the constituency. There are a host of possible institutional differences—term length, size of the chamber, and constitutionally assigned roles. It is hard to produce empirical realizations of these differences. My strategy here is a more indirect one: I try to determine whether, once other considerations are taken into account, institutional differences go away. Under the strong version of the political setting argument made earlier, when all relevant differences in diversity of interests, media market efficiency, and partisan balance are controlled for, variables representing institutional differences should have no impact on campaign activity, candidate quality, or voter learning and choice. From a pure measurement perspective, I represent all the rich literature on Senate/House institutional differences with a simple dummy variable.

There is another way that institutional convergence can be revealed via my analyses. Institutional arrangements may modify the way that political settings affect campaigns and the way that campaigns affect voters. Thus, the structure of explanation could be similar across the institutions while the relative impact of particular variables changes. For example, I would use the same set of variables to predict competitiveness in the House and Senate but would not place the same weights on the various pieces of information I collected.[16] The presence or absence of institutional effects, independent of differences in political settings, will be revealed via these analyses.

I cannot escape the charge, then, that my specification of institutional differences is sparse. A fine example of what a grander theory of institution might encompass is contained in Grier and Munger's comparison of PAC contributions in the Senate and House (1993). Even there, however, "institution" is primarily understood in terms of committee assignments, voting patterns, party, and seniority, along with what might fall into my "setting" category, electoral security. While I would argue that their representation of electoral effects is limited, they would surely accuse me of short changing institutions.

In my defense, my focus here is more on carving out boundaries—what does *not* seem to count as an institutional difference—than on providing a complete specification of all the categories in figure 2.1. I do not think that institutional differences count for nothing. At the same time, I do not believe

---

16. In the language of regression, the set of significant variables is the same across the House and Senate even if the coefficients vary. I would estimate such a model by interacting the dummy variable representing institution with each of the other variables in the model. This also allows me to identify which subset of coefficients changes across the House and Senate and which remain the same.

that they count for everything.[17]

Stage Two: Campaigns and Candidates

Stage two of the election process is the campaign: candidates and their campaign activities. Scholarly research on congressional candidacies and campaigning abounds. There are well-established ways to measure the quality of congressional challengers and their levels of campaign activity, and I take advantage of these where I can. Most importantly, however, I add one set of causal relationships and empirical findings. Following the three-stage models, I explore the *causes* of campaign spending or candidate quality, as a consequence of the political setting, rather than just looking at their effects, typically on incumbent reelection. Intracampaign dynamics—candidates responding to each others' behavior—are weighed against the setting as competing explanations of campaign spending and candidate quality. This way I can assess what helps us understand campaigns better: the relative levels of heterogeneity, media market efficiency, and so on of states and congressional districts or something inherent to House and Senate campaigns. As before, I allow for remaining institutional differences in the levels of activity and quality. Directly comparing three sets of explanatory variables—setting, intracampaign effects, and institution—helps me to identify the degree to which higher levels of candidate quality and campaign activity in the Senate are really a product of the relative attractiveness of the office and not a consequence of running in what are, on average, larger and more heterogeneous electoral districts.

Candidate quality influences the competitiveness of a campaign independent of other campaign effects. Experienced candidates know when to contest a seat and when to take a pass (Canon 1990). Higher quality candidates can more easily overcome the recognition hurdle (Hinckley 1981; Mann and Wolfinger 1980). Success rates in the general election are far higher for experienced or prominent candidates (Jacobson 1997, 1990b; Canon 1990). Candidate quality is included in my model of the campaign process.

Campaign activity is also part of my model. Campaigns inform voters about candidate names, policy positions, and leadership qualities. Campaign activity should reflect, as much as is feasible, all steps taken toward informing the voter and winning the election. As such, campaign activity includes both information flow—the information output of the campaign as reflected in such things as spending levels, candidate activities, and media coverage—and content—the relative weight given in the campaign and media coverage to

17. Recent articles by Grofman and his colleagues, most of which compare House and Senate elections, wrestle with these same issues: Grofman, Brunell, and Koetzle 1998; Grofman, Griffin, and Berry 1995; and Grofman, Griffin, and Glazer 1990.

issues, candidate features, and other campaign topics. Flow increases the likelihood that voters will be exposed to campaign information. Content reflects the mix of issues that campaigners are stressing and presumably has some impact on the kinds of considerations that voters employ. I include measures of flow in this study, but for practical reasons I ignore campaign content.[18]

I claim that candidates and campaigns react to the political setting. If this is true, then campaign activity and candidate quality will covary in systematic fashion with district diversity, media market efficiency, political balance, and institutional arrangements. The first step in the analysis of campaign activity and candidate quality is descriptive: are there enough *similarities* between House and Senate candidates to allow me to *contrast* institutional and other explanations of campaign outcomes? This may seem contradictory, but it is not. *Overlaps* in the distributions of candidate quality and campaign spending are necessary if one is to proceed with a comparative mode. For example, high spending by the challenger in House elections is associated with a variety of other events such as high levels of spending by the incumbent, relatively higher levels of voter information, and increased turnout (Jacobson 1997). I express spending in terms that are comparable across Senate and House races and examine whether high spending *in general* is associated with higher levels of voter information or whether this effect only occurs in the House. This comparison is not possible without House and Senate races with relatively equal spending levels. Discovering whether overlaps exist is taken up in chapter 4. The second step in the analysis of campaign activity and candidate quality is to see whether they are associated in systematic ways with variations in political settings. The expected pattern of these relationships are discussed next (the empirical tests are in chap. 5).

From Setting to Campaign

There is a wealth of research that suggests that candidates and campaigns respond to the political environment. I know, for example, that candidates for Senate seats are on average more experienced, more prominent, and spend more money (Abramowitz 1980; Ragsdale 1981; Hinckley 1980b; Westlye 1983, 1986). National political tides (popularity of the sitting president, the state of the national economy) enter into the candidate's decision about whether to run for office (Jacobson and Kernell 1983). It is also probable that candidates attend to features of the political district (such as ease or difficulty of gaining recognition, partisan balance, and diversity) when making the decision to run or choosing campaign strategies. In a heterogeneous political setting, it

18. Content measures for all contested House and Senate races from 1982 to 1996 would be very time consuming to collect.

should be more difficult for a representative to solidify his or her support since more interests to alienate and more opportunities for challengers to construct competing support coalitions. Media market efficiency pushes in the opposite direction, allowing candidates to spend less money and get the same message across. An even split of partisans encourages quality challengers and should be associated with higher spending levels by both sides.

I also expect that candidate quality varies with the makeup of the electoral district. One obvious time when this occurs is after redistricting. Redistricting reduces incumbent margins (Jacobson 1997) and is positively associated with challenger quality (Canon 1990, chap. 4). I do not examine redistricting effects here and only mention them because they can be thought of as another example of how changes in political settings can impact electoral outcomes. Instead, I concentrate on the influence of district diversity, media market efficiency, and partisan balance. I predict that more diverse settings, more efficient markets, and more evenly balanced numbers of partisans should be associated with higher quality challengers.

There are two additional components to my model of candidate quality and campaign activity. First, a model of campaign spending is woefully incomplete unless intracampaign dynamics are included. Political candidates respond to the activities of their opponents. Much of the driving force behind campaign spending levels is reactive; if you have a high-spending opponent, you will spend more, all other things being equal.[19] Thus, I include the opponent's spending in my models of campaign spending, employing appropriate estimation techniques (see chap. 5 for more information).

Second, since, I estimate my models for the House and Senate together, institutional effects must be considered. There is good evidence indicating that campaign spending and candidate quality can be profitably compared across the House and Senate (Krasno 1994; Canon 1990). According to Krasno, once those features that supposedly differentiate the Senate from the House are controlled for—campaign intensity and challenger prominence—Senate and House campaigns appear surprisingly alike: "(D)ifferences in the aggregate largely exist because Senate campaigns are much more likely to be intense, and Senate candidates are more likely to be formidable" (1994, 114). Canon (1990) finds that the same set of "structural and institutional variables" (the makeup of the primary system, the size of the state legislature, the permeability of the political structure, and the "shape of the political opportunity structure") help account for the appearance of quality challengers in both the House and Senate. Both results, while highly suggestive, have limits. Krasno only examines one year (1988), while Canon does not estimate a pooled model, nor

---

19. A large number of authors make this point; see, for example, Erikson and Palfrey 1998; Palfrey and Erikson 1993; Jacobson 1985, 1997; and Green and Krasno 1988, 1990.

does he speculate much on what might be the cause of the different patterns that do appear between the House and Senate. Still, Krasno's and Canon's results indicate that a pooled model of political campaigns in the U.S. House and Senate is not only possible but promising.

Stage Three: Information, Evaluations, and Choice

The final stage of the electoral process is voting. If political and institutional settings form the stage upon which the main electoral actors (candidates, parties, interest groups, and the media) play their roles, then voting is the final act in this drama. The story line for House and Senate as well as presidential elections has been much the same—economic growth and decline, presidential popularity, and rally events such as wars and scandals are strong determinants of aggregate electoral patterns. Thus, one might expect that voters evaluate candidates in a similar fashion and employ a similar set of considerations when voting across offices. These are only aggregate findings, however. The decision rule used by individual voters seems to vary by the office being contested. Where presidential voters rely upon a combination of partisanship, candidate evaluations, and issue opinions, House voters more frequently cite constituency service, casework, and candidate issue opinions when explaining their preferences. Incumbency plays as central a role as partisanship. Studies of Senate voting are an odd blend, some claiming that national policy and issue stances are more important for Senate candidates and others including a House-like set of contact and constituency variables.[20] What seems most likely is that the main difference between presidential and House voting is *information.* The presidential voter is exposed to a far larger amount of information (Alvarez 1999), and thus the presidential voter employs a more complex decision rule. The impact of information on the decision rule can be used to compare and contrast voting for the House and Senate.

First, I examine the level of information that survey respondents have about Senate and House candidates. There may be significant differences in *how much* voters know (are some House candidates as well known as the typical Senate candidate?) as well as in the *content* of that information (do voters feel differently about Senate and House incumbents and challengers?). My expectation is that once I control for a set of independent variables (heterogeneity, partisan balance, market efficiency, candidate quality, and campaign spending) information levels will not look all that different across institutions. After showing how settings, institutions, campaigns, and candidates combine to affect voter information levels, I describe my expectations about voting. I

---

20. Compare the series of articles by Abramowitz (1980, 1988) and Abramowitz and Segal (1990, 1992) to Krasno (1994).

argue in chapter 6 that a pooled model of the vote is not only possible but reveals similarities between House and Senate voting that have been previously disguised. The pooled model, however, must take into account the diverse electoral settings from which voters come as well as particular pairings of candidates and their associated campaigns.

Voter Information, Evaluations, and Choice

Independent of institution, I expect that more active campaigns will result in greater amounts of information held by the voters. The kinds of information that are critical to candidate success are easily identified: recognition and trust. Therefore, the first way I compare voter information is by comparing relative levels of recognition and "likes and dislikes" across the Senate and House. Following the same analytical path as in previous chapters, I start by asking how distinct levels of recognition and candidate evaluations are across the institutions. If there is no overlap, the enterprise cannot proceed. Next, I test whether variations in recognition and trust are associated with variations in campaign activity and candidate quality regardless of whether I am looking at the House or Senate. Thus, I estimate a series of regression models, with voter information levels as the dependent variable, and my setting and campaign measures, along with individual characteristics, as independent variables.

Next, I turn to the actual vote choice. Perhaps Senate and House voters employ similar voting rules when the flow and content of political information are similar over the two institutions. This indicates that the place to look for comparisons is among comparable campaigns: voters in low-intensity Senate campaigns compared to the average House voter and voters in high-intensity House campaigns compared to the average Senate voter. Suppose for a moment that all citizens were exposed to the same level and mix of political information. In this case, only individual tendencies to seek out political information will determine how much an individual will know about politics. The distribution of voting rules will be shaped like a bell curve, where at one extreme you would find highly involved and interested citizens who take into account a wide variety of policy positions, character assessments, and even institutional roles into account when voting. At the other end, you would find citizens who are uninterested in politics, who vote at relatively low rates, and whose votes are determined by a few broad-gauge cues: party, incumbency, and the nature of the times.

This is obviously a caricature, but it is a useful illustration of the impact of increased information flow. It does not change the underlying distribution of citizens' political interests but shifts the distribution to the right, exposing more citizens to a greater amount of campaign information. Thus, in a high-flow environment I would expect the less interested voter to behave like an average voter in a low-flow environment. In information poor environments, I would expect to find most voters relying on simplified cues, party or incumbency. In an information rich environment, voters still might rely on this simplifying device. However, with more information to draw upon in the campaign environment it is more likely that more voters will draw upon a larger set of considerations when they make their choices.[21]

The hypothesis for a Senate/House comparison is therefore straightforward. Under the "institutional differences" hypothesis, I should observe distinctive voting patterns, even after I have controlled away other effects. Under the "no difference" alternative, Senate and House voting will look quite similar once candidate quality and candidate spending are controlled for. If the latter hypothesis is confirmed, then observed differences in voting are more a function of the higher competitiveness of the average Senate contest.[22]

While this will not eliminate the very real difference in Senate and House voting, it does place it in a different light. Theoretically, if we could somehow improve the candidate quality and campaign finances of House candidates, voting choice for the House might resemble voting choice for the Senate. This is in fact in the same spirit as those campaign finance reformers who, via a public-financing mechanism, want to bring House challenger spending up to the level of incumbent spending. The assumption is the same that I make here: if we can equalize the information flow about the candidates, then House campaigns will be far more competitive (i.e., more incumbents will lose).

Conclusion

Paul Allen Beck, reviewing a quarter century of electoral research, called for a reintroduction of context into the theory of voting:

---

21. See Alvarez 1999 for a similar approach.

22. The interaction between individual-level characteristics and information flow is quite a bit more complex than this model allows for. Zaller (1992) shows that individual responses to external information flows is the result of an interaction between the individual's political preferences and attentiveness, and the amount and partisan bias of the information stream. This turns out to be difficult to replicate in a comparative model of the House and Senate. Zaller assumes that information flow in House campaigns is pro-incumbent, thus allowing him to use the simpler one-way information model. The same cannot be assumed about Senate campaigns: neither pro-incumbent nor pro-challenger information dominates. So, while my model reflects Zaller's idea that individual and contextual factors interact during the voting decision, I do not employ his exposure-acceptance model here.

No theory of vote choice is complete without specification of the impact of context. The Michigan approach to electoral studies and its revisionist competitors have identified almost every conceivable component of the electoral decision. Both the ordering of these components and their empirically based weights undoubtedly vary with contextual factors. Until this research path is beaten by many scholars, though, our understanding of the effects of context will be woefully incomplete. (1986, 269)

And Charles Franklin, reflecting on Senate campaigns, Senate candidates, and voter learning and choice, recognizes the interplay, and distinction, between institutions and politics:

These results should remind us of the dominance of politics over institutions. ... [P]oliticians exploit the loopholes, as much as they are bound by the constraints, of institutions. (1991, 1210)

My study of campaigns and voting in the U.S. House and Senate builds from these two observations. Any comparison of the House and Senate has to take into account contextual variation within and across these institutions. Up to now, most studies have appealed to contextual effects without really specifying their impact. I attempt to do so here. By carefully laying out what is meant by "political setting," I can assess its contribution to political outcomes independently of institutional effects. Context cannot be studied in isolation, however. Unless we also understand how actors pursue their self-interest within the constraints of district contexts and institutional settings, we are left with an incomplete picture of the electoral process. Heeding Franklin's call, I hope to discover to what degree candidates for the U.S. House and Senate are constrained by, and to what degree they act independently of, contextual and institutional boundaries.

Settings, institution, campaigns, candidates, and voters have not been ignored by electoral scholars. Nor is this the first study to suggest comparing Senate and House elections. Where does my study stand apart? I bring previously disparate approaches under a single theoretical and empirical umbrella.

Some students of the Senate suggest that attributes of the political setting—population size, heterogeneity, and media market efficiency—result in different levels of competitiveness in Senate elections. Other scholars compare Senate and House elections, concluding that institutional arrangements explain different patterns of voting behavior. A third school eschews background features altogether, preferring instead to focus on the strategic decisions of campaigns and candidates. They conclude that Senate candidates are more visible, have more money, and simply run better campaigns than House candidates do.

It is impossible to identify the unique contribution context, institutions, candidates, and voters make to electoral outcomes unless we disentangle their separate effects. This book integrates what is known about district heterogeneity with our understanding of campaign spending and candidate quality. It links campaign activity to voter learning and decision making and directly confronts an institutional and sociological explanation of elections. It points to the possibilities of developing a broader understanding of how locality, institutions, campaigns, and voters interact to produce a final outcome.

The confusion surrounding institution versus setting epitomizes the central question of this book: to what degree is a comparative model of elections, one that will apply across elective institutions, possible? In order to determine the relative merits of an institutional versus a setting explanation, institution must be *separated* from setting. Without comparative analysis, our models might be institution specific. In line with Fenno's (1982) call for a bicameral perspective in congressional studies, studying elections across the House and Senate forces me to be explicit about what kinds of institutional arrangements lead to certain electoral outcomes. Aggregate data analysis cannot answer this question because aggregate analysis does not allow me to explore the *interplay* among the three stages—settings and institutions, campaigns and candidates, and voters. So, while I may be able to describe the different electoral outcomes in large and small states (e.g., Hibbing and Brandes 1983), I can only speculate about the reasons why population size affects elections. Many past studies that compared the House and Senate failed to *disentangle* the impact of institutional variation from variations in settings, campaign activity, and candidate quality. It is time for a fresh look at campaigns and elections in the House and Senate, using the schematic outlined in figure 2.1.

CHAPTER 3

The Setting: Political "Districts" in the U.S. House and Senate

The conventional wisdom is that Senate and House represent a host of differences in settings, institutional arrangements, candidates, campaigns, and voters. But is the conventional wisdom regarding Senate and House elections an accurate description of reality? One might suspect that it is not: Westlye (1983) points out that some differences between Senate and House challengers (e.g., Abramowitz 1980; Hinckley 1980a; Mann and Wolfinger 1980) are an artifact of sample design. In fact, many Senate challengers look just like House challengers. I show in this chapter that differences in political settings also have to be reexamined. When arrayed on a series of demographic, media market, and partisan measures, many congressional districts look like states while many states look like congressional districts. This means that neither senators nor House members automatically confront particularly more "complex" arrays of political interests when they run for office. States and congressional districts *are* different but not in the ways that might have been expected.

This chapter is primarily descriptive, but the results form the foundation for all subsequent analyses. My working hypothesis, outlined in chapter 2, is that Senate and House districts are *not* electoral settings. State/congressional district is not a dichotomy but a way of identifying two *distributions.* Each has a midpoint and a spread, as any distribution does. A complete comparison of the political settings in the House and Senate must take into account both aspects of the distributions. These comparisons will reveal whether or not institution and setting are collinear. If they are, then no statistical analysis, no matter how creative, can hope to disentangle their relative effects. Overlaps, on the other hand, provide an opportunity to test the political-setting explanation of elections. Under the strongest version of the political-setting argument, when I select out similar political districts, regardless of the institution, candidate quality, campaign spending, voter information, and voter decision rules ought to look quite similar.

I compare states and congressional districts on those politically charged demographic characteristics (race, income, education, occupation, and ethnicity) that form long standing cleavages in national and local American politics. I improve on previous comparisons by keeping these demographic categories separate rather than lumping them into a summary measure.[1] To these I add a set of indicators that are surrogates for ease of information dissemination in the district: population density and television market efficiency.

With these measures in hand, I ask how different, and how similar, states and congressional districts really are. States and congressional districts turn out to be very similar on measures of demographic diversity. States are not more heterogeneous than congressional districts. Instead, the most homogeneous *and* heterogeneous election settings are congressional districts. Where states and congressional districts do differ is in the information environment and partisan balance. Congressional districts are on average much smaller and denser, with less efficient media markets and skewed numbers of Republicans or Democrats.

In the next section, I describe the measures that I use to characterize congressional districts and states. The reasons *why* we would care about diversity were explicated in chapter 2, especially in the section entitled "Politics and the Locality."

Diversity, Partisan Balance, and Media Market Efficiency

Any explanation of the political process must begin with a description of the terrain. Individual actions—running for office, selecting a campaign strategy, spending campaign funds, learning about politics, and choosing among competing candidates—take place within an electoral setting. For candidates, this terrain is what Hershey (1984) calls "the environment of political campaigns." One aspect of the political setting is the number of distinct political interests in a electoral district, what I operationalize as political diversity. A second feature of the setting that constrains campaigners is the ease or difficulty of communicating political information. I measure this by the efficiency of media markets. Finally, I add the balance of partisans in the district—how skewed the district is toward Democrats or Republicans. While not a comprehensive summary of the ways that one might think about the political setting, no major categories are excluded from this survey.

---

1. Grofman, Koetzle, and Brunell (1997) and Lee and Oppenheimer (1999) independently reached this same conclusion. They allow different kinds of demographic cleavages to have differential impacts of competitiveness.

Diversity of Interests in States and Congressional Districts

There is a multitude of demographic divisions that might matter to Senate and House candidates. I reduce this to a manageable set by means of two decisions. The first is guided by methodological considerations. Reliable opinion measures for congressional districts are unavailable. Ideally, I would have survey data on ideological, partisan, and policy opinions in states and congressional districts, but these are only available for states (e.g., Erikson, Wright, and McIver 1993). Good measures of public opinion within congressional districts either do not exist or are difficult to obtain.

I substitute *demographic diversity* as a surrogate for diversity of interests. Demographic categories tap into at least some part of the way that members of Congress, and the Senate, view their constituencies. Fenno claims that some part of "home-style" activity is oriented toward the "geographic constituency, [a] district's internal makeup using political science's most familiar demographic and political variables: socioeconomic structure, ideology, ethnicity, residential patterns, religion, partisanship, stability, diversity, etc." (1978, 2). Bond et al. (1985), Bond (1983), and Bullock and Brady (1983) have all used a summary measure of heterogeneity based on a set of demographic measures under the assumption that demographic characteristics "provide the basis for political cleavages" (Bond et al. 1985, 516). Others use a weighted set of demographic categories in order to simulate or otherwise characterize public interests in congressional districts. A combination of race, income, some measure of social class, education, urban/rural, and sectionalism are most often used. For all their hoary quality, race, income, class, and education perform admirably in summarizing the political cleavages politicians face.[2] I select a small set of demographic categories in order to characterize states and congressional districts as more or less diverse.

The second decision is what categories to include. I choose a small set of characteristics that reflect long-standing political divisions in American society: social class, race, ethnicity, and urban/rural. This has the advantage of both reducing the number of categories and making it less likely that I will be distracted by the idiosyncrasies of any one election.[3]

---

2. Jackson and King (1989) use income levels as a surrogate for opinions on tax policy and education as a surrogate for political informedness. In a different vein, Page et al. (1984) use regression to determine a set of weights to apply to demographic measures in order to simulate district opinion. Kingdon (1968), Froman (1963), and Turner and Schneier (1970) all characterize districts using a small set of demographic and party indicators such as metro/rural, ethnicity, race, sectionalism, and competitiveness.

3. The list of characteristics selected by Grofman, Koetzle, and Brunell (1997) matches the list I chose.

The first cluster of variables comprise the components of socioeconomic status or social class: income, education, and occupation. Class divisions have not been as great in the United States as in other advanced industrial democracies (Beck 1997, chap. 6), but they still help us to differentiate Democratic and Republican convention delegates (Stone et al. 1990) and voters (Beck 1997). In general, higher SES is associated with higher levels of voter turnout (Rosenstone and Hansen 1993) and political activism (Verba, Schlozman, and Brady 1995). Finally, SES bears some relationship, tenuous perhaps, to New Deal economic and social policies, a set of issues that has dominated American elections in the postwar era (Rosenstone 1983).

Race has played a central role in American politics for the half century since the New Deal (Rosenstone 1983) and beyond (Sniderman and Piazza 1993). Racial divisions of all kinds (white vs. black, black vs. Hispanic, white vs. Hispanic) have been regularly prominent in national and local elections. Controversy surrounding the 1982 Civil Rights Act and 1992 redistricting have focused specifically on the legitimacy of racial gerrymandering and racial voting (Grofman and Davidson 1992). Relatedly, white ethnicity has remained an important consideration for congressional candidates. In many urban centers, Polish, German, Irish, and other ethnic groups retain distinctive patterns of voting (Pinderhughes 1987, chap. 4; Gove and Masotti 1982). I tap into the racial and ethnic dimension in two ways, first by measuring racial diversity (the categories are white, black, Hispanic, and Asian American) and second by measuring the percentage of foreign stock, in an attempt to reflect white ethnic diversity.

Measuring Diversity

For theoretical reasons, means and medians are not the best way to compare states and congressional districts. Means do not tell us whether there are states that look like congressional districts or vice versa. Second, my conceptual construct is diversity of interest. I want to measure diversity of a setting in a way that reflects both the midpoint and the spread of the demographic distribution.[4] Thus, I need some estimate of the level of variation *within* an electoral district. Two estimators are employed here. Variance is an appropriate measure of dispersion for continuous variables (such as income and education). A derived measure of variation is applicable to nominal variables. I refer to this derived measure as a diversity score.

The derived measure comes from the work of Sullivan (1973) and has been employed by Bond (1983), Bond, et al. (1985), Bullock and Brady (1983),

---

4. A more technical treatment of this topic is contained in appendix A.

Grofman, Koetzle, and Brunnell (1997), and Koetzle (1998). All of these authors (save Koetzle) calculate a summary measure of heterogeneity, lumping race, income, occupation, and education together. I take a different tack. There is no good reason to pool ethnic, economic, and residential diversity. It is quite possible that the political import of racial diversity, for example, is different from that of economic diversity (in fact, partisan differences on class are far smaller than partisan divisions on race). Therefore, I present both the summary measure for comparison with Bond's calculations and separate diversity scores for racial, occupational, foreign stock, and urban/rural diversity. Since these are measures of variation *within* settings, I am also able to calculate variation in the diversity scores across the population of settings. With a mean diversity score and a variance in diversity scores across all states and congressional districts, I can test for the likelihood that the state and congressional district distributions have different means.

Does diversity mask more than it reveals? In a recent study of Senate elections, Lee and Oppenheimer (1999) claim that it does. First, they believe that diversity measures contradict our common sense because states such as Mississippi rank as more diverse than Pennsylvania (chap. 4). They also criticize the limited variation in the diversity scores, ranging from only .40 to .55 in a recent updating (Morgan and Wilson 1990, see also appendix A, table A.3). Finally, the repeated failure of diversity scores to explain electoral dynamics calls their utility into question. I disagree with Lee and Oppenheimer on each count. First, remember that the researcher chooses what to include in the diversity score and how to calculate it. In this book, I have chosen to keep the scores "unpacked." Treating all political divisions equally is misleading. This does not mean, however, that I need to abandon a focus on diversity.

Second, and related, the range and standard deviation of the summary score depend on what the researcher chooses to include. As I demonstrate in appendix A, both mathematically and empirically, if you keep a large number of demographic categories, you increase the range of diversity scores. Since the diversity score represents the probability that a random pair of individuals will differ on any combination of characteristics, then the linkage between the number of potential categories and the range of the scale is obvious. The more possible variations that are possible, the probability that a randomly selected pair will match is lower and the variance between relatively homogeneous settings and relatively heterogeneous settings is larger. Besides, a limited range does not in and of itself indict the diversity scores. It may be that small movements on the scale have large political consequences.

Since scholars have typically chosen a limited set of variables (race, occupation, urban residence, and foreign stock) and have collapsed across categories, it is not surprising that states such as Mississippi and Hawaii rank high on a diversity measure. This is almost completely a product of equal racial and urban/rural divisions in these two states. Mississippi is more diverse than Pennsylvania if by diverse you mean the likelihood that a pair of individuals will differ in terms of race or type of residence. Arguably, this kind of variation is quite important to campaigners. Thus, the drawbacks quite rightly pointed out by Lee and Oppenheimer are not a drawback of the theory but rather of the way scholars have constructed and used the diversity measure.

Partisan Balance

The number of Democrats, Republicans, and independents in a district is, prima facie, central to the level of political competition. Partisan balance requires no special metric. A measure should indicate the level of competitiveness between the major political parties and be purged of incumbency advantage and national forces. Survey measures of partisanship and vote choice would be ideal but are unavailable for congressional districts and states. Election results must be used. That raises a second question: which results? A running average of the last four results is a good alternative for congressional districts.[5] This is a long enough period to smooth out spikes due to particularly odd years. It includes two off-year and two on-year elections. For the Senate, I cannot average the past four elections, since that would necessitate averaging 24 years of data, far too long a time during which to claim some average level of partisan support. Instead, I take the mean normal vote score across all the congressional districts in the state and use this as statewide partisan balance.[6]

Measuring the Information Environment: Media Market Efficiency

In chapter 2, I argued that the ease with which political information can be disseminated in an area is a second important feature of political settings. In locations where media markets and electoral districts are highly contiguous,

---

5. A problem with these variables is that they are based on congressional elections and therefore combine partisan with incumbency advantage. One way to overcome this problem for states would be to code and average election results from a wider variety of elections (e.g., Bond et al. 1985). Palfrey and Erikson (1993) suggest a measure that is purged of incumbency advantage. This measure is only defined for districts where incumbents faced challengers, thus significantly reducing the House sample by 100 cases, nor have they developed a state equivalent of the measure.

6. A partisan vote measure is first calculated, running from 0.0 (pure Democratic district or state) to 1.0 (pure Republican). My partisan balance measure runs from 0.0 to 1.0, where 0.0 represents a completely non-competitive district (either 100 percent Republican or Democratic normal vote) and 1.0 represents a perfectly divided district (essentially the vote measure folded about its midpoint, then multiplied by two.)

or where advertising (or other distribution) costs are lower, we would expect elections, ceteris paribus, to be more competitive.[7]

Potential routes for information dissemination include television, radio, newspaper, and interpersonal communication. Data are readily available for only one: television markets. Therefore, I rely on information about television markets in order to describe media structure in political settings. My measures of the information environment reflect two broad features of the television market that affect the strategic thinking of political campaigners: cost and efficiency.[8] As an additional, indirect measure of the communication environment, I compare population density in states and congressional districts.

The drawbacks to this decision are obvious. Although television market structure may be a valid standard of comparison for states, it is a much less obvious one for congressional districts. Senate candidates rely on television for many reasons. It is an efficient means of communicating with large, widely scattered populations (Jacobson 1997; Fenno 1982). Senate candidates have more money to spend and thus a greater ability to spend on television advertising. Senators receive more free television coverage than representatives do (Fenno 1982; Hess 1986; Foote and Weber 1984). Previous research has shown that the efficiency of television markets affects how much Senate candidates spend and how much voters learn (Stewart 1989a; Stewart and Reynolds 1990).

More surprising, perhaps, is a parallel finding for congressional districts (Campbell, Alford, and Henry 1984; Niemi, Powell, and Bicknell 1986; Fowler and McClure 1989, chap. 2). One explanation is provided by Niemi and his colleagues: television market efficiency predicts information levels because television markets serve as surrogates for other media markets (radio and newspaper): "the correlation between newspaper-district congruence and television-district congruence is probably very high" (1986, 195). Other researchers respond that newspapers are the main source of information in House campaigns. Goldenberg and Traugott stress the relative infrequency of television advertising in House campaigns (1984, 117). Westlye suggests that even in Senate races information dissemination occurs mostly through newspapers (1986, chap. 3). It would be reassuring if television markets are surrogates for newspaper markets. My suspicion is that they are not. This does not explain how the findings of Goldenberg and Traugott and Niemi can be reconciled. Nor does it answer the question of whether using television market data is a

---

7. I am grateful to Charles Stewart for substantial help with this section.

8. The formulas used to calculate the cost, contiguity, and dominance measures are contained in appendix A.

meaningful way to characterize congressional districts. Practical considerations dominate this decision. A measure based on television markets is the only alternative available for all congressional districts and states. I use cost and efficiency measures of the television markets for states and congressional districts.[9]

Television markets are not the only way to represent the information environment. A different angle on information dissemination is this: the more dense a district is, the more likely it is that a variety of communications channels will emerge, including traditional mass media, local media sources, and interpersonal communication. I also compare states and congressional districts on population density. My assumption is that the more dense a district is, the easier it will be for candidates to reach a large number of voters. They can afford to be relatively less active in dense districts.

Similar or Different? Comparing States and Congressional Districts

How similar or how different are states and congressional districts on measures of demographic diversity, media market efficiency, population density, and partisan division? It comes as no surprise that states, on average, are larger and more populous than congressional districts. Still, greater size does not necessarily translate into greater diversity. As I will demonstrate, unlike the archetypal description, on most demographic measures there are substantial overlaps, with *both* the most homogeneous and most heterogeneous districts being congressional districts. At the same time, states have substantially more efficient media markets. Finally, Senate candidates face a more balanced partisan environment. The consequence of this latter difference could be substantial. Even if states and congressional districts are not distinctive demographically, they may be politically. In a final section, I attempt to sort out this finding and discuss its potential consequences for campaigns and elections.

A Most Similar Comparison: Demographic Diversity

The geography of congressional districts is designed to encourage more personalized and localized politics. Congressional districts are much smaller and

---

9. *Contiguity* represents the relative degree of overlap between the electoral district and the Arbitron area of dominant influence (ADI), a categorization of counties as television markets. Contiguity runs from zero, or one ADI for every county, to one, or a perfect overlap between district and ADI. *Dominance* represents the degree to which a district is served by a few (a single ADI results in a value or 1.0) or many (closer to zero) ADIs. Finally, *per capita cost* and *average cost* are measures that represent the relative costs of advertising on the six o'clock news across a district. See appendix A for more complete information.

less populous than the average state. The smallest state comprises more than a thousand square miles, while the smallest congressional district is only seven. State populations are a magnitude larger. The size difference, in particular, looms large. Nonetheless, as shown in the last two columns of table 3.1, differences in size do not necessarily translate directly into more diverse constituencies.

On all measures, a congressional district is both maximally and minimally diverse (at least as reflected in the minimum, maximum, means, and standard deviations). The variation among congressional districts is larger than the variation among states (see col. 3). States are not substantially more heterogeneous than congressional districts when the measure of heterogeneity relies on racial, occupational, percentage urban, income, or educational variability. On all measures, states are slightly more diverse than congressional districts, but the differences are neither statistically nor substantively significant. When appeals to heterogeneity are made in order to account for Senate/House differences, political scientists should be aware that *demographic diversity* cannot be what is meant.

As I have argued at multiple points, descriptive statistics, particularly the mean, can be deceptive. Do these results hold up when I use a more nuanced measure of diversity? I answer this question in some detail by looking at racial diversity. I deal much more quickly with the other characteristics since the conclusions are exactly the same: there is little or no basis upon which to argue that states are uniquely diverse political settings. In this case, at least, the simple descriptive statistics were not deceptive at all.

Figure 3.1 is a histogram of racial diversity for states and congressional districts (CDs). The horizontal axis of this figure represents the diversity score calculated for either a state or a congressional district. On the vertical axis, I have plotted the percentage of total election districts (435 congressional districts or 50 states) at that level of diversity.[10] Below this, I report the mean variance and standard deviation (of the diversity measure) for states and congressional districts, and a test statistic that tells whether the two distributions are statistically distinguishable.[11] Empirically, the most diverse districts tend to be congregated in urban areas with high concentrations of both blacks and Latinos (Los Angeles, New York, Dallas, and Houston) as well as cities with

---

10. The diversity measure can be interpreted as the probability that a randomly selected pair of individuals would differ on the characteristic in question.

11. The Kolmogorov-Smirnov test compares means and variances of two samples. The associated probability level tests whether the Senate and House variances are *the same*. Thus, a high p-value implies a high probability that the cases (states and congressional districts) are drawn from identical (or at least similar) distributions (Blalock 1979, 266–69).

TABLE 3.1. Demographic Characteristics of Election Districts

Characteristic		Mean	Standard Deviation	Min	Max
As of 1970					
Population	States	3,702,914	3,915,537	302,173	19,953,134
	CDs	464,769	27,296	302,173	617,761
Black	States	0.082	0.094	0	0.37
	CDs	0.105	0.144	0	0.889
Blue collar	States	0.353	0.06	0.21	0.468
	CDs	0.361	0.079	0.073	0.592
Urban	States	0.529	0.263	0	0.927
	CDs	0.681	0.343	0	0.1
Income	States	9,166.28	1,473.21	6,068	12,441
	CDs	9,630.04	2,121.00	826	17,102
High school	States	0.531	0.081	0.378	0.673
	CDs	0.522	0.106	0.246	0.803
As of 1980					
Population	States	4,518,143	4,715,042	401,851	23,667,902
	CDs	519,327	25,040	316,619	690,768
Black	States	0.091	0.092	0.002	0.352
	CDs	0.114	0.149	0.001	0.921
Blue collar	States	0.319	0.051	0.227	0.416
	CDs	0.322	0.072	0.112	0.524
Urban	States	0.506	0.204	0.15	0.847
	CDs	0.613	0.328	0	1
Income	States	16,778.00	2,415.00	12,271	24,967
	CDs	17,105.00	3,672.00	7,461	29,806
High school	States	0.693	0.067	0.562	0.818
	CDs	0.682	0.09	0.41	0.874

relatively high proportions of Asians (Honolulu, San Francisco, and Los Angeles). An expert observer's impressions of at least one district corroborates the diversity measure. For example, in the 1980s California's Thirty-First District ranked as the most racially diverse in the country. There was a 67 percent chance that a randomly drawn pair of individuals would be of different races. *Politics in America* agreed, describing the Thirty-First District as "a working-class suburban district with more ethnic and racial diversity than is found in almost any district in the state" (Duncan 1989, 188).

TABLE 3.1. (continued)

Characteristic		Mean	Standard Deviation	Min	Max
As of 1990					
Population	States	4,960,979	5,454,770	453,588	29,706,021
	CDs	568,886	47,326	57,184	970,902
Black	States	8.646	8.384	0.3	31.6
	CDs	11.055	15.295	0.1	72.4
Blue collar	States	26.608	4.14	20.5	1,330.4
	CDs	26.663	6.989	8.5	51.6
Urban	States	67.404	15.698	28.7	92.6
	CDs	75.012	22.073	13.1	100
Income	States	34,332.24	6,054.34	24,448	49,199
	CDs	35,983.52	9,397.56	16,683	64,199
High school	States	31.992	10.435	15	98.5
	CDs	30.099	6.263	15.4	60.8

Source: 1970, 1980, and 1990 Censuses.
Note: The congressional district data are post-redistricting (1972, 1982, and 1992). The figures do not take into account lines that may have been redrawn later in the decade. Income figures represent median income.

It is apparent from the two distributions shown in figure 3.1 that states are not more racially diverse than congressional districts are. The most noticeable characteristics are the large overlap and the fat right tail of the congressional district distribution. The tail indicates that, among states and congressional districts, congressional districts are the most racially diverse. Of the 50 most diverse political settings, only two (Mississippi and Hawaii) are states. The mean values of racial diversity bear out the same point. The average congressional district is marginally more diverse on race than the average state. Overall, the two distributions are statistically indistinguishable.[12]

A series of additional comparisons reinforce this conclusion: states are just marginally more heterogeneous than congressional districts. As shown in figures 3.2 through 3.5, states contain a wider variety of occupational groups, show more variability in urban/rural residents, and vary more in income and

---

12. The means reported in each figure are not weighted by population size. I treat 50 states and 435 congressional districts as two independent samples of political settings. Although the assumption of independence is obviously incorrect, it is reasonable here. The whole point is to determine whether states, as a sample of political settings, differ from congressional districts as a sample of political settings. If I weigh the state values for diversity by their relative population sizes, the means for the 50 states and the 435 congressional districts would be identical.

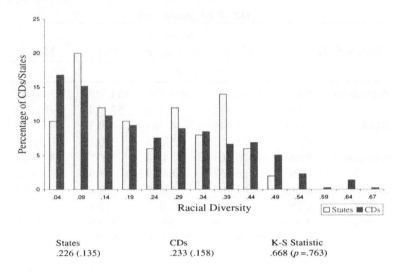

Fig. 3.1. Diversity in racial makeup, states and congressional districts

education levels. Congressional district populations, on average, vary more only on measures of racial diversity and foreign stock. On two summary measures, state populations are more diverse.[13] The tails of all the histograms are dominated by congressional districts, while states cluster in the center. The most heterogeneous and homogeneous political settings are congressional districts, not states.

It is misleading to claim that Senate candidates as a group face more heterogeneous electorates than House candidates do. This assertion overlooks an important conceptual feature of heterogeneity: it has a variance as well as a mean. These measures (race, income, education, etc.) are distributions with significant overlaps across these institutions. Put another way, heterogeneous/homogeneous and state/congressional district are not collinear. Some Senate states look more like congressional districts, and some congressional districts look like states. This means that it is possible to disentangle the political impact of district diversity from the impact of institutional makeup. What remains to be seen, though, is whether this conclusion—some differences with substantial overlaps—holds for other aspects of the political setting.

---

13. These results, which update the figures reported in Bond 1983, are reported in table A.3 in appendix A.

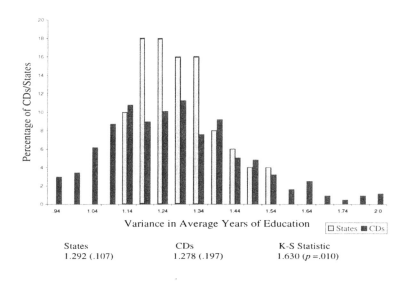

States	CDs	K-S Statistic
1.292 (.107)	1.278 (.197)	1.630 ($p = .010$)

Fig. 3.2. Variance in education levels, states and congressional districts

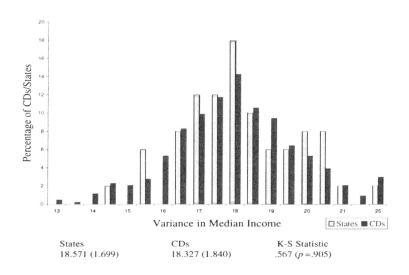

States	CDs	K-S Statistic
18.571 (1.699)	18.327 (1.840)	.567 ($p = .905$)

Fig. 3.3. Variance in income levels, states and congressional districts

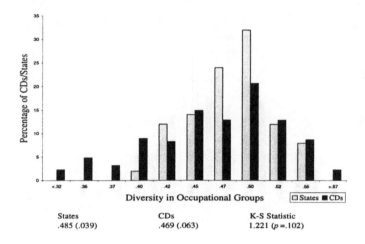

States	CDs	K-S Statistic
.485 (.039)	.469 (.063)	1.221 (p =.102)

Fig. 3.4. Diversity in occupation, states and congressional districts

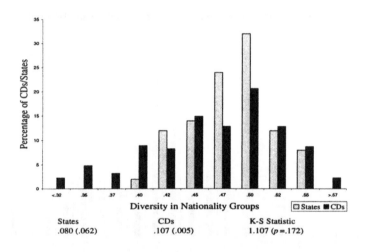

States	CDs	K-S Statistic
.080 (.062)	.107 (.005)	1.107 (p =.172)

Fig. 3.5. Diversity in nationalities, states and congressional districts

A Most Different Comparison: Media Markets and Partisan Balance

In contrast to demographic diversity, the media markets of states and congressional districts differ dramatically. In a congressional district, it is relatively easy to decide in which market to advertise—most are enveloped in a single media market (ADI).[14] However, free media time is difficult to obtain for members of the House, since high dominance is paired with low contiguity: the congressional district population makes up a small proportion of the total ADI population. For states, the situation is reversed: states are seldom dominated by a single ADI, but the contiguity of ADI and state borders is generally quite high. However, there are some notable exceptions. A few states have dominance scores that place them squarely among congressional districts and a very few district boundaries are highly contiguous with ADI boundaries. Advertising costs follow the same pattern. It is much more expensive per capita to advertise in congressional districts than it is in states. Yet the advertising costs in a few states (e.g., Delaware and Wyoming) are quite high. The only measure of the information market that shows substantial overlap between the House and the Senate is population density.

If you are campaigning for a seat in the House, it is often quite easy to decide in which television market to advertise. Forty-eight percent of the congressional districts (206 out of 432, excluding Hawaii and Alaska) have dominance scores of 1.0 (the congressional district is enveloped within a single ADI). Another third have scores ranging from .50 to .98 (see fig. 3.6). States are rarely dominated by a single ADI. Fifty percent of states have dominance scores ranging from .14 to .32, with an overall mean almost one-half the congressional district mean. States show a wider range of variation than congressional districts do. Six states have dominance scores greater than .70. All this might lead me to conclude that House candidates rely on television advertising more the Senate candidates, since the House markets are usually dominated by a single or small number of media markets.

This conclusion is obviously wrong because it fails to take into account other aspects of television markets: contiguity and cost. The population of a typical congressional district makes up a small proportion of the typical ADI. If I were to fold the dominance scale at its midpoint, I would obtain a rough approximation of contiguity (fig. 3.7). Congressional districts are not very contiguous with ADI boundaries (mean contiguity score = .264); states, in contrast, are highly contiguous with ADI's (mean score = .767). If a news

---

14. If a county is in an ADI, it means that over 50 percent of the television households receive signals from that market and so that the market is the "dominant" (most commonly received) television signal in the county.

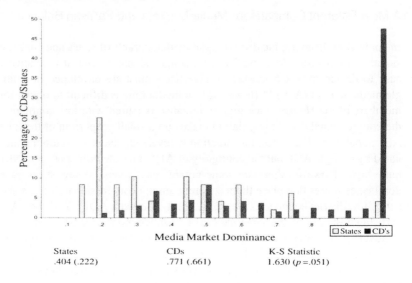

States	CDs	K-S Statistic
.404 (.222)	.771 (.661)	1.630 (p =.051)

Fig. 3.6. Media market dominance of electoral districts

editor were to take nothing into account to measure newsworthiness other than the contiguity of his ADI and a political district, the vast majority of Senate races would be "newsworthy." Challenger recognition and voter information are conditioned in large part by the amount of information provided by the mass media; therefore, Senate candidates have a distinct advantage over their House counterparts.

Advertising costs also differ in dramatic fashion between states and congressional districts. Mainly because of the efficiency of state media markets, the per capita cost of advertising is lower. Employing a television strategy, it has been suggested, is a necessity in today's competitive Senate campaigns. It is also much cheaper for a Senate candidate to employ this strategy. As is shown in figure 3.8, the per voter cost in the average congressional district is four times as great as in the average state.[15] Only 12 percent of congressional districts have a per capita advertising cost below one dollar, whereas 79 percent of states do. At the other end of the scale, it costs more than two dollars per capita to advertise in 58 percent of the congressional districts, whereas these

---

15. Notice that this is still true even though I set a threshold beyond which per capita costs cannot rise. Some of the congressional district/ADI overlaps are so small, approaching 100 households, that this threshold is a necessity in calculating reasonable cost figures.

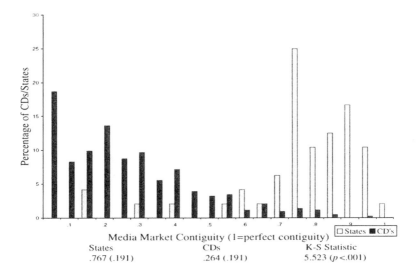

Fig. 3.7. **Contiguity of media markets and electoral districts**

advertising rates are broached in only three of 48 states. Within the Senate, there is a wide variety of advertising costs; within the House, almost all candidates face daunting advertising prices. The large populations that a Senate candidate is trying to reach combined with relatively inexpensive advertising makes it unsurprising that Senate campaigns have relied more and more on mass media appeals. On the basis of cost measures alone, one would expect that Senate candidates would have an easier time getting their names before the voters by employing television advertising.[16]

Population density further complicates the picture. In figure 3.9, I array states and congressional districts on a horizontal scale of population density (population per square mile). The data show that House members on average represent districts without the widely scattered populations that many states exhibit. If population density is a reasonable approximation for difficulty of information transmission, this indicates that, ceteris paribus, House candidates will have an *easier* time communicating with their constituents than Senate candidates do. Based on well-known findings about the recognition levels of Senate and House candidates, I know that this is not true. At least I know

---

16. A crucial test would be whether House districts where markets are efficient also rely more on television advertising relative to other sorts of campaign appeals. Since the Federal Election Commission does not require campaigns to report a breakdown of how money was spent, this cannot be explored without more detailed information about specific campaigns.

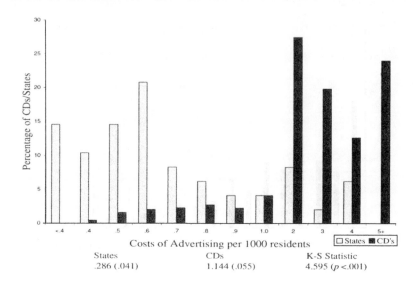

Fig. 3.8. Per capita advertising costs in electoral districts

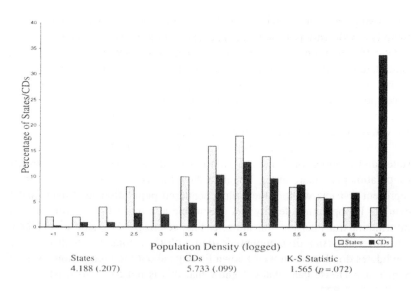

Fig. 3.9. Population density in states and congressional districts

that low recognition rates for House candidates are not a result of sparsely populated House districts. What these data do not tell me is whether low information levels are due to a lack of funds, bad candidates, or uninterested voters. Once again, this points to the necessity of considering these competing explanations simultaneously.

On average, senators will have an easier time gaining free media coverage independent of greater attention due to any increased importance of the Senate (Hess 1986). Television advertising will probably be an inefficient proposition for most members of the House, since the TV audience is not predominantly made up of their constituents, while most senators can rest assured that their campaign advertisements are viewed by eligible voters. Senators are disadvantaged by larger and less dense electorates. On the other hand, states are much more efficient media markets—they are served by fewer television stations, the boundary lines between states and ADIs are more contiguous, and it is far cheaper to advertise (on a per capita basis) in most states. Nonetheless, on all of these distributions there are interesting cases that allow me to test the theoretical assertions laid out in chapter 1. There are House districts that look like states on measures of media market efficiency and vice versa. If media market structure has the effects that I suspect it does, these cases in particular ought to reveal these effects.

There are at least two caveats to these results. First, a recent dissertation (Lipinski 1998) shows that members of the House engage in a wide variety of communications strategies. Even something as seemingly disposable as "franked" mass mailings significantly improve incumbents' images among their constituencies. Obviously, I have no leverage on these sorts of communications in this study. Second, recent changes in the information environment, specifically the emergence of cable television and the Internet, may eventually fundamentally change how voters learn about political candidates. Research results at this point, however, are preliminary (e.g., Baum and Kernell 1999; Adler et al. 1998).

The final measure of the political setting that I consider is the most explicitly political of them all: partisan balance. As with media markets, states and congressional districts are quite distinct on measures of partisan balance. Unlike media markets, however, the advantaged chamber is the House. Representatives are able to take advantage of skewed partisan distributions in their districts. Sitting senators are much more likely to represent an evenly split state.

I contrast states and congressional districts on two measures of partisan balance: average vote and partisan split. The partisan split measure is simply the average vote measure folded about its midpoint. As shown in figures

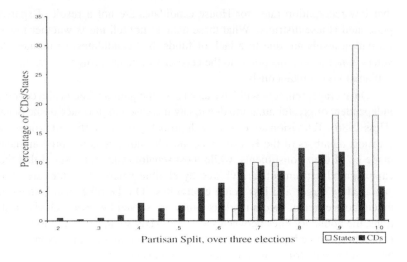

Fig. 3.10. Partisan competitiveness in electoral districts 1982–88

3.10 and 3.11, many more states are evenly split than are congressional districts. This is a direct indication that states, and Senate races, will be more competitive on average.[17]

These figures reproduce a familiar finding: elections in the Senate were more competitive in the 1980s and had been for a number of decades. The incumbency advantage has had a much smaller impact in Senate than in House elections (Kostroski 1973; Abramowitz 1980; Hibbing and Brandes 1983; Gross and Breaux 1989; for a dissenting voice, see Collier and Munger 1994). Partially confirmed, then, are the assertions of those who appeal to setting differences between the House and Senate. There is greater competitiveness in states, but it does not seem to be due to demographic diversity. Instead, vigorous party systems and balanced numbers of party loyalists are far more likely to be found in states than they are in congressional districts. Competitiveness may also be a function of more efficient media markets.

---

17. I reproduced the House distribution using a partisanship measure purged of incumbency advantage (Palfrey and Erikson, 1993). There were no obvious differences in the distribution. There are no state equivalents for the Palfrey and Erikson measure.

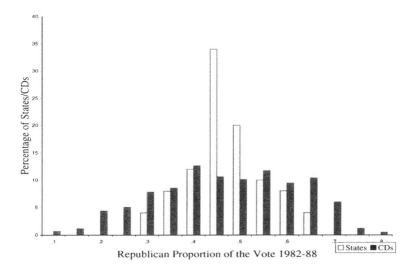

Fig. 3.11. Normal Republican vote in electoral districts 1982–88

A Sidenote on Racial Redistricting and District Diversity

It is important to consider the impact of the 1992 redistricting on district heterogeneity. Constitutional provisions, as well as a series of Supreme Court decisions, mandate that congressional district lines be redrawn following each decennial census. Not surprisingly, the results of redistricting are far from politically neutral. A craftily carved plan can cement one party's control of the legislative delegation and may even provide party control where it is undeserved. The results of redistricting can help or hinder current officeholders and future aspirants to federal office (Gronke and Wilson 1999).

The situation after the 1990 census was further complicated by the requirement for minority-majority districts, which was laid out most explicitly in the 1982 amendments to the Voting Rights Act and the 1986 *Thornburg v. Gingles* decision. Clearly, the 1992 reapportionment gave rise to powerful political struggles throughout the nation, particularly in the South. Many southern states witnessed an uneasy alliance of Republicans and black activists, each with a shared interest in creating minority-majority seats but each realizing their differences on many other political matters. These differences, and the impact of racial redistricting on the representation of black interests, are laid out most carefully by David Lublin (1997).

Nonetheless, did these significant changes in redistricting modify the relative levels of heterogeneity in the House and Senate? In fact, they did not. As shown in table 3.1, there was no substantial jump in racial homogeneity in the 1990s. The requirement for equal population districts (required since the 1960s) led to more heterogeneous congressional districts (making them more comparable to states) (Baker 1995, chap. 4). Ironically, creating minority-majority seats had the same impact. Remember that *balanced* demographic divisions lead to higher scores on the diversity measure—and balanced divisions are precisely what the Justice Department and the Court require (Gronke and Wilson 1999; Lublin 1997). Racial redistricting created some less heterogeneous districts, as blacks were removed from districts that were controlled by Democratic incumbents. It also created some that were more heterogeneous, primarily minority-majority districts with just over 50 percent black populations. The 1990 redistricting had a substantial impact on the political dynamics of particular districts and on the membership of state and the national legislatures. Racial redistricting did not have a significant impact on the relative levels of heterogeneity and diversity of congressional districts and states.

Conclusion

Political setting includes both the constituency features (who lives in a district, what they want from government) and the structural features (size, shape, lines of communication) of an electoral district that influence campaigners and election outcomes. A politician or candidate seldom views his or her constituency as composed of individuals. They rely on simplifying cues, just as voters do. Group memberships—racial, ethnic, and economic categories—are the dominant way that a politician identifies interests in his or her constituency (Kingdon 1968, 1988). Furthermore, politicians recognize that constituencies display variances—it is not just the "average" voter but the variety or heterogeneity of a district that has to be represented (see Fiorina 1974 for the most completely developed theoretical description of this relationship). Finally, the electoral district has certain structural features that constrain candidate actions. These features include the ease of reaching individual voters.

What I have done here is reorganize the contents of these categories. To political setting, I have explicitly added structural features of the district such as media market efficiency and population density. Partisan diversity is important enough to deserve separate treatment. I have shown that states and congressional districts differ but not in ways that would be expected. There is a large amount of overlap on demographic measures of diversity, with averages that are statistically indistinct. On media market measures, states and congressional districts are clearly different, with media markets in states being much more efficient and the costs lower. Partisan balance is another way that congressional districts and states differ. There are very few states that are skewed to one end or another on partisanship.

Ross Baker, in his important study *House and Senate* (1995), suggests that the most notable difference between congressional districts and states is the loss of "intimacy" among states. The kinds of personal relations that are possible in relatively small, geographically contiguous, congressional districts are inconceivable in the typical state. Baker also points to a number of other ways that states differ from congressional districts—states are more heterogeneous, media markets are less efficient—but in the end he returns to a theme of "loss of control." Senators simply cannot comprehend all the diverse interests and groups in a typical state.

This chapter takes Baker's observations on district geography and subjects them to a careful test. In some ways, they remain unchallenged. Size and scope are two undeniable differences between Senate and House electoral environments. From the perspective of an electoral analyst, in contrast to Baker's more institutional viewpoint, similarities emerge as frequently as differences do.

States and congressional districts are not as different as a superficial view would have us believe. States are not exceptionally heterogeneous, nor are congressional district unusually homogeneous. Rather than asserting that states are simply more complex, I need to attend to the shared features of states and congressional districts and to other ways in which they might diverge. The overlap of media markets and election districts is more efficient in most states. It is no great insight to realize that in some ways congressional districts and states look similar and in other ways they differ. If, however, characteristics of a political district operate to constrain the actions of campaigners, these effects ought to be observed across institutional settings. If they are not, then the political context cannot be cited as a cause free of institution. With a set of measures of the political setting that are truly comparable in states and congressional districts, I can test several hypotheses about the relationship between political settings, institutional arrangements, and campaign dynamics.

CHAPTER 4

The Campaign: Quality Candidates and Campaign Funding

House and Senate candidacies include quixotic efforts by unknown challengers, poorly funded campaigns by reputable challengers, well-funded efforts by political novices, and, of course, incumbent and challenger operations that rival small corporations. Our political system is highly permeable, marked by the ability of new elites to enter at all levels, even contesting the presidency. One step back from the idiosyncracies of individual candidates and campaigns broad patterns emerge. It is the task of this chapter to unearth these broad patterns over the past two decades and assess their stability across the U.S. House and Senate.

My claim, laid out in chapter 2, is that House and Senate campaigns are driven by four factors: the nature of the electoral districts, attributes of political institutions, the natures of the candidates, and their political campaigns. I showed in chapter 3, that many states that look like congressional districts and many congressional districts look like states. Consequently, following the hypotheses laid out in chapter 2, there should be *Senate campaigns* that look like *House campaigns* and vice versa. Furthermore, I should be able to explain and predict these similarities.

In this chapter, I examine whether Senate and House campaigns are really different. I compare them on three dimensions—candidate quality, campaign spending, and campaign intensity. Senate elections typically feature highly qualified candidates, comparatively high expenditures, and intensely fought campaigns. House elections, in contrast, are characterized as noncompetitive, low-spending affairs with inexperienced challengers. As I have argued, however, focusing on the average case is misleading. Averages alone cannot help answer these questions:

- What relative proportion of Senate and House candidates are of high quality?
- Are Senate campaigns more expensive once the larger size of Senate electorates is taken into account?

61

- Once I control for different levels of campaign intensity across institutions, do institutional differences disappear?

All of these touch on the core questions of this book: what are the similarities as well as differences between House and Senate candidates and campaigns, and can they be brought under a single analytic umbrella?

I proceed by describing my data and measures. The discussion of candidate quality is brief, given the widespread agreement about its importance and measurement. Campaign activity is substantially more complicated. In order to simplify the analysis, I choose to examine one measure of campaign flow—campaign spending—and avoid content measures altogether. I discuss the implications of this decision later. Finally, I compare candidate quality and campaign spending levels in House and Senate races from 1982–96. I close with a discussion of an alternative measure of campaign activity—campaign intensity—and show how it is really a product of spending and candidate quality.[1]

The evidence demonstrates, as will not be surprising to anyone familiar with U.S. elections, that Senate campaigns are more intensely fought, with higher levels of campaign spending and more experienced challengers. Nevertheless, Senate and House campaigns can be arrayed on a common metric. There is substantially more overlap on measures of candidate quality, campaign spending, and campaign intensity than might be expected. In particular, once campaign expenditures are adjusted on a per capita basis—a wholly reasonable procedure given the larger populations of many states—Senate and House candidates spend comparable amounts of money. In hard-fought campaigns, in fact, there are few differences between House and Senate in either rates of spending or quality of opponents. In the typical, low-profile candidacy—most often House contests—competitors suffer from poor political skills, poor resources, and, as I will show in later chapters, poor name recognition and little chance of success. On the other hand, in the most intensely fought races during the 1980s and 1990s, Senate and House campaigns look quite similar. The obvious expectation is that campaign dynamics and voter choice will display equal similarities. Those matters are deferred until chapter 5.

---

1. Campaign intensity deserves special attention because recent studies of Senate campaigns (Kahn and Kenney 1997; Westlye 1989; Sinclair 1990) and a comparative study of Senate and House campaigns (Krasno 1994) all rely heavily on an intensity measure.

Campaign Activity and Candidate Quality

As with chapter 3, this chapter is primarily concerned with description and measurement. The theoretical background and hypotheses were presented in chapter 2 and will not be repeated here. First, I explain how I determine what races to look at and how I measure candidate quality and campaign spending. Then, in a set of graphical and tabular displays, I show how the apparent dissimilarity of Senate and House campaigns is misleading. This leads naturally to chapter 5, where I bring together stage 1 (setting and institution) and stage 2 (campaigning) of the electoral process.

What Races?

The first decision that I have to make is what kinds of races to examine. Congressional contests fall naturally into three categories: unopposed (almost all incumbents), open seats, and incumbent/challenger. One set of races can easily be eliminated—unopposed. There is no point in comparing campaign spending and challenger quality levels when there is only one candidate.[2] Open seats are a more problematic category. On the one hand, if the aim is to select out a set of comparable contests, then open seats can be revealing. They are almost always fiercely contested in the Senate and quite often in the House. Unfortunately, they are rare enough in both chambers that any comparisons will be tentative at best (273 House and 45 Senate seats from 1982 to 1996, an average of only 33.0 House and 5.5 Senate seats per election cycle). I adopt a mixed strategy. I exclude open-seat races from most of the structural models that are estimated in later chapters, but include them in the descriptive analyses reported in this chapter.

That leaves incumbent/challenger contests as the primary focus in this study. I do not eliminate any cases based on either the amount of spending by the challenger or the final vote margin. As long as there is a challenger who is a Republican or Democrat, who reports some campaign expenditures, and who receives some votes in the general election, the race is included in the sample.

---

2. On average, 15 percent of House seats go uncontested (Jacobson 1997). The almost total lack of unopposed seats is a distinguishing feature of the modern Senate. During the period covered by this study, only four Senate seats went uncontested—all in 1990—even with incumbents like Sam Nunn (D-GA) and Spark Matsunaga (D-HI) rolling to victories in the 1980s and Charles Grassley (R-IA), Daniel Ikaka (D-HI), and Orrin Hatch (R-UT) posting 70 percent margins in the 1990s. This observation by itself is evidence of greater competition in the Senate.

Measuring Candidate Quality

A "high-quality" candidate can mean many things. A candidate might "fit" particularly well with the district. It might refer to fundraising prowess or a high public profile. One would hope that "quality" candidates also have a desire to improve government and formulate superior public policies. For my purposes, candidate quality is a way of capturing those features of a candidate that are likely to increase his or her chances to win the election—features that make someone a strong contender. It encompasses both previous political and elective experience and celebrity status, notoriety, or other features that lend him or her particular prominence. I include previous political experience because experience demonstrates at least some experience with organizing a campaign, appealing to donors and voters, and, hopefully, winning an election. I also consider celebrity status or great wealth, since these also help candidates gain recognition (or, in the case of celebrities, indicate that they are already well recognized) and attract campaign donations. Following conventional practice, I report both a dichotomous measure indicating whether the candidate has held previous office (Jacobson 1997, 1990a; Abramowitz 1988; Bianco 1984) and a more elaborate, four-point scale (Canon, 1990). There are more complex alternatives, some of which adjust for the proportion of overlap between previous elective office and current office.[3] Krasno and Green (1988), the leading example, employ a six-point scale, but this complex measure considers 11 separate criteria. They worry about bias in the measure because some races may be more closely covered than others. Unfortunately, this concern has become more serious given recent changes in the coverage of congressional campaigns by the *Congressional Quarterly,* the most commonly used source. I discuss this problem later.

The dichotomous measure is coded one when the candidate has held any previous elective office and zero otherwise. Unlike Squire (1989), I give credit for any elective office, not just officeholding during recent years. The four-point scale, adapted from David Canon's work, has levels for any elective office, other political appointments or employment (legislative assistants, party workers, etc.), ambitious amateurs (previous attempts at public office, previous success in primaries, great personal wealth), and others.[4]

---

3. In theory, this can be calculated for the House, but it would be practically impossible without sophisticated geographical mapping software. Squire's measure has only been reported for the Senate; see Squire 1989, 1992; and Smith and Squire 1991.

4. I am grateful to Gary Jacobson and David Canon for allowing me access to data for 1980–86, and to Patrick Sellers for House candidate data for 1992–96. All data for 1988 and 1990, and Senate data for 1992–96 were coded by the author. Reliability checks were performed on 25 percent of the data coded by Canon and recoded by the author or research assistants. All

Measuring Campaign Activity

The nature of the candidates is one part of the campaign; the campaign itself is the other. I need to distill out some subset of the category "campaign activity"—I cannot measure every punch and counterpunch in over 2,000 campaigns across eight election cycles. In chapter 2, I argue that campaigns can be defined by flow and content. To simplify matters, I compare the House and Senate on only one measure of campaign flow: campaign spending.

In our candidate-centered election system, the bulk of campaigning is performed by candidate organizations.[5] A measure of organizational activity will probably also be a good measure of campaign activity. My primary measure is money. Most of what campaigns do—travel, advertise, coordinate activities, pay staff, raise additional funds—costs money. Furthermore, it is straightforward to find out how much money is being raised and how much is being spent. Since the passage of the Federal Elections and Campaigns Act, candidates for federal offices have to file periodic financial reports with the Federal Election Commission.[6] I deflate spending to 1982 dollars and adjust it to a per capita figure in order to take into account variations in state and congressional district populations.

Campaign spending is my measure of campaign activity. How much does it miss? One can easily imagine a situation in which there is lots of spending

coding disagreements centered on the definition of *celebrity.* For example, is Hillary Clinton's brother a celebrity? There were only 14 total cases in which there was disagreement. The four-point scale is described in more detail in Canon 1990, chapters 3-4. Canon's scale runs from 1 to 5 for Senate candidates and 1 to 4 for House candidates (with 5 being awarded for Senate candidates who had previously been in the Senate or the House or had held statewide office). To make the data comparable across the House and Senate, I collapsed levels 4 and 5.

5. While party organizations have reemerged in recent decades by some measures, they mainly play a service role in federal contests. Money, consulting expertise, and poll information is provided to candidate organizations. The amount of independent campaigning performed by parties is quite low (Herrnson 1995; Sorauf and Wilson 1990). Moreover, most party, political action committee, and individual activities—mainly in the form of fund raising—are channeled through candidate organizations.

6. The leading protagonists in the debate over campaign spending (Jacobson 1997, 1990a, 1985; Green and Krasno 1990, 1988) use early release Federal Election Commision (FEC) data taken from press releases after the election or published in the *Almanac of American Politics* or *Politics in America* (which also use early release information). Candidates have years to make amendments to these numbers, as new bills appear, old bills get paid, and the books are finally balanced. The discrepancies I found between the final FEC figures (as reported in data files archived at the Institute for Political and Social Research at the University of Michigan) and the figures reported in the volumes cited earlier are sometimes in the hundreds of thousands of dollars (though these large discrepancies are unusual). I do not know whether these discrepancies make any difference in the results reported by Jacobson and Green and Krasno. In order to avoid such discrepancies, I rely on the final release FEC data.

without much information. In 1988, Congressman Dan Rostenkowski of Illinois, then the powerful chair of the House Ways and Means Committee, spent $428,000, while his opponent's spending was too low to be reported. There are many reasons why Rostenkowski spent at such high rates: to discourage quality opposition (Jacobson and Kernell 1981); to boost his margin in order to impress colleagues in the House; and, last but surely not least, simply because the money was there. As chair of the main tax-writing committee in Congress, "Rosty" faced no shortage of willing campaign contributors. Does this indicate an information-rich campaign environment in the Eighth District of Illinois? I have my doubts. In contrast, during most of his storied career, Senator William Proxmire of Wisconsin often spent less than $1,000 on his reelection bids, yet he won handily. William Natcher, cited in the opening chapter, routinely spent one-tenth as much as his opponents, yet he did not face a serious electoral challenge for decades. In still other instances, a challenger may spend a large amount without ever gaining measurable voter recognition. To further complicate matters, the disbursements reported by the Federal Election Commission only represent *total* spending. Administrative and organizational costs are lumped in with information-providing expenditures.

This discussion raises a number of red flags about campaign spending. It is an incomplete measure of campaign activity and should be complemented by other measures when possible. Voters draw upon past experiences with the candidate as much as, and in many cases more than, the current campaign. Models of voter information levels need to take previous elections into account.[7] Finally, because spending is not broken into functional categories, the relationship between spending and voter information will be attenuated.

A Digression: Identifying "Intense" Campaigns

Are there alternative measures for campaign activity besides campaign spending? Many scholars code campaigns according to their *intensity*. Westlye's pathbreaking analyses show that the intensity of a campaign is a key determinant of challenger success or failure. Intensity strongly influences voter information levels as well as the vote. Campaign intensity is obviously an important criterion for understanding Senate contests (Kahn and Kenney 1997; Krasno 1994; Westlye 1991, 1986). The problem is that there is no agreed upon way to gauge campaign intensity and the data source most often used to determine the coding has been changing over time.

Westlye codes campaign intensity by collecting descriptions about the races from various published sources and coding races as "hard-fought" or "low-key" based on this information. His main source for descriptions of the

---

7. This comes into play in chap. 6.

race is the semiannual special election report published by the *Congressional Quarterly* (CQ), supplemented with other written descriptions when necessary (such as the *Cook Report* or the *National Journal*). This is obviously a complicated procedure, although one that draws on a wide array of available information. Barbara Sinclair (1990) suggests a simpler surrogate for intensity: recode the "calls" of House and Senate races made by the same political observers at CQ.[8] If either of these measures of campaign intensity performs well, they will be useful complements to campaign spending.

Unfortunately, there are serious problems with both. Westlye's measure is based on published information that has been changing in both quality and quantity over time. Prior to 1986, the *Congressional Quarterly Weekly Report* provided a brief description of every House and Senate race. Starting in 1986, only the competitive or interesting House races were described. For example, in 1988, 90 races receive special mention, whereas by 1996 only a few dozen merited close coverage.[9] A measure based on the CQ descriptions will become less reliable as coverage of House races is reduced.[10]

Sinclair's alternative fails validity tests. She validates her use of the CQ call in 1988 by means of a favorable comparison with Krasno 1989(one disagreement out of 27). It performs far less favorably in additional years, as is shown in table 4.1. The basic problem is that Sinclair measures the wrong thing. The CQ reporters gauge the closeness and intensity of the race as well as the likely outcome. While it is true that close races will tend to be more intense, it is not necessarily true that all intense races are close.

The ratio of incumbent to challenger spending is a third alternative measure of campaign intensity.[11] This takes advantage of what is already known about campaign spending—candidates spend reactively (Jacobson 1990a, 1997; Green and Krasno 1988, 1990). Ratios close to 1:1 indicate an active, vigorous

8. The "call" is a seven-point scale, running from safe Democratic to safe Republican. Sinclair (1990) recodes this as a dichotomous intensity measure.

9. One possible course to follow would be to assume that contests not explicitly covered by CQ are low-intensity races. This does not seem unreasonable.

10. Starting with the 1998 election cycle, two alternative online sources have become available. Campaign coverage on the *National Journal* web site, http://www.nationaljournal.com, does not approach the elaborate coverage in the pre-1988 CQ, but it is more extensive than that in the printed copies of *Congressional Quarterly Weekly Report* or the *National Journal*. The problem with National Journal site is that the content changes daily or weekly, so scholars need to monitor updates to the site. Second, Project Vote Smart http://www.votesmart.org, while it does not provide information relevant to campaign intensity, has a wealth of biographical and other candidate information that is no longer available in the printed weeklies or online sites maintained by the *Congressional Quarterly*.

11. Westlye (1991) and Krasno (1989, 1994) employ the ratio rule when their readings of other information on campaign intensity are inconclusive.

TABLE 4.1. Comparison of Intensity Codings: Three Sample Years

Year	Race Type	Westlye (1991)	CQ Call	Spending Ratio
1980	low-key	11	14	11
	hard-fought	17	14	17
1982	low-key	15	7	11
	hard-fought	15	23	19
1984	low-key	19	16	20
	hard-fought	9	12	8

Source: Westlye 1991; CQ call measures and campaign spending ratios calculated by the author.
Note: Races are categorized into low-key or hard-fought. Westlye (1991) codes are taken from the appendix to his book. CQ call follows the coding scheme proposed by Sinclair (1990). The spending ratio rule is to code a race low key when the incumbent or one candidate in an open-seat spends more than twice what the opponent spends.

challenge, whereas ratios greater than 2:1 suggest an incumbent swamping the challenger. The *ratio* is thus the gauge of campaign intensity.[12] This measure takes into account the variation across states and congressional districts in population size, media market efficiency, and heterogeneity. Westlye (1991), who proposes this measure, also notes some of its faults. By his reading, at least three Senate races between 1972 and 1986 are incorrectly categorized.[13] Still, the ratio rule has much to recommend it. The data are readily available. The measure can be calculated as either a dichotomy or a continuous variable. If Westlye's intensive reading is taken as a guide, the spending ratio measure performs far better than an alternative based on CQ call (see table 4.1). Spending ratios also reflect in a more direct way the intensity of campaign competition.

12. In open-seat races, a spending ratio less than 2:1 qualifies as an intense race. In races involving challenges to incumbents, a ratio of incumbent to challenger spending under 2:1 qualifies as an intense race. Note the latter standard means that *any* race in which the challenger spends more than one-half the incumbent qualifies as intense.

13. These are Virginia, 1978, Warner versus Miller, in which John Warner spent "far more" than his opponent yet Westlye identifies this as a hard-fought race; and Wisconsin, 1976, 1982, William Proxmire in which Proxmire spent only $692 and zero in his two races. As a result, the ratio of incumbent to challenger spending would identify these races as highly intense, whereas they were "among the lowest of low-key" (Westlye 1991, 23). William Natcher's House races would also be incorrectly categorized. For the period 1972–1988, the spending ratio and intensive reading agree 81 percent of the time (23). Four of the 19 discrepant cases were analyzed more intensively by Westlye. For these four cases, he feels the CQ reading was more accurate and the spending ratio classification would have been incorrect.

For all of these reasons, I opt for spending ratios as my principal measure of campaign intensity. I retain the untransformed version of the CQ call measure as a gauge of the closeness of a race.

Similar or Different? Comparing Senate and House Campaigns

Senate campaigns are generally described as more competitive, with higher levels of spending and higher quality candidates. Is this really the case? The average Senate challenger is more likely to have previous political experience than the average House challenger. On average, Senate candidates spend more money than their House counterparts, although once spending is adjusted to a per capita basis the gap between the Senate and the House narrows considerably. And the average Senate challenger is more likely to have previous political experience. The answer seems clear: the Senate and the House are obviously distinct electoral arenas.

The distributions, in contrast to the averages, tell a very different story. Many House challengers are politically savvy, high-spending candidates, just like the typical Senate candidate. Not surprisingly, the most experienced, best-funded House candidates are concentrated in the most competitive races. Similarly, as Westlye discovered in the late 1970s and early 1980s, candidates in low-intensity Senate contests are often just as inexperienced and underfunded as their House counterparts. By looking at the distributions rather than just the means, I show that Senate and House candidacies and campaigns are eminently comparable in the essential meaning of that term. They are not identical, but I can *compare* them on a common metric. I demonstrate this point in the next two sections.

Candidate Quality in the House and Senate

The distribution of candidate quality is reported in table 4.2. Higher quality candidates run for the U.S. Senate. Over the eight election cycles considered in this study, Senate candidates were nearly three times as likely on average to have held elective office (compare the "elective office" column in table 4.2).[14] The least-experienced set of Senate candidates over this period ran in 1982 (though 1992 came close), yet even then over half had held previous elective office. In 1988, almost 65 percent had, compared to less than a third of House candidates. The much vaunted year of the outsider, 1994, was not a year in which candidates had particularly low levels of political expertise; it was just a year in which Republican challengers in the House knocked

14. Entries in table 4.2 include open-seat races as well as races involving incumbents. Uncontested elections are excluded.

TABLE 4.2. Challenger Quality in the Senate and House, 1982–96

	Insti- tution	Amateur (1)	Ambitious Amateur (2)	Political Office (3)	Elective Office (4)	$\bar{x}$
1982–90						
All races	Senate	.10	.09	.35	.46	2.87
	House	.68	.04	.15	.13	1.74
High	Senate	.06	.06	.29	.58	3.37
intensity	House	.42	.05	.21	.32	2.43
Low	Senate	.19	.21	.30	.30	2.71
intensity	House	.76	.03	.13	.08	1.53
1992–96						
All races	Senate	.24	.02	.15	.59	3.09
	House	.67	.07	.10	.16	1.75
High	Senate	.14	.03	.14	.69	3.38
intensity	House	.34	.15	.17	.35	2.55
Low	Senate	.39	.02	.15	.44	2.64
intensity	House	.78	.04	.07	.10	1.47

Source: Calculated by the author (all 1990–96 data, House candidate quality for all years); David Canon (Senate candidate quality, 1982–88).
Note: The table covers races from 1982 to 1996. Entries are the mean value on Canon's four-point candidate quality scale. High and low intensity are defined by the ratio of challenger to incumbent spending. Entries in columns 3 through 6 are the proportion of challengers falling into each level of candidate quality. The final column contains the mean candidate quality score.

off many Democratic incumbents (although the crop of House challengers in 1994 was also of particularly high quality—see Jacobson 1996). Senate challengers similarly took up the anti-Washington cudgel. On the four-point scale, competitors for Senate seats during the 1980s ranked a full point above House competitors and a point and a quarter in the 1990s (final column of table 4.2). Overall, 54 percent of Senate candidates in 1982–96 (in all races, not just incumbent/challenger) had no previous political or elective experience versus 86 percent of House candidates. Krasno (1994) found similar results. Employing a six-point measure, he reports that "just 10 percent of House challengers were rated as 5's or 6's. ... [M]eanwhile, 55 percent of 27 Senate challengers rated in the top quality groups, while just 11 percent were in the lowest" (94). Similar findings are reported by Jacobson (1997, 1996) and Mattei (1996). The Senate is a more attractive institution; it clearly attracts higher quality, more experienced (and, as I will show, better funded) candidates.

These results are unsurprising. Conventional wisdom states that the average Senate candidate is more experienced and better known than the average House candidate. One way to challenge the conventional wisdom is via a simple control for campaign intensity. Although large gaps remain in the quality of the average Senate and House challenger, there may be significant numbers of low-quality Senate challengers clustered in low-intensity contests. High-quality challengers, in contrast, may cluster in high-intensity races regardless of the institution. This is exactly what would be predicted based on the strategic politicians model of Jacobson and Kernell (1983), Schlesinger's (1966) ambition theory, and the candidate emergence model of Canon (1990). Experienced politicians choose races in which the chances of winning are higher; their fund-raising and other political abilities thereby create more competitive contests. The strategic politician and ambitious politician models are not limited to a single institution—neither should many of our electoral theories be.

A closer look at table 4.2 confirms these expectations. Many candidates do not fit into the convenient cubbyholes of conventional wisdom. In high-intensity races, there are substantial numbers of House challengers who meet the high standards normally associated with Senate contenders. Low-intensity contests, in contrast, are far more likely to feature low-quality challengers regardless of the institutional setting. From 1982 to 1996, 79 percent of the low-quality Senate challengers and 72 percent of the low-quality House challengers were competing in low-intensity races.[15] Krasno (1994) found even more extreme distributions for 1988: *all* low quality Senate challengers and 94 percent of low-quality House challengers were competing in low-intensity races. There have been some shifts in recent years—like Mattei 1996 (40-42), I find that challenger quality in Senate races increased after 1990, especially when the seat was open.

Perhaps these figures are skewed by the impact of incumbency. Since campaign intensity is driven in large part by whether or not an incumbent is running, institutional differences may be more evident in open seats, where House/Senate differences in incumbency are not involved and the contest is more competitive for both parties. The patterns of candidate experience in open-seat contests, shown in table 4.3, bely this suggestion. There is little to distinguish the House and Senate throughout this period (I have merged the data from the 1980s and 1990s) other than the higher proportion of "no office" among House candidates (14 percent vs. zero percent) and the lower proportion of races in which both candidates previously held elective office (15 percent of races or 31 percent of candidates vs. 26 percent in the Senate). Senate candidates in open-seat races are of high quality, rating about a point

---

15. Low quality is defined here as categories 1 and 2 in the four-point scale (never held an elective or appointive political office).

TABLE 4.3. Candidate Quality in Open-Seat Contests, 1982–96

	Both No Office	Democrat No Office	Republican No Office	Both Held Office	Four-Point Scale
Senate	.00	.26	.21	.53	3.73 (0.65)
House	.14	.30	.22	.31	2.25 (1.39)

Source: Calculated by the author (Senate previous office, intensity); Jacobson (House, previous office); Canon (candidate quality).
Note: Challenger quality is the average value on a five-point scale. Standard errors are in parentheses.

higher than the average Senate candidate and about 1.5 points higher than their House counterparts. Still, the quality level of House candidates for open seats over the past 20 years approaches that of the typical Senate candidate (2.25 for the House in open seats vs. 2.88 for all Senate candidates). Given a highly competitive political situation—most open seats and high-intensity races involving an incumbent—differences between House and Senate candidates are substantially reduced.

What of institutional differences? In low-intensity contests, challengers are of relatively low quality in both institutions but far more so in the House. In competitive races, House challenger quality improves dramatically but still trails the rates observed in the Senate. Overall, then, Senate challengers are much better candidates for office than are House challengers based on what we believe leads to success in the general election. Controlling for intensity reduces the differences substantially, but important institutional differences remain. Excepting high-intensity contests in the 1990s, the average quality level of a Senate challenger is always a full point or more higher than that of the average House challenger. Another way to highlight the difference is to note that average House challenger quality under what might be deemed the best circumstances—a high-intensity election—is roughly comparable to average Senate challenger quality under the worst circumstances, a low-intensity contest. Even in low-intensity contests, 60 percent of Senate challengers were rated high quality, whereas approximately 52 percent of House candidates in *high-intensity* contests were equally ranked. Obviously, the Senate attracts more experienced challengers, in part at least because the Senate is a higher profile, more attractive institution (Baker 1995). It would not be surprising if the same patterns I observed are paralleled in campaign spending.

Change and Continuity: The Politics of 1994 and Beyond

The 1994 elections ushered in a new era in party politics, one so important that some suggest that the United States is in the midst of a party realignment (Aldrich 1999; Aldrich and Niemi 1996). The dynamics of congressional elections changed in this period as well. Redistricting and the creation of minority-majority seats, alluded to in chapter 3, significantly increased the number of African Americans, Hispanics, and women elected to Congress. These changes in district lines, combined with increasing Republican strength in the South, emboldened the Republican Party and led, in 1992, to the best crop of challengers in recent memory (22 percent of challengers in 1992 had previously held office; see Jacobson 1997, 155). From the state house to Washington, Republicanism was on the march. Furthermore, the anti-Washington sentiment of the Reagan era saw its full flowering in the 1992 campaign of Ross Perot. An era of the "angry American" voter seemed destined to fundamentally change our electoral system (Tolchin 1996).

There are many reasons to be skeptical of these claims. In large part, careful analyses of the 1992 presidential election have shown that economic discontent played the dominant role (and, relatedly, Clinton's reelection in 1996 was driven by economic content; see Alvarez and Nagler 1998). With regard to *who runs for Senate and House,* nothing in the decade of the 1990s changes my conclusions. Challenger quality declined somewhat in 1994, and declined even further in 1996. As we have seen, the end result, when aggregated across the post-1990 era (shown under 1992–96 in table 4.2), is an overall level, and comparative level, of candidate quality unchanged from the 1980s through the 1990s. As important as it was, 1994 should not mislead us. The apparent success of amateurs, read in the media as the flowering of the Ross Perot, Jesse Ventura, anti-politician, anti-Washington fervor, was mainly a consequence of a few high-profile, amateur victories in the Senate, a wisely chosen Republican strategy to "nationalize" the midterm race, and anti-Democratic sentiments throughout the electorate.[16]

Campaign Spending: The Per Capita Solution

Candidate quality provides the first really significant gap between the House and the Senate. The gap is attenuated once campaign intensity is taken into account, but it still remains. Campaign spending is another area where, according to common wisdom, House-Senate gaps are unbridgeable. Campaign spending levels in the Senate are of an order of magnitude greater than in the House

---

16. These points are made throughout the articles in Klinkner 1996, including Jacobson 1996 and Mattei 1996.

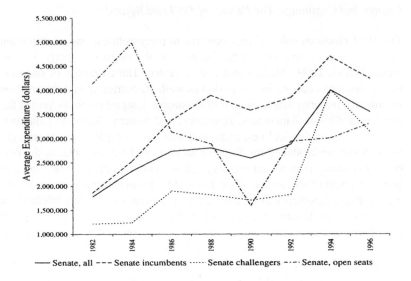

Fig. 4.1. Senate campaign expenditures, 1982–96

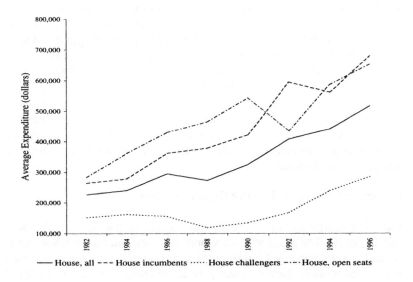

Fig. 4.2. House campaign expenditures, 1982–96

(see table 4.4), and this gap has not been reduced over the past two decades. The growth in campaign expenditures is less evident in table 4.4 because, to simplify the presentation, I report only two illustrative years.[17] In figures 4.1 and 4.2, the upward trend in overall spending over the period is clearly demonstrated. There are interesting patterns in spending—for example, the decline in Senate open-seat spending from a high point in 1984 and a less pronounced dip in House open-seat spending from 1990 to 1992. I leave these patterns aside here, for they are the purview of far more sophisticated analysts of campaign spending (e.g., Erikson and Palfrey 1998; Kenny and McBurnette 1994). What these plots illustrate are, first, the dramatic difference in levels of spending across the two institutions. If plotted on the same chart, the House figures would appear as horizontal lines at the bottom of the graphic. Second, these charts show, via rough eyeballing, that trends in spending follow the same path across institutions. Overall spending climbed at a fairly steady rate. The two series are correlated at .85, and the House series has a steeper slope.[18] For both institutions, challenger spending lags incumbent spending significantly (excepting 1994 in the Senate). Open-seat spending dipped for both, though more severely for the Senate.

I have shown in previous chapters, however, that some House/Senate differences are a function of nothing more than size. This is probably in large part due to differences in the electoral setting: states are, on average, much larger and more populous than congressional districts.[19] Whether these constitute a significant *institutional* difference is, of course, open to debate (see Baker 1995 for a strong argument that they do). Congressional campaigns, however, are at least in part an attempt to convince a fixed set of voters, regardless of whether they be 50 million Californians or 500,000 Nevadans in the First District. How much do Senate and House candidates spend per voter?

When campaign spending is expressed on a per capita basis, the House and Senate gap is dramatically reduced. In figures 4.1 and 4.2, House and Senate had to be plotted separately because the scales were so disparate. In figure 4.3, I can easily plot House and Senate together. Throughout the period, spending in Senate campaigns was approximately twice as great as spending in House

---

17. Neither was chosen because it represents a particularly distinctive year for spending. In chapter 6, 1988 is one of the two years examined intensively, and 1994 is the most recent midterm year (at the time of this writing) for purposes of comparison.

18. Assuming that the two are fixed at an order of magnitude, the House slope should be one-tenth the Senate slope. The predicted increase in spending during each two-year election cycle, based on these figures, is $40,000 for the House and $250,000 for the Senate.

19. Within the Senate, campaign spending is positively correlated with population size (.474 for Democratic candidates, .431 for Republican candidates).

TABLE 4.4. Campaign Spending in the Senate and House (in dollars)

	Senate	House
1988		
All Candidates	2,802,118	273,811
Democrats	2,934,817	287,560
Republicans	2,669,420	258,441
Incumbents	3,898,821	378,316
Challengers	1,816,113	118,877
1994		
All candidates	4,000,274	441,378
Democrats	3,395,629	487,493
Republicans	4,604,919	396,411
Incumbents	4,691,617	561,441
Challengers	3,997,104	240,188

Source: Ornstein, Mann, and Malbin 1998.

campaigns (see also col. 1 of table 4.5). Furthermore, just as we discovered when examining candidate quality, House incumbents look an awful lot like Senate challengers once campaign is adjusted. Finally, although it is risky to project too far into the future, the trends in the lines indicate that House incumbent spending is approaching Senate incumbent spending, while Senate challenger spending is approaching House challenger spending.[20]

Still, the standard deviations attached to these figures, reported in the second column of table 4.5, suggest that substantial numbers of House members will spend at Senate rates and vice versa. Figures 4.4 and 4.5 reinforce this point. The *distribution* of total spending is roughly comparable in the Senate and House, except for the larger proportion of Senate races with spending rates over two dollars per capita, and there are significant overlaps in both directions.

Spending by incumbents and challengers in the Senate and House follows many of the same patterns we saw in chapter 3. While Senate candidates spend two to three times as much as their House counterparts, with much wider variations in Senate spending, the highest spending contest was in the House, $9.50 per capita by incumbent Newt Gingrich (R-GA) in 1996. His opponent, Michael Coles, spent $3.3 million, $5.66 per capita. Given that most members of Georgia's Sixth District already recognized Gingrich's name and knew

---

20. In fact, what is happening is that Senate spending in all races, once adjusted to a per capita basis, basically has been flat since 1988, while House spending continues to increase.

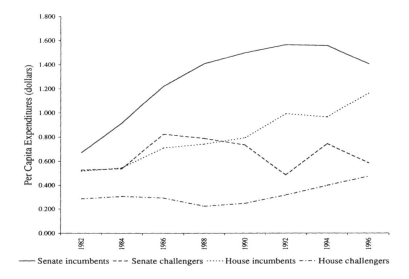

Fig. 4.3. Per capita campaign expenditures, 1982–96

TABLE 4.5. Per Capita Campaign Spending in the House and Senate

Institution and Race Type	Per Capita Spending	(Standard Deviation)	Min.	Max.
1982–1988				
House Incumbents	.633	.465	.009	5.074
House Challengers	.221	.367	.008	4.447
Senate Incumbents	1.066	.938	.001	4.937
Senate Challengers	.644	.924	.000	6.184
1990–1996				
House Incumbents	.917	.627	.000	9.487
House Challengers	.326	.522	.000	8.229
Senate Incumbents	1.539	1.181	.196	5.721
Senate Challengers	.657	.759	.001	3.331

Source: Calculated by the author from Federal Election Commission and Census data.

his positions, one wonders about characterizing this campaign as "information rich." Just to compare, the highest spending Senate candidate on a per capita basis in this period was challenger Tom Daschle (D-SD) who spent $5.50 per

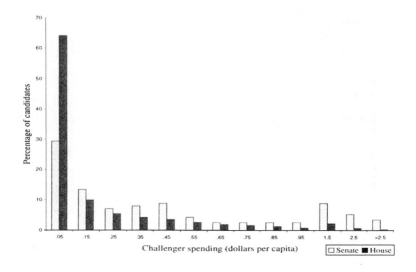

Fig. 4.4. Campaign spending for challengers, 1982–96, per capita

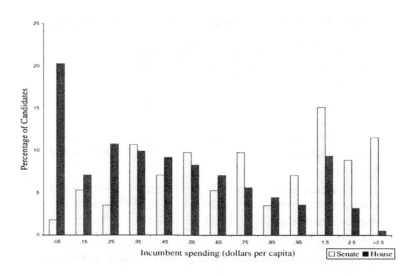

Fig. 4.5. Campaign spending for incumbents, 1982–96, per capita

capita in 1986; the highest spending incumbent was his opponent, Republican Senator James Abdnor ($4.94 per capita).[21]

The gap between House and Senate challenger spending was larger than the gap between House and Senate incumbents. On average, Senate challengers spent 140 percent of what a typical House challenger spent, with the gap increasing to over 250 percent in since 1988. Considering that these figures *already* take into account the larger size of a typical Senate electoral district, the gaps are large indeed. Furthermore, there is an undeniable difference across institutions in the distribution of incumbent and challenger spending (shown in figs. 4.4 and 4.5). Nearly 20 percent of House incumbents have the luxury of spending minimal amounts. Less than 15 percent of House incumbents spend more than one dollar per capita. Senate incumbents seldom have this freedom—more than a third of Senate incumbents spend more than a dollar per capita. The same institutional distinction applies to challengers—there are more House challengers spending at minimal levels and more Senate challengers spending at high levels. It appears, then, that the same differences I observed in candidate quality reemerge for campaign spending. The next step is to apply controls for open seats and campaign intensity.

A brief look at spending in open-seat races fails to dispel the conclusion that Senate campaigns are harder fought than House campaigns. The comparative spending rates in open-seat races, shown in table 4.6, are surprisingly similar to the rates for all races. Once transformed into a per capita measure, relative spending by Senate and House Democratic candidates for open seats retains the pattern observed earlier, although the gap is smaller. Democratic candidates for open Senate seats spend 53 percent more than Democratic candidates in the House. Republican Senate candidates, however, spend only 20 percent more than Republican House candidates. Both of these sets of figures are much closer than what I observed overall (table 4.5), but of course examining open seats is analogous to a sample of the most competitive races. Roughly speaking, the set of open-seat races in the House and Senate look "more alike" than the set of all races in the House and Senate.

What does this mean? Do open-seat contests have special features that tell me something about the ability to compare House and Senate campaign dynamics? Open-seat races are among the most competitive. Average spending is higher (compare table 4.4 to rows 1 and 2 of table 4.5). Candidates for

---

21. The overall spending record is held by Michael Huffington, whose losing California Senate contest, in 1994, reported expenditures of nearly $30 million. Dianne Feinstein was the victor ($14 million). Since California has almost 30 million citizens, the per capita expense was relatively low. The most spent ever per capita by a losing candidate was in the House. In 1994, Republican Gene Fontenot spent $4.6 million in a losing effort to unseat incumbent Ken Bentsen (D-TX), who spent a paltry $972,688.

TABLE 4.6. Open Seat Spending (in dollars)

	Senate	House
Democrats, 1982–96	3,745,380	356,691
Republicans, 1982–96	3,471,070	383,646
Democrats, per capita	1.062 (1.367)	.692 (.545)
Republicans, per capita	.888 (.744)	.744 (.544)

Source: Federal Election Commission.
Note: Entries are average spending in contested open-seat races over the 1982–96 period, deflated to 1982 dollars.

open seats tend to be of higher quality and are better liked than candidates who are challenging incumbents (Canon 1990; Jacobson 1997). Margins in open-seat elections are much smaller than in elections involving incumbents. Open-seat contests, then, are among the most hotly contested races, exactly the characteristics that Westlye (1991) calls "hard-fought."

Senate/House differences in per capita spending are reduced substantially once I select out open-seat races. The logical extension of this result is that Senate/House differences on a wide variety of campaign measures (campaign spending, candidate quality) and potentially voting measures as well (information levels, decision rules) will disappear once campaign intensity is taken into account. I showed in chapter 3 that the likely sources of differences in *campaigns* between the Senate and House are partisan divisions and media market efficiency. Other measures of demographic diversity provided little empirical purchase as a way to discriminate between or within the institutions. The results in this chapter indicate that campaign intensity is a likely source of differences in *voting* between the House and Senate.

The Intensity Puzzle

Campaign intensity matters—this is no surprise. As electoral analysts, however, we are left on the horns of a dilemma. Candidate quality, campaign spending, and campaign intensity are all endogenous. High-intensity races, almost by definition, feature high-spending candidates. If both candidates spend a lot of money, the race will probably be defined as "intense." Elections are more competitive *because* higher quality candidates are running. Candidates can raise more funds *because* they pose a serious challenge. As Jacobson has argued (1990b), Republican prospects in the House during the 1980s were poor in large part because Republican challengers were of low quality: "[Y]ou can't beat somebody with nobody." This does not undermine the validity of comparing Senate and House races, but it does make the findings less clear. It is not surprising to find higher quality challengers and higher spending in more competitive races—the challengers and their spending are what made them competitive.

What does this mean for the qualitative coding of campaign intensity? Westlye (1983, 1996, 1991) and Krasno (1994) draw on a number of features of the campaign in order to determine intensity. Suppose that a candidate is taken seriously by the electorate if he or she passes one of two thresholds, either spending at least half what the opponent is spending or having previous political experience. This means that "hard-fought" races are a product of the interaction of spending and candidate quality. We have no way of knowing whether a campaign is coded "hard fought" because of a highly qualified contender, successful fund raising by one or both candidates, a particularly vulnerable incumbent, or some combination of these. A model that includes intensity, candidate quality, and spending ratios might be misspecified.

I can test for this possibility. If intensity is largely a function of candidate quality and spending ratios, I should be able to predict intensity codings with a high level of accuracy. In table 4.7, I do precisely this, regressing intensity on quality and spending for the House in 1988 (eq. 1), the Senate in 1982-84 and 1988 (eq. 2), and the House and Senate pooled. The dependent variable is the intensity codes reported in Krasno 1994 and Westlye 1986. The results in equation 1 reinforce my suspicions: intensity is strongly associated with candidate quality and the ratio of spending. All coefficients meet conventional levels of statistical significance and are signed correctly. This is not a surprising result. CQ's political columnists look at candidates and spending levels when they write their descriptions of a campaign. The second and third models are less conclusive. While candidate quality and campaign intensity are both strongly associated with Senate campaign intensity, the second model predicts only 75 percent of the cases correctly. The fit of the third, pooled model is driven mostly by the ability to predict House campaign intensity. Furthermore, the appropriate standard of comparison is the level of accuracy reached by a naive model: always code Senate races hard fought and House races low key. This naive coding would correctly predict 90 percent of Krasno's coding of House races and 45 percent of Krasno/Westlye Senate coding.

Campaign intensity undoubtedly summarizes a lot of information about political campaigns. Political scientists, media commentators, and politicians implicitly rely upon it when describing the strategic situation in campaigns and attempting to make sense of results. The implication is that House and Senate campaigns will look increasingly similar as the races become increasingly intense, even converging, perhaps, at some threshold level. I can illustrate some of these changes by comparing House and Senate spending rates for different

TABLE 4.7. Predicting Campaign Intensity

Sample	Maximum Likelihood Estimate
House only, 1988	
Spending ratio	−.803 (.124)
Challenger quality	.483 (.101)
N of cases	329
Percentage predicted	92.7
Senate only, 1982, 1984, 1988	
Spending ratio	−.297 (.007)
Challenger quality	.294 (.007)
N of cases	96
Percentage Predicted	75.0
All Data	
Spending ratio	−.751 (.107)
Challenger quality	.435 (.008)
Institution (dummy)	.726 (.393)
N of cases	425
Percentage predicted	91.7

Source: Intensity codes for the Senate in 1982, 1984, and 1988, Westlye 1991; intensity codes for the House and Senate, in 1988, Krasno 1994; spending taken from Federal Election Commission data; challenger quality is Canon's four-point scale.

Note: Standard errors are in parentheses. The equations were estimated via maximum likelihood probit. The dependent variable in each case was campaign intensity (1 = hard fought, 0 = low key). The pooled equation includes House races from 1988 and Senate races from 1982, 1984, and 1988.

ratios of incumbent and challenger spending. In table 4.8, I display the average spending ratios for the House and Senate in 1982–96 over an increasingly "intense" subset of contests. More intense here is defined as a lower ratio of incumbent to challenger spending. For example, in row 1 the average spending ratio for all contested Senate races ("full range") was 11.98, with a standard deviation of 35.84. Moving right, the average spending ratio decreases from 3.87 (for spending ratios in the range −25 to 25), 3.27, and so on. By the time I reach the final column, the ratio of incumbent and challenger spending is only about 15 percent higher in the Senate than in the House. Relative levels of spending by incumbents and challengers *do* coverge as I select out an increasingly intense subset of contests.

Furthermore, note how the ratio declines as I remove more and more of the high-spending contests. When I eliminate only the least-competitive races (in col. 2 of table 4.8), House incumbents still spend more than five times as much as House challengers do, with a high standard deviation. The comparable rates for the Senate are 1.4 points lower, with a smaller standard deviation. As I move to more and more competitive races, the House incumbent spending advantage disappears. In the final two columns, in the most competitive subset of races, the Senate spending ratio is higher than the House ratio.[22] This is to be expected; spending ratios in noncompetitive contests in this period were skewed because of high-spending Democratic incumbents. Note also that as the range is truncated the proportional reduction in races is greater in the House than in the Senate (proportions of races are in parentheses for each row). As I select out more competitive races, I lose 10 to 15 percent more of the House contests. This is a simple indication that on average Senate elections are more competitive. Still, I retain only 6 percent fewer House races in the most competitive category (43 vs. 37 percent).[23] Once we isolate the most competitive races, Senate and House campaign spending ratios are virtually identical. Institutional differences may be of little consequence in these races.

Campaign spending is a barely acceptable measure of campaign activity. An alternative measure—campaign intensity—tells a lot about House and Senate campaigns, but it is difficult to measure in a reliable fashion. Some alternatives are more easily accessible and are comparable across years and institutions (previous political experience, candidate quality, spending). Others draw upon a more inclusive set of considerations (intensity coding). While campaign intensity is clearly a central concept in the study of House and Senate elections, there is also much room for additional theoretical and measurement work in this area.

Conclusion

Senate and House *campaigns* are more distinct than Senate and House electoral *districts*. On average, Senate races are on average harder fought, with more money spent by higher quality challengers. However, as Westlye first noticed, many Senate races look like the typical House race and vice versa (1983). Westlye was able to show that challenger visibility in low-intensity Senate races fell to levels typically associated with the House. This same

---

22. In fact, spending ratios are more alike than is shown here. Once I select out hard-fought races, the party ratios of relative spending by Democrats and Republicans (including both open and incumbent seats) also converge.

23. These figures are certainly too high for the House. This shows once more that campaign spending alone is an error-prone measure of campaign activity and intensity.

TABLE 4.8. Spending Ratios in the Senate and House

	Full Range	$R < 25$	$R < 15$
Senate	11.98 (35.84)	3.87 (4.39)	3.27 (3.03)
Proportion of races	1.00	.92	.88
House	15.06 (24.06)	5.27 (6.13)	3.35 (3.26)
Proportion of races	1.00	.80	.70
		$R < 5$	$R < 2$
Senate		2.02 (1.00)	1.37 (.27)
Proportion of races		.72	.43
House		1.86 (1.08)	1.22 (.30)
Proportion of races		.55	.37

Source: Federal Election Commission data.
Note: Entries in each column are the mean spending ratios (R) for a given range. Standard deviations are in parentheses.

logic applies to the campaign environment. In low-intensity Senate races, I observe spending and candidate quality levels that I would typically associate with House races; in hard-fought House races, I observe high levels of both spending and candidate quality. Once again, concentrating on averages is a misleading way to look at things. It disguises interesting patterns within these institutions. While I care about the average level of competitiveness in the House and Senate, it is just as important to know how many House incumbents face stiff challenges and how many Senate incumbents can breeze to victory. At a minimum, this provides a more nuanced picture of electoral competitiveness in the U.S. Congress. More broadly, our attitudes toward reform of the campaign finance and election system, and opinions about the possibility that members, and institutions, respond to electoral pressures, will be affected not just by the typical candidate experience but by the experiences of all House and Senate candidates in both competitive and non-competitive races.

The first step in comparing the Senate and House is to generate comparable measures. Campaign spending must be adjusted on a per capita basis. Obviously, a candidate running in a state with 25 million people has to spend more than a candidate running in the typical House district of 500,000. Nonetheless, if we are interested in the probability that a citizen will be exposed to campaign information, then higher spending by the Senate candidate may actually provide less information. A per capita adjustment is one way to allow comparisons across widely disparate electoral settings. Candidate quality measures, in contrast, have generally drawn on two pieces of information: previous elective experience and other notable political assets. Both are easily obtained for the House and the Senate.

The last part of the puzzle, campaign intensity, remains the most contentious to define and most difficult to operationalize. I have reviewed a series of competing measures of intensity, none of which is ideal. However, I am blessed with multiple realizations of campaign intensity. In subsequent chapters, I continue to utilize each of these scales.

Senate and House campaigns and candidates, like states and congressional districts, are not as different as a superficial analysis might lead us to believe. Candidates for the U.S. Senate spend, on average, 10 times as much as their House counterparts. But we know that states are larger than congressional districts. Once adjusted by population size, the distributions of Senate and House spending show considerable overlap. Spending in Senate campaigns anchors the high end and spending in House campaigns anchors the low end, yet there are many cases with the same levels. These are the cases I want to isolate for analysis.

Senate candidates also rank higher on measures of candidate quality. Previous experience and overall candidate quality are higher in Senate races. Again, I remain interested in those numerous cases in which the Senate challenger quality is well into the typical House range or in which the House candidate is actually quite experienced. If experience level *causes* competitive campaign situations, then this effect should be evident independent of institution.

In fact, once I isolate the most intense or competitive races, per capita spending rates and challenger quality levels begin to converge. This indicates that some Senate candidates look like House candidates and vice versa. Once the effects of campaign intensity, along with political setting variables such as media market efficiency, population diversity, and partisan division, are taken into account, we might find that candidate quality and campaign spending really do not differ across the House and Senate.

The next step is to determine why these differences persist. Is there is something inherently different in the House and Senate or do Senate *districts* happen to have certain features that, when they appear in House races, make House campaigns look like Senate campaigns? This requires a multivariate analysis of campaign spending, challenger quality, political settings, and institutions. I take up this task in the next chapter.

CHAPTER 5

From Setting to Candidates to Campaigns: Tracing the Causal Chain

In the two preceding chapters, I showed that Senate and House districts and campaigns share significant similarities. States, as a class, are not more heterogeneous than congressional districts. Senate candidates may have more political experience and spend more money than the average House candidate, yet many House candidacies look like Senate candidacies and vice versa. In this chapter, I bring these two empirical regularities together in causal models of candidate emergence and campaign spending. I treat campaigns as a *dependent* variable, examining whether spending and candidate quality vary in systematic ways across more and less heterogeneous settings, with more and fewer partisans and efficient and inefficient media markets. I pay special attention to campaign spending, comparing the impact of intracampaign variables—spending in reaction to the opponent—to the exogenous influence of the political setting. I allow for institutional variations in these models, providing a direct test of the relative influence of the political setting, institutions, and intracampaign influences.

The analyses are directed toward answering these questions:

- To what extent are Senate and House campaigns explicable by a similar set of district attributes?
- What is the relative influence of intracampaign effects and exogenous, "background" variables on candidate quality and campaign spending?
- Do institutional differences disappear when settings and intracampaign effects are taken into account?

However complex some of these models may be, the analysis is guided by a quite simple claim: those features of the political setting that make a seat more or less competitive will also be the features that are positively associated with higher quality challengers and greater campaign spending *independent* of the institutional setting.

87

I begin by discussing the theoretical relationship between settings, candidate quality, and campaign spending. Next, I show how the decision making of challengers, at least inasmuch as it is reflected in observed variation in challenger quality, responds *only* to the long- and short-run competitiveness of the seat. Despite my theoretical expectations, which were laid out in chapter 2, and the claims of other scholars, the political setting (heterogeneity, market efficiency) plays no significant role, nor do characteristics of the incumbent. "Strategy and choice in congressional elections," to borrow the title of Jacobson and Kernell's modern classic of congressional campaigning (1983), is predominantly concerned with a favorable competitive environment.

Next, I explore the relationship between the setting and campaign spending, with much the same result. Partisan balance and the competitiveness of the current race, along with spending by the opponent, largely determine the spending levels undertaken by both the incumbent and the challenger. District heterogeneity and media market efficiency fail to account for variations in campaign activity across states and congressional districts. Candidates react to each other much more than they do to any fixed characteristic of the setting. This calls into serious question any appeal to district heterogeneity as an explanation of Senate/House differences in campaign activity (see Lee and Oppenheimer 1999 for a contrasting view).

A second, perhaps more important result emerges from the analyses. While district characteristics may not play a great role in determining the activity of House and Senate campaigns, the overall influences on both House and Senate candidates are remarkably similar. The relationship between partisan balance, member characteristics, candidate quality, and campaign spending are relatively stable across institutions and over time. Although the political setting may not be a part of a generic language of elections, a generic account is still a possibility. It includes the partisan makeup of the district, the profile of the member, the quality of the opposition, and spending by both candidates. I close by suggesting how these revisions modify the theoretical presentation made in chapter 2.

Settings, Institutions, and Intracampaign Effects

There is a wealth of evidence suggesting that candidates and campaigns respond to their political environment. I know, for example, that Senate candidates are on average more experienced, more prominent, and spend more money than their House counterparts (Abramowitz 1980; Hinckley 1980a, 1980b; Ragsdale 1981; Westlye 1983, 1986; Abramowitz and Segal 1992; Lee and Oppenheimer 1999). National political tides (e.g., the popularity of the sitting president and the state of the national economy) enter into the candidate's decision about whether to run for office (Jacobson and Kernell 1983). It is also probable that candidates attend to features of political districts, such as communication patterns, partisan trends, and political interests, when deciding to run or choosing a campaign strategy. This is the foundation of the three-stage model presented in chapter 2.

In this section, I discuss ways that district diversity, media market efficiency, partisan balance, and institutional makeup might constrain the activities of candidates and campaigns. I start by describing the basic way that I think the political setting relates to these campaign measures, briefly recapitulating the links from figure 2.1, in light of the descriptive results in the last two chapters. Next I complicate the world a little, adding variables representing institutional differences and over-time effects. Then I complicate the world a lot, showing why a reasonable model of campaigns must include features of the incumbent (seniority, age, previous electoral record) and intracampaign effects (candidates reacting to each other's actions). While this more nuanced account is more realistic, it also makes it significantly more complicated to parse candidate from campaign from political setting.

Settings and Campaigns

Quality challengers and campaign dollars are drawn to competitive races. What features of the setting—exogenous, pre-campaign features—are positively associated with competitiveness? One is easily identified: partisan balance. In an evenly balanced district, elections will be closer, spending will be higher, and better challengers will run.[1] An efficient media market means that it will be easier and cheaper for a challenger to get his or her name before the voting public and overcome the recognition hurdle. Therefore, I expect to find a positive relationship between market efficiency and candidate quality. The expectation for campaign spending is somewhat different. Market efficiency should be *negatively* associated with campaign spending because a challenger will be able to spend less and still overcome the recognition hurdle. Similarly, incumbents will be able to maintain satisfactory media exposure at a lower cost in an efficient media market, all else being equal.[2]

The impact of district diversity on candidate quality and campaign spending is more complex. I expect that candidates react strategically to the makeup

---

1. A small victory margin in the previous race and relative levels of partisan division are associated with high-quality challenges (Bianco 1984; Bond, Covington and Fleisher 1985) and higher levels of incumbent spending (Green and Krasno 1988, 1990; Jacobson 1990a, 1985).

2. Stewart (1989a, 1989b) and Stewart and Reynolds (1990) did not test these relationships, but they did find that market efficiency was positively related to voter information levels (for 1988 Senate races).

of the electoral district.[3] There are a number of different plausible reasons why heterogeneity makes it more difficult for incumbents to get reelected. For example, heterogeneity might make it more likely that an incumbent will alienate one interest or another. It is more difficult to satisfy a heterogeneous set of constituency interests (Fiorina 1974). Heterogeneity can also make it more difficult for both incumbents and challengers to communicate with voters because multiple appeals have to be made and appeals to one group might not be "heard" by another (or, worse, they could alienate another). It might also be true that politics in complex, heterogeneous districts takes on a different flavor, either more impersonal (Baker 1995) or less individualistic and constituency oriented (Lee and Oppenheimer 1999). In general, then, I expect that heterogeneity will be positively related to both incumbent and challenger spending.

A Fuller Model of Campaigns: Institution, Time, and Intracampaign Effects

There are four additional parts to my model of candidate quality and campaign activity: institutions, incumbents, time, and intracampaign effects. Institution indicates nothing more than what I have already presented in previous chapters: do significant differences remain between the House and Senate once other variables have been taken into account? By time, I simply mean estimating these models from 1982 to 1996 (i.e., pooling the data). Intracampaign effects represent the influence that candidates have on each other: incumbents spending more because they face quality challengers and incumbents and challengers spending more in reaction to their opponents' expenditures. Finally, incumbents are vulnerable for other reasons: their ideological leanings, voting records, time in office, and ages. I describe each of these below.

The first complication in the model has to do with institutional differences. Ideally, the effects of political settings, candidate quality, and intracampaign dynamics on campaign spending, if not identical across the House and Senate,

---

3. Redistricting illustrates how the setting may alter the strategic calculations of politicians. Redistricting, on average, hurts incumbents. It is negatively associated with incumbent margins (Jacobson 1993) and positively associated with challenger quality (Canon 1990, chap. 4) in large part because incumbents are less familiar with the new setting. Redistricting could work in an incumbent's favor: Fowler and McClure (1989) found that uncertainty due to redistricting dissuaded a highly qualified candidate (Louise Slaughter), but this could be an unusual case. I have discussed redistricting in previous chapters, but because it did not effect the comparability of House and Senate districts I do not explicitly consider redistricting here. Postredistricting shifts in campaigns and elections remain a prime example of a political setting effect (see Niemi and Abramowitz 1994; Hill 1995; and Lublin 1997 for more detailed treatments of this topic.)

will display substantially similar patterns. There is good evidence indicating that campaign spending and candidate quality can be profitably compared across the House and Senate (Krasno 1994; Canon 1990).[4] When differences in setting, candidate quality, and fund-raising are taken into account, institutional differences should disappear.

I test this hypothesis by pooling Senate and House races and adding a variable that is coded one for Senate contests and zero for House races. If the coefficient on this variable is zero, there are no remaining House/Senate differences not already represented in the model. More likely, this coefficient will remain statistically significant, reminding me that there are institutional differences between the House and Senate that are not incorporated into the analysis. This provides a rough test of the size and relative influence of institution when district diversity, media market efficiency, partisan balance, challenger quality, and campaign spending are taken into account.[5]

The second addition to the analysis is time. As noted in chapter 1, estimating these relationships over time increases the sample size (a particular concern for Senate races), improves the efficiency of statistical estimates, and decreases the likelihood that my results will hinge on a particular year and election.[6] Over-time effects can be grouped under a "nature of the times" heading. Some years are good for the party in power; others are not. In good years for Republicans, such as 1978 or 1994, high-quality Republican candidates run for office and Republican candidates spend more money (Jacobson 1990b). In poor years for Republicans, such as 1982, high-quality Republican candidates are discouraged from running and high-quality Democratic challengers emerge. I try to capture these year to year effects with a dummy variable for

---

4. Krasno shows that Senate and House campaigns appear surprisingly alike once the features (campaign intensity and challenger prominence) that supposedly differentiate the Senate from the House are controlled for: "Differences in the aggregate largely exist because Senate campaigns are much more likely to be intense, and Senate candidates are more likely to be formidable" (Krasno 1994, 114). Canon finds that the same set of "structural and institutional variables" (the makeup of the primary system, the size of the state legislature, the permeability of the political structure, and the "shape of the political opportunity structure") help account for the appearance of quality challengers in both the House and Senate (1990, chap. 4).

5. I allow for differential intercepts, estimating a coefficient for the dummy variable, and test for the existence of differential slopes, interacting the dummy variable with each of the independent variables. This latter analysis is identical to a Chow test of the stability (or equality) of the slope coefficients across the House and Senate samples (Johnston 1984, 220–28, 507–8). See appendix B for more information

6. I assume that political setting measures such as racial heterogeneity, income variance, and media market efficiency stay constant throughout the decade. Campaign spending and challenger quality obviously change from district to district and election to election.

each year, also known as a least-squares dummy variable (LSDV) specification.The dummy variables also have the beneficial effect of reducing serial correlation to insignificant levels.[7]

Finally, I need to consider the reasons why incumbents might attract well-qualified, well-funded challengers regardless of their past electoral performances. In general, I expect that members who have been in office longer, are older, or occupy extreme ideological positions will appear ripe for a primary and general election challenge.[8]

Intracampaign Effects and Campaign Spending

In order to account for variations in campaign spending, one more complicating element enters the picture: intracampaign dynamics. If voters are not fools, neither are candidates. Politicians are strategic actors par excellence. At a minimum, they are political junkies and at a maximum seasoned political activists, elected officials, and previous House members and senators. It is not surprising to observe strategic behavior among such an intelligent and highly motivated set of competing individuals. In the campaign context, this means that candidates will spend in reaction to their opponents, real and perceived.[9] Thus, I expect a positive relationship between incumbent and challenger spending and Democratic and Republican spending in open seat contests.

Strategic actors also try to anticipate the moves of their opponents. Candidates, therefore, react to the quality of the opposition. Is he or she experienced or a rank amateur? Do I have to worry about his or her ability to tap into celebrity status or personal wealth or is this opponent invisible in the district? And, for the challenger, how much effort is this incumbent expending on the race? Has he or she built up an enormous war chest or can I compete dollar for dollar (Box-Steffensmeier 1996)? Green and Krasno (1988) suggest that incumbents spend directly in response to the quality of the opposition. I

---

7. I attempted to include variables with more political punch: the change in real personal disposable income and the popularity of the sitting president. The economy and presidential popularity both explain a great deal of aggregate variation in presidential voting. They would also be expected to affect the strategic decisions of campaigners (e.g., Jacobson and Kernell 1983). The overall fit of the model when these variables were included was worse compared to a model including just the straight year dummies.

8. Ideological positions are measured using data from two sources, the ratings of the Americans for Democratic Action (ADA) and one-dimensional D-Nominate scores (Poole and Rosenthal 1985, 1997).

9. Jacobson and Kernell (1983) claim that early spending by incumbents discourages quality rivals, which is a kind of reactive spending. The equations presented by Jacobson (1985, 1990a) and Green and Krasno (1988, 1990) illustrate the strong relationship between incumbent and challenger spending.

think this relationship works indirectly: quality challengers are able to raise more campaign funds, and incumbents then react directly to higher rates of spending. Why expend a great deal of effort raising funds, or, more accurately, spending those hard-won dollars (I only consider actual campaign expenditures, not money raised) when your opponent is expending little effort in the race? The statistical implication is that challenger campaign spending, but not challenger quality, is a cause of incumbent campaign spending. Since I have two dependent variables in this system—incumbents react to challengers and challengers react to incumbents—there are two dependent variables and the campaign spending model is estimated as a system of equations.

This system is estimated via two-stage least squares. The challenger-spending equation is underidentified—there is nothing in my data that I can reasonably argue affects incumbent spending and does not also affect challenger spending.[10] As argued earlier, I exclude challenger quality from the incumbent-spending model under the assumption that differences in challenger quality are reflected in higher levels of challenger spending. Unfortunately, there are no exogenous variables related to incumbent spending that are not directly related to challenger spending. This is why the incumbent-spending equation is identified, with results reported later, but the challenger-spending equation is not.

On the positive side, in many situations involving simultaneous effects, good instrumental variables are unavailable. This is not the case here. Current incumbent spending is strongly related to previous spending and vote margins. Green and Krasno call the former the "incumbent's propensity to spend" (1988, 897). Relatedly, challenger spending in the previous race (and the current race) probably reflects in some respect the competitiveness of the district and the vulnerability of the incumbent. However, I cannot argue that lagged challenger spending represents "the *challenger's* propensity to spend." After all, in most cases the challenger in the current race is a different candidate from the one in the previous race. The implication is that my instrumental variable equation for current incumbent spending will have explained a higher proportion of variance than the instrumental variables equation for challenger spending. Again, this reinforces my decision to report estimates only for the incumbent-spending model.

---

10. A requirement of two-stage least squares is a set of variables that are related to the endogenous variables in the system, in my case incumbent and challenger spending, but are unrelated to the residual terms associated with the predictive model (exogenous variables). In addition, in order to make the system identified, each equation must exclude at least one exogenous variable (Greene 1993, chap. 20).

Some Caveats: What Is Not Included?

What is *not* included in this model? Particular features of the incumbent's record that might make him or her vulnerable would be a good addition. Banks and Kiewiet (1989) identify three things that dissuade quality challengers: the incumbent's voting record, incumbent casework, and incumbent exposure. Mann (1978) also found that voters penalize incumbents for unpopular votes. I have included some surrogates for these, including the incumbent's ideological position and previous vote margin. Second, more explicitly political features of the district certainly affect the decision-making process of potential candidates. In the most comprehensive study of candidate emergence in the House and Senate, Canon (1990) shows how potential candidates respond to a similar set of state and congressional district attributes when deciding to run. Campaign variables (the previous challenger's vote and the existence of some scandal involving the incumbent), national-level variables (real income and unemployment), and structural/institutional variables (normal vote, candidate "supply," redistricting, and the number of candidates in the primary) all have statistically significant impacts on the challenger's political quality. While my measures of the district's political terrain are not as rich as Canon's, my models do have the advantage of explicitly comparing Senate and House dynamics.

Finally, using lagged values of spending reduces substantially the number of cases for each year, so severely that estimating this system for the Senate is very difficult. I discuss the causes and consequences of this in appendix B. Second, I recognize that total campaign expenditures may misstate the actual campaign effort undertaken by candidates. Unfortunately, detailed breakdowns for every election in this period are not available. The unequal proportions of expenditures devoted to communications and "general" campaign activities reported in Ansolabehere and Gerber (1994) are a point of concern. It is not clear whether their findings cause problems for the models of campaign spending reported in this chapter or just for the voting models that are typically reported in the literature.

In summary, the data reported here are primarily intended to address the influence of district heterogeneity, media market efficiency, and institutions on campaigns and elections. Many of the specification problems that have occupied many congressional scholars are not relevant here because the dependent variable is campaign spending not vote totals. By focusing on heterogeneity and institution, this study may overlook many of the more explicitly political variables such as those Canon or Kiewiet and Banks collected. Future data collection efforts could augment the results reported here.

A Guide to the Results

The data used in this chapter span almost two decades of elections and have been gathered from many different sources. I include tests of my own central theory, presented in chapter 2, as well as comparative tests of alternative theories. I simplify the presentation by presenting the empirical results in a sequential fashion. The candidate-quality models are reported first, followed by the campaign-spending models. I open with a direct test of the main hypotheses of chapter 2. These tables include measures of district diversity, media market efficiency, partisan balance, and an institution dummy. Next, I conduct a separate test of the impact of candidate (incumbent) features: ideology, age, seniority, previous electoral outcome, and, again, an institution dummy variable. Then, to reassure the reader that the estimated coefficients are stable across these two specifications, I merge these two tables into a single estimation. As will become clear, the results are stable across these different specifications, as they were across many alternatives, noted later, but not reported in the interest of space. The short lesson from the long set of results is clear: once sufficient controls are added, institutional differences all but disappear.

When Do Good Candidates Run for Office?
The Determinants of Candidate Quality

The estimates from my model predicting candidate quality in the House and Senate are shown in table 5.1. The most important predictors in the model, not surprisingly, are those associated with the general competitive situation. As congressional scholars have long recognized, better quality candidates emerge when the competitive situation looks favorable (where competitiveness is represented here by the closeness of the race and a favorable partisan balance).

The consistently strong impact of partisan balance confirms previous results (Bianco 1984; Bond, Covington, and Fleisher 1985). The size of the estimated coefficient is large and negative for both institutions, as was expected (see col. 1 of table 5.1) and remains robust when I control for the incumbent's previous vote margin, a variable obviously correlated with partisan balance (compare tables 5.1 and 5.3). Excluding "closeness" from the model increases the estimated impact of party, but this should not be surprising. Party balance is part of the long-term competitive environment, whereas closeness reflects both long- and short-term influences.[11] The size of the effect is impressive:

---

11. I interpret "closeness" as a summary of short-term political forces, including the current state of the economy, the popularity of the incumbent's party, particularly controversial votes, and congressional and personal scandals. I am assuming that closeness reflects these; at least in a rough way. "Partisan balance" is a summary of long-term competitive trends such as population

TABLE 5.1. Challengers and Diverse Districts

Variable	Coefficient	Coefficient
Closeness	1.532 (.087) **	—
Partisan Balance	−1.833 (.308) **	−3.468 (.312)**
Contiguity	.270 (.148)	.284 (.160)
Dominance	.006 (.125)	.046 (.135)
Income variance	−.030 (.020)	−.053 (.021)*
Education variance	.166 (.179)	.459 (.192)*
Racial diversity	−.287 (.180)	−.235 (.193)
Urbanness	−.211 (.150)	−.190 (.161)
Foreign stock	−.559 (.343)	−.788 (.369)*
Institution	.762 (.115) **	.987 (.123)**
Constant	3.098 (.388) **	4.364 (.408)**
N of observations	2,482	2,482
R^2	0.301	0.184
Root MSE	0.998	1.078

Source: Data from the 1982–96 elections.
Note: Challenger quality data collected by the author (Senate, House 1982–1990) and courtesy of Patrick Sellers (House 1992–1996). Demographic data collected by the author. See Appendix for variable coding information. Standard errors are in parentheses.
$*p$ = significant at the .05 level $**p$ = .01 level.

a movement of .5 in the incumbent's favor in partisan balance (one-half the full range) is associated with a 1.8 point drop in challenger quality, nearly 50 percent of the range, and a 3.4 point drop when closeness is dropped. My second measure of competitiveness, closeness, is also strongly associated with the appearance of a quality challenger. On average, a unit of increase in closeness (the scale runs from zero, or safe seats, to three, races "too close to call") causes a unit and a half of increase in candidate quality.

Most impressive of all, the magnitude, size, and statistical significance of these relationships are remarkably stable across years and institutions. Across years and institutions, the estimated coefficient falls no more than two standard deviations from the value reported here only once, a 1988 Senate estimate. The relationship between closeness and candidate quality failed to reach the 95

---

growth, migration, economic development and decline, and other changes that affect the partisan coloration of an area.

percent level of statistical significance level only in the 1984 and 1982 Senate equations.[12]

The impact of district diversity, on the other hand, is disappointing. I expected to observe more quality challengers in more diverse districts, since there would more opportunities to construct a competing coalition. The negative coefficients for all but education, even though seven of 10 fail to reach conventional statistical significance levels, indicate the opposite: challenger quality is *negatively* associated with diversity. The impact of foreign stock, a measure of ethnic diversity, is especially strong relative to other variables in the model (although note, from chap. 3, that most of the diversity measures vary from 30 to 70, so the effect across the variable's full range does not approach that of institution or the other measures of competitiveness). Perhaps the difficulty of running in a diverse district discourages opponents and overwhelms any positive impact that diversity might have. On the other hand, my expectations regarding media market efficiency are borne out. Although the coefficient for contiguity only passes a one-tailed significance test, it does imply that higher quality challengers appear in districts with more efficient media markets.

Finally, note that controlling for differences in the competitive situation and the political setting reduces the explanatory power of institution from 60 percent.[13] Furthermore, there are no differences in the impact these variables have in the House versus the Senate.[14] Senate challengers rank roughly a point higher ($b = .987$) on the four-point scale of candidate quality using the estimate from the second model, the one least favorable to my theory. The most likely explanation for this remaining difference is that the Senate is a more attractive prize, drawing experienced and ambitious politicians like moths to a flame.

Banks and Kiewiet (1989) propose a theoretical model to predict why "sure losers" might challenge incumbents and, by implication, when experienced politicians will run for office. In part, a candidate's calculation is driven by the attractiveness of the prize (Senate vs. House vs. other offices), but, drawing on a substantial literature in congressional research, the calculation also turns on the condition of the incumbent (Jacobson and Kernell 1983;

---

12. I estimated all equations reported in this chapter separately by institution, year, and year and institution, a total of 18 different subsamples. Other changes were made and are described later.

13. The bivariate regression coefficient on institution (regressing challenger quality on institution and a constant term, estimated for the same set of 2,482 cases) is 1.654, compared to an estimated effect here of .762.

14. When I ran a model with the institution dummy variable interaction terms on all variables, *none* of the coefficients met the 95 percent statistical significance level using the more generous one-tailed test.

TABLE 5.2. Challengers and Incumbents

Variable	Coefficient
Ideological extremity	.232 (.079) **
Age of member	.002 (.002)
Seniority of member	−.010 (.002) **
Vote $(t-1)$	−.009 (.001) **
Institution	.184 (.349)
Constant	4.301 (.482) **
N	2,482
R^2	0.137
Root MSE	1.085

Source: Data from 1982–96 elections. Member data courtesy of Philip Ardoin.
Note: Standard errors are in parentheses.
$*p = .05$ $**p = .01$

Baker 1995; Abramowitz and Segal 1992). In table 5.2, I consider the condition of the incumbent, his ideological position, age, seniority, and previous vote margin. Holding all else constant, more ideologically extreme members attract more qualified challengers, with a fairly robust effect on predicted quality (.232 ∗ 100 = two points on a four-point scale). Seniority deters challengers, confirming previous results, and a relatively poor performance in the past election encourages challengers. The substantive impact of the latter two, however, is quite low, less than half a point on the quality scale.

As before, I have reestimated this model in separate years, separately for institutions, and in the fully dummied out specification. The coefficients are robust and consistent in their impact, allowing for some variation across years. Institution remained insignificant in all pooled analyses, specified either as a separate dummy variable or an interaction term.

The results again call into question any claims of institutional differences—differences, that is, that cannot be captured in the modeling process. Once I control for features of the incumbent, *no institutional differences remain.* If these findings are consistent under alternative specifications, then I have "unpacked" the observed gap in challenger quality between the Senate and the House. This fundamentally changes the way political science describes, and theorizes about, differences in campaigning across these two institutions.

In the next analysis, I unite these accounts of challenger emergence. By considering the demographic, competitiveness, and incumbency variables in a single equation, I can reassure the reader that there are no serious collinearity

TABLE 5.3. District Diversity, Incumbents, and Challenger Quality

Variable	Coefficient
Closeness	1.476 (.092) **
Partisan balance	−1.162 (.347) **
Contiguity	.345 (.151) *
Dominance	.000 (.128)
Income variance	−.029 (.020)
Education variance	.053 (.184)
Racial diversity	−.305 (.186)
Urbanness	−.358 (.156) *
Foreign stock	−.497 (.358)
Ideological extremity	.265 (.071) **
Age of member	.005 (.003)
Seniority of member	−.005 (.003)
Vote $(t-1)$	−.007 (.002) **
Institution	.162 (.115)
Constant	3.137 (.417) **
N of cases	2,482
R^2	0.392
Root MSE	0.991

Source: Data from 1982–96 elections.
Note: Standard errors are in parentheses.
$*p = .05$ $**p = .01$

issues that could undermine one or another of the analyses (e.g., are more conservative members predominantly clustered in particular kinds of districts?). I already know that the results shown in tables 5.1 and 5.2 are robust over two decades and across institutional settings. Are they similarly robust when combined?

The answer is strongly affirmative. Nothing in table 5.3 detracts from the conclusions already reached. Challengers clearly act in a strategic fashion, selecting races in which the competitive situation is move favorable. These are, in the main, races in which the partisan balance is more likely to be in their favor and signals foretell a competitive contest. A strategic actor will also consider the quality of the opposition—in this case, the condition of the incumbent. Ideologically extreme members, and members who performed poorly in the last election, attract high-quality challengers, which is consistent with the results reported here. Once I control for the competitive nature of the district, however, the effect of seniority falls below statistical significance, indicating that junior members, on average, come from more competitive settings. Finally, there is no real pattern to estimated impact of demographic diversity. I suspect that the estimate for media market efficiency is accurate—this variable barely fell below statistical significance in previous estimations. The other demographic estimates fluctuate. Members from congressional districts and states that are more urban face lower quality challengers, on average, yet this result was not evident in earlier analyses (although the direction of the effect is consistently negative). Income, education, and foreign stock fall below conventional significance levels, with the coefficient on education less than 10 percent from the first analysis. Overall, I place more stock in a regularly negative effect than in the statistical significance of any particular measure.

What of institution? In chapter 4, I observed a large gap in challenger quality between the House and Senate (1.5 points; see table 4.2). After controlling for district diversity and the competitive environment, this gap was reduced by half (.762). After controlling for characteristics of the incumbents and the electoral environment, the gap was almost one-tenth (.162) and no longer statistically significant. House/Senate differences in challenger quality, then, are a product of differences in the competitive nature of states, the higher level of the media market efficiency of states, and the ideological position and previous electoral performance of Senate incumbents, not anything distinctively attractive about the Senate as an institution.

Endogeneity in Campaigns? Looking More Closely at Closeness

The estimated impact of the closeness of the race merits further examination. Remember that closeness is the *Congressional Quarterly* "call" of the race (running from safe Democratic to safe Republican) folded about its midpoint. These calls are made in mid- to late October, when the identity and "quality" of the challenger is a known quantity. Closeness and challenger quality are in many respects inseparable. Thus, reverse causality could apply: closeness is a function of candidate quality rather than quality being a function of competitiveness (as reflected in the closeness measure). The dilemma here, as in all models of candidate quality and campaign spending, is rampant endogeneity. I lack variables that both reflect short-term influences on candidate decision-making and are not themselves products of my dependent variables.[15]

---

15. Canon tries to solve this problem, including the state of the national economy, the Watergate scandal in 1974, and whether there were any significant scandals involving the incumbent in his model of candidate emergence. None of these variables is available in this study. Even with a set of measures collected specifically to understand challenger emergence and success, Canon was able to explain only 25 percent of the variance in challenger quality in the House and 21

I tested this by removing closeness from the equation. These estimates were reported in the second column of table 5.1. Happily, they do not change the conclusions. The estimated impact of partisan balance increases substantially. This comes as no surprise, since closeness and partisan balance are two measures of district competitiveness. More importantly, most other coefficients do not change. The estimates for the demographic diversity measures increase somewhat, with income and education nearing statistical significance. There is undoubtedly some interaction between Senate and House candidate quality and the short-term competitive situation (see also Jacobson and Kernell 1983; Bianco 1984; Bond, Covington, and Fleisher 1985; and Banks and Kiewiet 1989), but this does not undermine the results reported in tables 5.1 to 5.3.

Discussion

Candidate emergence is a key part of the elections puzzle. The dynamics of presidential primaries have been a focus of many studies (e.g., Aldrich 1980; Bartels 1988). Candidate emergence in the House and Senate has received less attention. Canon (1990) attempts to explain the behavior of amateur politicians in American politics, and the decision to run is an important part of that explanation. Fowler and McClure (1989) perform an intensive analysis of the decision to run, identifying all the contending candidates, interviewing them about their perceptions of the district and the race, and following a single district from incumbent retirement to open seat contest to second-term defeat. Still, this study is limited to a single congressional district.[16]

In this section, I tested one part of my broad model of campaigns and elections: how candidate decision making, at least as reflected in candidate quality measures, is conditioned by the makeup of the political setting. The political setting and the institution serve as the backdrop to House and Senate

---

percent of the variance in the Senate (1990, chap. 4), roughly the same amount as here. Other possible sources of exogenous variables might be the polls taken by candidate organizations, national campaign committees, and media outlets at various points in the campaign or campaign contribution lists with dates attached. The inferential problems associated with these data, most of which are collected after the campaign is over, resurface throughout this chapter. As of the time of this writing, another possible source has emerged on the Internet. As was mentioned in chapter 4, the *National Journal* web site has extensive coverage of state and national campaigns. This site is the first publicly accessible source that I know of in which races are "called" *throughout* the campaign season. Thus, a researcher can track which races are "too close to call" as early as February and how these elite evaluations change during the election year as opponents are determined, campaigns raise funds, and the election evolves. This feature has only been available, to my knowledge, since 1998.

16. One group of congressional scholars is working to remedy this deficit (see, e.g., Canon, Schousen, and Sellers 1996; Kazee 1994; and Fowler 1993).

campaigns. Politicians respond to the setting, deciding that some districts are potentially competitive and others are not. Their decisions are determined, I suggested, in part by the diversity of the district, the efficiency of the media market, the partisan behavior of the voters, and particular events that make incumbents more or less vulnerable. This hypothesized relationship between political settings and candidate quality was not borne out. There are no statistically discernible relationships between my measures of heterogeneity or media market efficiency and the quality of challengers. Instead, challenger quality is most related to competitiveness measures: partisan balance and closeness.

The decision to run for office is often idiosyncratic and unpredictable. In the next section, I examine whether the decision to spend can be more systematically related to the backdrop of political campaigns. While the decision to run may be idiosyncratic, the decision of how much to spend might be less so since it is determined by other actors such as political action committees, the national congressional and senatorial campaign committees, state and local parties, and individual donors, all of whom may react in tandem to the political makeup of the district, the efficiency of the local media market, and the activities of competing candidates.

How Much Do Candidates Spend?
Complexities in Campaign Spending

In table 5.4, I present the estimates from a two-stage least squares model predicting incumbent campaign expenditures in House contests involving incumbents from 1984–90, 1994, and 1996.[17] The primary hypothesis tested in this table is that candidates respond to the strategic situation when making the decision to run, regardless of whether they are choosing to run for the Senate or the House. Observed differences in campaign spending, reported in chapter 3, should disappear once we control for characteristics of the district. Given the strategic nature of campaigns, we should not be surprised to discover that the most important determinant of incumbent spending is challenger spending. In contrast to my findings for candidate quality, however, the results reported here support my expectation that candidates react to the political setting. Incumbents spend more in diverse political environments. Media market efficiency also influences campaign spending but not in the ways I predicted. Candidates spend more when the district is dominated by a few media markets and less when market and political district are highly contiguous. I do not think these are contradictory findings and attempt to reconcile them later. Finally

---

17. The inclusion of lagged variables in the model means that 1982 and 1992 have to be dropped. Districts that were redistricted during other years were also dropped from the analysis.

TABLE 5.4. Campaign Spending, Incumbents, and Political Settings

Variable	Coefficient
Constant	−.765 (.366) *
Challenger spending	.289 (.064) **
Closeness	−.006 (.142)
Media contiguity	−.500 (.143) **
Media dominance	.236 (.120) *
Income variance	.006 (.019)
Education variance	.111 (.165)
Racial diversity	.064 (.168)
Urban diversity	.369 (.136) *
Foreign stock	.579 (.309)
Partisan split	−1.562 (.440) **
Ideological extremity	.128 (.367)
Member age	−.006 (.007)
Member seniority	−.005 (.008)
Vote $(t-1)$	.007 (.005)
Institution	.181 (.090) **
Constant	.927 (.388) *
N of observations	1,938
R^2	0.486
Root MSE	0.984

Source: Data from 1982–96 elections.
Note: All entries are 2SLS coefficients with robust standard errors (estimated in STATA 5.0). Incumbent and challenger spending are treated as endogenous. Standard errors are in parentheses.
$*p = .05$ $**p = .01$.

as would be expected, incumbents spend dramatically less when the partisan balance is in their favor.

Incumbents react most strongly to the competitiveness of the race, as reflected in challenger spending. A movement of 10 cents in per capita spending by a challenger, roughly $50,000 for the average congressional district and $450,000 for the average state, is associated with a 51 cent increase in incumbent per capita spending (all ceteris paribus). This means that a House challenger who spends only $50,000 more than the average candidate faces an incumbent who spends $257,000 more.[18] Since the full range of challenger spending runs from −6.9 (challengers who spent basically nothing) to 1.58, this is a potentially huge effect. Incumbents are also able to spend less when district partisanship leans in their favor. Moving from a perfectly balanced district to one that is 90:10 in favor of the incumbent's party causes a 49.5 cent drop in predicted incumbent spending, all else being held equal. These results confirm the conventional wisdom: incumbents spend more when faced with high-spending challengers and when the long-term partisan balance is not in their favor.

Surprisingly, the impact of my other measure of competitiveness—the closeness of the race—is indiscernibly different from zero. This seems odd until we recognize that the two-stage model includes lagged as well as current spending. Spending by candidates in both the current and previous elections already accounts for current and long-term competitiveness. There is nothing left for closeness to explain. Incumbent characteristics are statistically insignificant for the same reason. Once I control for past spending ("propensity to spend" in Green and Krasno's terminology) and the district's partisan balance, there is little additional variation in incumbent spending behavior.

Incumbents also spend in reaction to district diversity. While only one of the estimated coefficients is two times its standard error, all are signed correctly and the combined substantive impact of the diversity measures is substantial. A movement from the least to the most diverse setting on percentage urban is associated with a $1.39 increase in per capita spending ceteris paribus.[19] A similar movement from the least to the most diverse setting on percentage foreign stock is associated with an 89 cent increase.[20]

Finally, as hypothesized, incumbents can spend less in highly efficient media markets. The estimates from table 5.4 show that contiguity (how much media market lines and district boundaries overlap) is negatively associated with spending. This is as expected: candidates devote less money to advertising when each ad dollar is more efficiently targeted at voters. On the other hand, the results also indicate that incumbents spend more when their districts are dominated by a single media market. Put another way, when a district is served by many media markets this model predicts that incumbents will spend less money. It is possible that when there is a single obvious place to spend

---

18. Jacobson (1990a) argues that trying to increase challenger spending will not help competitiveness since incumbents can simply swamp high-spending challengers. These results lend support to his claim, though I do not estimate the marginal impact of a dollar's worth of spending on vote totals.

19. The urban diversity measure theoretically runs from zero to 1, but empirically it runs from .004 to .90.

20. These may seem large compared to the impact of challenger spending, but remember that challenger spending has a range eight times larger than these variables.

TABLE 5.5. Changes in Incumbent Spending as a Product of Diversity and Media Efficiency: Two Examples

	Wyoming	CA31
Diversity		
Urbanness	high	low
Spending relative to average	1.16	−.86
Foreign Stock	low	high
Spending relative to average	−1.04	1.11
Media markets		
Contiguity	moderate-high	low
Spending compared to average	−.93	.89
Dominance	low	high
Spending compared to average	−1.15	1.05

Source: Entries were obtained by substituting the actual values for each district into the estimates from table 5.4

advertising dollars candidates on average spend more. Incumbents may spend less in districts that are not dominated by a single media market because they are targeting nonmonetary resources, such as time, at activities that are more efficient for that type of district, such as newspaper interviews, personal visits, county fairs, and other types of personalized campaigning. These results are somewhat contradictory, however, and need further study and refinement.

Two sample districts illustrate the impact of district diversity and media market efficiency on campaign spending. Wyoming ranks relatively high on urban diversity because its population is evenly split between a few urban centers and a large rural sector, it has relatively small numbers of foreign born, and it has the *least* efficient state media market in the country. California's Thirty-First District (CA31) was cited in chapter 2; it is described in *Politics in America* as *the most diverse* congressional district in the United States, and it ranks at the top in racial, income, and foreign stock diversity scores. However, it is the least diverse in terms of the urban-rural split—the district is 100 percent urban. Finally, CA31 ranks at the top in market dominance (completely dominated by the Los Angeles market) but at the bottom in market contiguity (96 percent of the residents of the Los Angeles ADI do not reside in CA31).

The relative impact these variables have on the predicted level of the incumbent spending is shown in table 5.5. These two examples demonstrate the potentially large impact of the political setting. The predicted difference in spending is roughly two dollars per capita, solely as a product of differences in setting. At the minimum, in a typical House seat, this translates into $1 million in additional spending. Of course, this comparison is taken in isolation. In the real world, I would have to consider the state of the economy, both nationally and in particular states or regions; the vulnerability of the incumbent; the quality of the challenger; and other idiosyncratic features of the contests. Nonetheless, demographic diversity does seem to affect spending. A more complex district is harder to run in and requires a higher level of campaign activity.

Finally, I turn to institution. Large differences in campaign spending between the House and Senate were apparent in chapter 4. Ceteris paribus, the results in table 5.4 lead me to expect that Senate incumbents spend $1.31 more per capita than do House incumbents. Controlling for district diversity, media market efficiency, characteristics of the incumbent, and even per capita spending by the challenger does not make institutional differences go away, but they are substantially attenuated. The bivariate regression coefficient is .280, while the multivariate estimate is .181. As with the candidate quality models, the weights that are attached to these various measures remain constant across the Senate and the House.[21] Senate incumbents spend at a higher level than House incumbents do, but the *relative* spending levels among incumbents of both institutions are explicable by the same set of indicators and the same causal model.

Discussion: Explaining Campaign Spending

Unlike previous studies, this one models campaign spending as a result of intracampaign dynamics, the political context, and the institution. My expectation was that short-term forces would be captured by closeness and long term forces by partisanship. Neither of these expectations were met. Instead, it was found that the dynamics of incumbent spending in the U.S. Congress over the past 20 years depend mainly on current spending by the opponent and the competitiveness of the previous race. Spending is determined primarily by the strategic situation in the current contest and by long-term forces in the district such as heterogeneity, media market efficiency, and partisan balance.

The major findings from the results presented in table 5.4 are three. First, the "closeness" of the race has no discernible affect on incumbent spending. I think this is a product of other variables introduced into the two-stage setup that reflect long-run competitiveness. Second, other characteristics of the incumbent—his or her ideological extremity, age, and seniority—have no discernible impact on spending. Finally, and most importantly for our concerns

---

21. The dummy variable interaction terms were all statistically insignificant, but they need to be included in order to handle serial correlation in the data.

here, institutional effects are relatively weak. The inclusion of campaign, setting, and media market variables explain 75 percent of the observed gap in incumbent campaign spending; institution accounts for the remaining 25 percent.[22]

What does this teach us about the validity of House and Senate comparisons? Incumbent spending is related to the same set of variables across the two institutions. Political settings and media markets constrain campaigners in the ways I expected. But Senate and House differences persist. Even if the structure of explanation is stable across the two institutions, the level of many of the independent variables is dramatically different. Incumbents may react to increases in per capita spending by challengers at the same rates in the House and Senate, but a 10 cent growth translates into a predicted increase in spending that is eight times larger for the average state than for the average CD. Challengers are of higher quality and spend more money in the Senate. Nothing I have done makes this difference go away.

The comparisons here are hindered by the small number of Senate contests, even when they are pooled over two decades. One or two idiosyncratic races can skew the results for a whole year (although per capita and inflation adjustments help the situation). In appendix B, I discuss the dangers inherent in using two-stage least squares estimation for studying campaign spending generally, and especially in the Senate. The data loss can be severe.

I believe that these results argue in favor of a single theoretical approach and empirical model to describe and explain House and Senate campaigns. While coefficients vary from year to year, this is mainly due to small sample sizes in the Senate. The overall influences on House and Senate campaign spending are the same. House and Senate candidates react in similar fashion, and at similar rates, to spending by their opponents. On average, higher quality challengers in both institutions spend more than lower quality challengers. Incumbents and challengers both spend more when past voting patterns indicate a relatively even split between Republicans and Democrats (even when the competitiveness of the current year's race is controlled for). These patterns are independent of the office being contested.

A Unified Approach to House and Senate Campaigns?

A high hurdle stands in the way of comparative electoral studies: do the countries, states, or electoral units vary so greatly that everything falls into "differences" and nothing into "similarities"? I have shown that this is not an insurmountable problem when comparing the House and Senate. Another hurdle rises in its place: the small number of Senate races relative to those of the

---

22. As was already noted previously, I cannot discuss challenger spending because the spending equation is underidentified.

House. At first, this seems to be an imposing barrier. After all, there are 33 Senate races a year, so pooling over eight elections results in 250 cases. However, once I try to apply any of more demanding quantitative tools the number of Senate cases rapidly diminishes. The assumptions and data requirements of two-stage least squares analysis render any analysis of Senate cases suspect. Still, the results show that Senate and House campaigns respond to the same set of pressures: the opposing candidate and the political makeup of the district. This is an encouraging result for the political setting hypothesis and otherwise confirms in the Senate a series of findings about House campaigns and candidates (summarized well in Jacobson 1997).

There are improvements that can be made. First and most obvious, while I have an extensive set of demographic measures I fail to examine more prima facie political measures. David Canon included such variables as the number of seats held by each party in the state legislature, the "shape of the structure of political careers," strength of the local party organization, and the existence of significant primary opposition. The latter would obviously help us distinguish between high and low spending levels (since the spending figures include primary as well as general election spending). Another recent study, reviewing more than a century of electoral data, is able to discern district effects in the Senate (Lee and Oppenheimer 1999). The data requirements for a study such as mine, however, are tremendous. The starting point—a comparable set of measures in the House—is enough to dissuade any but the most dogged researcher. Second, I have been unable to operationalize potentially important patterns in these data. Perhaps modality is important: racial distribution is different in Illinois than it is in Virginia, even though they both have a 15 percent black population. Perhaps there are thresholds beyond which certain economic or racial groups have a significant impact.

The results here point more to the future than to the endpoint of comparative models of campaigns in the House and Senate. While my hypotheses surrounding the effects of the political setting fell short, the overall patterns are remarkably similar across years and institutions. Both Senate and House elections feature higher quality candidates when the strategic situation is promising. The Senate acts as an attractive lure for quality candidates above and beyond other factors that might make the race competitive. Campaign spending in the House and Senate is correlated with the same sets of indicators: opponent spending, challenger quality (in the case of challenger spending), and partisan balance. At least for incumbents, there are consistent indications that spending is higher in more diverse political settings. Setting matters. Your opponent matters. These lessons apply to House, Senate, and probably all competitive electoral contests.

CHAPTER 6

Voters in U.S. Legislative Elections

The U.S. House and Senate share many similarities in the electoral arena. On most measures, states and congressional districts are indistinguishable. During campaigns, robust differences are observed—contenders for Senate seats are more experienced, more prominent, and raise and spend more money—but these differences are substantially attenuated once campaign intensity and population size are taken into account. Is it also the case that voters use a common set of standards to evaluate and choose House and Senate candidates? In this chapter, I compare and contrast voter information and choice in the U.S. House and Senate in 1988 and 1990.

It is not my intent to develop a comprehensive model of voter learning and decision-making in congressional campaigns. Instead, the focus is on comparing voter behavior across the House and Senate with the aim of finding out whether the observed differences in voting are a consequence of observed differences in intensity or some function of institutional effects. I start with the assumption that the voter applies a fairly simple vote calculus in all elections, be they Senate or House or for that matter presidential, gubernatorial, or mayoral. The fundamental basis of the decision is identical. Yet we know that actual votes vary across institutions. How can my theory be reconciled with the empirical evidence?

What we observe, the final vote, is the output from a long and complex process. I tried to represent most aspects of that process in my three-stage model. It is quite possible that the inputs at the final stage (e.g., candidate visibility and political information flow) may vary across institutions while the voters apply a uniform decision rule. However, that is surely an oversimplification. Still, I believe that information operates like a rising tide that lifts all boats. There is variation among voters—some are attentive to every news item and candidate activity while others pay only passing attention to the evening news during dinner. But the high flow of information in high-intensity contests means that even the less attentive will be *relatively* more informed than might otherwise be the case. In a high-information setting, voters can more readily "turn on" variables such as policy and ideological positions and will rely less on prior beliefs such as partisanship or evaluations of the "nature of the times."

In this chapter, I disentangle institutional accounts of election outcomes from outcomes that are a product of coincidental distributions of quality candidates, campaign funds, and electoral settings. This thesis militates against explanations that focus on the uniqueness of the Senate or the House, instead focusing on shared features of voter information and behavior. If I can somehow identify House campaigns that look like Senate campaigns, I expect that voter information and behavior will look quite Senate-like. If I can identify Senate contests that are as low-key as a typical House election, then voters should display the same low levels of information and relatively simply decision rules that I associate with the House. I examine this thesis in three arenas: voter learning, voter evaluative standards, and voter choice.

Any study of voting starts with information. Many have asserted that differential information is *the* key difference between House and Senate races, so I compare the levels, and causes, of voter recall, recognition, and likes and dislikes about House and Senate candidates. I find, contrary to my theoretical expectations, that a significant gap between voter responses to Senate and House campaigns remains even after I control for campaign intensity. The results show that voters hold more information about Senate candidates even after candidate spending, candidate quality, and campaign intensity are taken into account.

Next, I ask whether voters have separate sets of expectations about representatives and senators. Is the job of the House and the Senate different (in the voter's mind), and does this difference modify the voting rule? Or is there a House and Senate "prototype" that feeds into the candidate evaluation process, similar to what has been found with regard to presidential candidates (Aldrich, Gronke, and Grynaviski 1999). For example, it might be that senators are held more responsible for foreign policy successes and failures while House members are expected to bring home the bacon. Thus, even if information flow and content were equal, different standards and expectations would result in different outcomes. I find, however, that voter standards and evaluations are independent of institution. If there is a prototype, it is for "legislator," not "senator" or "member of the House."

If political and institutional settings form a stage upon which the main electoral actors (candidates, parties, interest groups, and the media) play their roles, then voting is the final act in this drama. If voter expectations are converging, next I ask whether voter decision rules are as well. I provide good theoretical reasons to expect substantial similarity in voting across the House and Senate and present a simple model of voter choice that can be applied to U.S. legislative elections. I make explicit the links between stage two of the election process—candidate emergence and campaign activity—and stage three—voter information and choice. As in previous analyses, I always test for institutional differences, thus allowing me to evaluate the relative similarity and difference in House and Senate voting. I find that the set of considerations that voters use and the weight that they attach to these considerations look alike.

Virtually all my attempts to tease out institutional differences fail. The weights that voters attach are the same, but the levels of these variables, such as candidate quality, remain dissimilar. These variations in flow—in inputs to the system—result in large differences in observed outcomes, even though they are channeled through the same decision making "pipe." I close by commenting on the implications of my research for comparative electoral analysis.

A Brief Digression on Data and Methods

From 1988 through 1992, the National Election Study administered a unique Senate Election Study (NES/SES), designed to improve the scientific study of Senate elections. The many academic papers using these data testify to the study's success.[1] The survey covered all 50 states, providing a large and more geographically dispersed sample of House and Senate voters and thus avoiding the large state bias noted by Westlye (1983). The NES/SES also contained a battery of survey items for both the sitting Senator(s) and the Senator up for reelection, including candidate recognition, job evaluation, issue positions, and candidate "likes and dislikes." Identical questions had been asked of House candidates since 1978. These batteries, besides advancing the study of Senate elections, allowed for the first time the kind of comparative analysis that is presented here.

Even so, I limit my study to voting behavior in 1988 and 1990. This decision is driven mostly by practical considerations. The 1992 component of the NES/SES, for reasons of cost and complexity related to the 1992 redistricting, dropped many of the questions about House candidates. Still, I continue to feel confident about the generalizability of the results. First, remember that the two main justifications for pooling in chapters 3 through 5 were, first, to make sure that the explanation was not bound to any particular year and, second, to increase the number of hard-fought races, thereby producing efficient statistical estimates. The second problem is rectified in the survey data set. Even when limited to two years, the NES/SES has 6,494 respondents. The smallest theoretically important subset of respondents are those facing intensely fought

---

1. Virtually all studies of Senate elections published after 1982 draw on the NES/SES. Its legacy continues almost a decade after the initial release in books such as this one and a recent study of Senate representation (Lee and Oppenheimer 1999).

House campaigns in 1988, a relatively less competitive year. These total 13.8 percent of that year's sample, nearly 400 cases. The data cover one presidential and one midterm year, thus eliminating the possibility that a single type of election accounts for the patterns revealed here. In the end, any questions regarding the generalizability of my results must rest on an argument whereby the two electoral institutions are closely tied in the voters' eyes in 1988 and 1990 and are somehow more separate in other years. I can see no reason to sustain this argument.

Information and Context

A large difference between House and Senate elections is the amount of information that voters have about candidates. Differential information flows could be an underlying cause of observed differences in voting rules. Hinckley (1981) makes information the centerpiece of her theory of congressional elections. Zaller (1992) describes the House campaign as a "low-information environment in which a few people know the name of the incumbent and perhaps something about his or her record; many others can, with a prompt, recognize the incumbent's name ... and still others know nothing at all" (1992, 19). Ragsdale (1981) refers to challenger "invisibility" in the title of her article on House challengers. Maisel (1982) bemoans his own trip "from obscurity to oblivion" in a personal account of a congressional campaign. Where there are high levels of information flow, voters can include a wider variety of considerations when making their choices. In a low-information setting, most voters will have to employ a few simple cues such as party or incumbency. The first step in understanding voting, therefore, is to understand information.

Therefore, information is a key part of any House and Senate comparison. How much do voters know about Senate and House candidates? Are any differences a product of increased media attention paid to the Senate (Hess 1986; Foote and Weber 1984), higher interest among voters in Senate elections, or perhaps of campaign differences? Answering these questions requires that I first explore relative levels of knowledge about House and Senate candidates.

Voter Information about Senate and House Candidates

As in each of the previous chapters, I start with a well-established descriptive finding: voters are much more likely to recall and recognize the name of Senate challengers. They are also willing to provide an answer to a greater variety of informational and evaluative questions. These results are well established

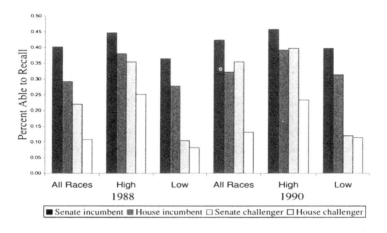

Fig. 6.1. Recall rates across institution and type of race, 1988 and 1990

and are only briefly recapitulated here.[2] Respondents report higher levels of recall and recognition, remember more contacts, and provide more "likes and dislikes" for Senate incumbents and challengers.[3] Just as campaigns are constrained by the political setting, however, voter information may also be conditioned by context. Perhaps I can disentangle the causes of higher information levels about Senate candidates. For example, we found in chapters 3 and 4 that Senate challengers involved in low-intensity races expended campaign funds at a rate comparable to that of the typical House candidate. Similar comparisons may be revealing for voter information. The first step, then, is to compare information over intensity as well as institution.

A visual inspection of recall rates in all races—the first and fourth sets of bars in figure 6.1 and the first four rows of table 6.1—suggests a step function.

---

2. More extensive treatments can be found in Jacobson 1997, 1990; Krasno 1994; and Abramowitz and Segal 1992, among others.

3. *Recall* refers to the ability of a respondent to provide, unprompted, the name of a candidate to the interviewer. On a "recognition" item, the respondent is provided a list of names and asked to identify the candidate. *Contacts* refers to the National Election Study candidate contact battery. Respondents are given a list of ways that they may have seen, heard, or been contacted by a candidate or his or her political campaign. "Likes and dislikes" are open-ended questions allowing respondents to freely cite things they like and dislike about the candidates. More information on these variables is contained in appendix B.

There are roughly three levels of respondent recall. Senate incumbents occupy the step, with roughly 40 percent of respondents able to recall their names without further prompting. Next come House incumbents and Senate challengers; respondent recall lags 5 to 10 percent behind that of Senate incumbents. House challengers bring up the rear. Less than 15 percent of respondents are able to recall these candidates' names without additional prompting.

The advantage enjoyed by Senate incumbents narrows when the more lenient recognition item is used.[4] Well over 90 percent of respondents recognized both Senate and House incumbents—so many, in fact, that I chose not to report the numbers in table 6.1. Yet, even when provided the name, only one-half of respondents in the NES/SES were able to recognize the House challenger's name. Compare that to the Senate, where more than 80 percent recognized the challenger. These are the sizable differences that first led analysts in the early 1980s to point to challenger recognition as the *key* difference between House and Senate elections (e.g., Hinckley 1980a, 1980b; Mann and Wolfinger 1980).

But appearances can be deceiving. I know that Senate races are more closely contested. Does this account for the advantage in name recognition? Apparently it does. I break the recall data down by race intensity, reported in the additional bars in figure 6.1 and additional columns in table 6.1. Once again, there appears to be a step function to recall, and this is encouraging. But the candidates have been reshuffled. In high-intensity contests, nothing much has changed. The highest step is still occupied by Senate incumbents (45 pecent), House incumbents and Senate challengers occupy the second step (much more clearly equal in both years, at 40 percent recall) and House challengers (25 percent) rank at the bottom. In low-intensity contests, however, the position of Senate challengers shifts. Only incumbents display high levels of visibility (with a significant advantage still held by senators), whereas challengers are equally *(in)visible,* regardless of institution.

These patterns are repeated in most respects in the recognition data (reported in the fifth and sixth rows of table 6.1). Thirty percent more respondents recognize the name of the average Senate challenger than recognize the average House challenger. The gap shifts as expected in high- and low-intensity contests, although in a less regular fashion. In 1988, there is almost no difference in high-intensity contests, whereas the gap in low-intensity contests is reduced from 30 percent to 22 percent. In 1990, the gap in high intensity contests declines from 28 percent to 22 percent, yet it is statistically indistinguishable in low-intensity contests. Note, finally, that in both years, the recognition (and

---

4. Mann (1978) argues that the recognition items more closely simulate the voting booth.

Table 6.1. Recognizing the Candidates, 1988–90

	1988			1990		
	All Races	High Intensity	Low Intensity	All Races	High Intensity	Low Intensity
Recall name						
House incumbent	0.292	0.380	0.277	0.322	0.392	0.313
Senate incumbent	0.402	0.447	0.364	0.424	0.458	0.397
House challenger	0.108	0.251	0.082	0.131	0.233	0.114
Senate challenger	0.220	0.354	0.105	0.354	0.397	0.120
Recognize Name						
House challenger	0.506	0.894	0.446	0.523	0.720	0.501
Senate challenger	0.813	0.954	0.666	0.801	0.938	0.542
Number of likes						
House incumbent	0.628	0.556	0.642	0.832	0.844	0.829
Senate incumbent	0.706	0.652	0.752	1.120	1.209	1.210
House challenger	0.163	0.413	0.118	0.257	0.388	0.217
Senate challenger	0.345	0.531	0.189	0.471	0.740	0.207
Number of dislikes						
House incumbent	0.179	0.341	0.149	0.321	0.359	0.309
Senate incumbent	0.177	0.174	0.179	0.284	0.535	0.235
House challenger	0.119	0.291	0.088	0.171	0.263	0.142
Senate challenger	0.122	0.224	0.035	0.177	0.277	0.079

Source: 1988–90 NES/SES.
Note: Entries for recall and recognition are the proportion correctly identifying the name of the candidate. Incumbent recognition rates are so high for both the House and Senate (over 88 percent) with minimal variation across intensity levels that they are not reported here). Likes and dislikes are the average number of mentions in each category, including zero mentions.

recall) rate for a Senate challenger in a low-intensity contest is equal to or higher than the rates for the *average* House challenger.[5] The figures are close, mathematically and empirically, because such a large proportion of respondents faced low-intensity House contests. The "average" House race is a low-intensity contest. Yet the comparison is valid, theoretically, because it identifies a very important institutional difference. Senate contests are harder fought on average, and as a consequence Senate challengers enjoy far higher voter recognition. Statistical controls are unlikely to diminish this gap much further.

Finally, I turn the the frequency of freely mentioned "likes and dislikes" about the candidates. These survey items allow a respondent to summon up almost anything he or she thinks about a candidate for office, from personality to partisanship to policy and much in between. They are useful because they allow a more fine-grained look at the level and content of respondent information and reactions to political candidates. Respondents are not asked to simply identify a name but have to expend the additional effort required to express a like or dislike. These items also allow me to discriminate between respondents who recognize the candidate's name but have nothing substantive to say (and are coded zero on these items) from those who provide one or more distinct mentions (up to five are coded by the NES staff). As will become clear, I can also use the likes and dislikes items to test specific hypotheses about institutional differences (e.g., whether respondents are more likely to mention district benefits when describing House candidates and foreign policy when listing Senate candidates). Here I am only concerned with raw information levels—how much respondents say about Senate and House candidates. Furthermore, I focus mainly on the "likes" mentions since, as is clear from both figure 6.2 and the last eight rows of table 6.1, respondents are far more willing to tell survey interviewers things they like about candidates than things they dislike.

Most importantly, as shown in both figure 6.2 and table 6.1, the now familiar three-step pattern emerges once more. For all races, respondents have the most to say about Senate incumbents, trailed closely by House incumbents. Respondents had only half as much to say, on average, about Senate challengers, followed by another drop of 50 percent for the typical House challenger.[6] Also once again, discriminating by means of race intensity reveals a far more complex picture. Senate incumbents still lead the pack but

5. For example, 10.5 percent of the respondents recalled the name of the Senate challenger in a low-intensity contest in 1988 compared to a 10.8 percent recall rate for House challengers in all races.

6. For unknown reasons, more likes and dislikes were mentioned in 1990 than in 1988. This may be because the NES subcontracted the survey in 1988 but conducted it in-house in 1990. Perhaps the outside contractor failed to record the open-ended responses carefully or did

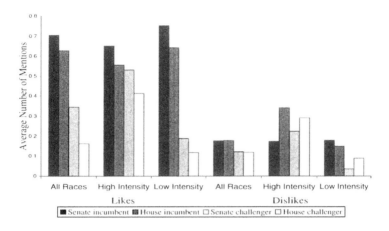

Fig. 6.2. Likes and dislikes across institution and type of race, 1988

by a very slim margin, with House incumbents and Senate challengers being virtually indistinguishable. In low-intensity contests, the most mentions are made about Senate incumbents, followed by House incumbents, with Senate challengers and House challengers again mired in virtual invisibility. As mentioned, respondents are less willing to provide the reasons why they dislike a candidate. Even so, the same pattern obtains across all three comparisons: in high-intensity contests, Senate challengers and House incumbents look alike, whereas in low-intensity contests Senate and House challengers look alike.

To summarize, roughly half of the difference between average level of recall and recognition is explained by intensity and the other half is explained by institution. Institutional differences, although still evident, have been substantially reduced. A persistent, three-step pattern to candidate recognition emerged. One set of candidates (Senate incumbents) enjoyed high levels of recognition and another set (always including House challengers) suffered low levels of recognition. The relative placement of House incumbents and Senate challengers depended on the intensity of the contest. This proves that the level of information that voters are exposed to about challengers is as much a function of the intensity of the campaign as it is something unique to the House and Senate.

---

not prompt as persistently as the NES interviews did. Fortunately, the patterns are the same, albeit at higher levels, in 1990.

TABLE 6.2. Information, District Diversity, and District Size

Recall Name	All	Low	Moderate	High
Diversity				
House incumbent	.292	.288	.297	.292
Senate incumbent	.402	.481	.378	.336
House challenger	.108	.079	.133	.112
Senate challenger	.220	.296	.189	.164
Size: population				
Senate incumbent	.402	.442	.340	.418
Senate challenger	.220	.192	.194	.273
Size: square Miles				
Senate incumbent	.402	.422	.313	.424
Senate challenger	.220	.299	.167	.175
Size: population density				
Senate incumbent	.402	.442	.369	.401
Senate challenger	.220	.333	.118	.227

Source: 1988 NES/SES.
Note: Entries are the proportion correctly identifying the name of the candidate. The categories (low, moderate, high) break the sample into thirds.

If intense campaigns lead to well-informed voters, perhaps other features of the context function the same way. I speculated in previous chapters that a candidate will have a more difficult time placing his or her name in front of the public when the district is particularly heterogeneous or media markets are inefficient. Analysts have noticed that Senate contests in large states tend to be more closely contested, thus leading to the obvious question of whether voters in these states tend to be more highly informed.[7] In fact, these relationships hold (table 6.2) but only for the Senate. About 15 percent fewer respondents in the most diverse states recall the names of the Senate incumbent and challenger than do respondents in the least diverse states.[8] Similarly, residents of more populous states seem to have a harder time learning the names of their Senate candidates, at least as reflected in the recall figures. There is no relationship between diversity and recall rates within congressional districts.

---

7. Abramowitz and Segal (1992, chap. 2) found that voters in large states were more informed about Senate candidates, while Hibbing and Alford (1990) found no relationship between state population and recall, recognition, or electoral support.

8. I use the summary index of diversity (see chap. 3). The categories break the sample into thirds.

The process that generates these results is difficult to envision. A heterogeneous district is often described as more difficult to campaign in because there are more interests to alienate (Fiorina 1974; Fenno 1982). Senate races in large states are more competitive because large states are more heterogeneous (Lee and Oppenheimer 1999; Abramowitz and Cribbs 1989). One problem with this hypothesis is that heterogeneity and population size are not linearly related, as I show in chapter 3. The first six rows of table 6.2 shed some additional light on this hypothesis. Neither "size" as population size nor square miles is consistently related to voter information.[9] Some interaction of population and size is what seems to matter: dense states make communication easier (it is easier to meet voters, to attract coverage in wide-circulation newspapers and on large-market television and radio stations, and to get voters to talk to each other), and sparsely populated, media inefficient states make campaigning particularly difficult. Abramowitz and Cribbs (1989), in contrast, speculate that *less dense* states are more amenable to competitive contests since they encourage a different, personalized style of campaigning that challengers can more easily accomplish (see also Baker 1995). The data here are inconclusive on this point: both challengers and incumbents are most widely known in the least-dense states. The relationship breaks down, however, when we examine the other levels of population density. Institutional differences in respondent knowledge persist even after controlling for variations in political settings.

I have examined some simple descriptive measures of candidate information in the House and Senate. The results highlight substantial institutional differences in the amount of information about challengers, thus replicating results from two decades of congressional voting research (now in the Senate as well as the House). Once campaign intensity is taken into account, respondent information levels about Senate and House challengers are closer, although Senate challengers are still better known. The consequences for the electoral outcomes that we observe in November should be clear. Because Senate challengers are far more likely to be recognized than their House counterparts, voters are far more likely to learn about, and vote for, Senate challengers. The observed differences are real, but their causes are more than just institutional.

To close the section, I examined a few of the more popular reasons given to explain higher levels of information about Senate incumbents and challengers. Neither diversity nor "size" (expressed as either population or square miles) has any relationship with knowledge about the incumbent. There does appear to be some tendency for respondents in the smallest and least-dense states to

---

9. One might suspect that these figures are skewed because there are few states fall into each category. However, since I have broken the sample into thirds, and the NES/SES has rough parity among state sample sizes, there are respondents from between seven and 10 states in each category.

have higher levels of recall of Senate challengers. While not eliminating the heterogeneity or population size argument, these results do call them into question.[10]

In chapter 2, I laid out a three-stage model. Some of those pieces have fallen into place, but there are still gaps to be filled. I eliminated the political setting as a cause of campaign activity and now as a cause of informational differences. The information gap remains. Different levels of respondent knowledge across the Senate and House may be a function of differential visibility of the two institutions or greater prominence of the average senator—the institutional explanation—or they could be a function of the relatively higher campaign spending levels, harder fought campaigns, higher quality candidates, and more efficient media markets evident in states. Controlling for individual level, campaign, and institutional influences on voter information lets me zero in on the causes of informational differences. In the next section, I propose a causal model of respondent information and test it using the 1988 and 1990 NES/SES data.

The Correlates of Voter Informedness

Why do voters know so much more about Senate than House challengers? What are the causes of higher or lower levels of voter information about political candidates and do they help me understand the differences observed here? To answer these questions, I must attend to both individual and contextual influences on voter learning. Individual correlates of informedness—political interest, media usage, and education—all will increase the probability that an individual will recall or recognize a candidate's name. Individuals are also affected by the political context in which they live. I discovered that more intense political contests result in higher levels of voter information. Varying levels of campaign spending, candidate quality, and campaign intensity, along with institutional controls, also need to be included in my model of voter information.

Models of political perception focus on the interaction between an individual's ability and desire to learn about politics and the way that the political environment supplies information. At the individual level, a generally attentive and politically interested respondent will be more likely to recall the names of political candidates and to make substantive comments about their characters,

---

10. Two ways to extend these tests would be expand the sample over time, adding recognition and recall tests for other years, and over institutions, obtaining district size measures for congressional districts or looking at governors and other statewide officeholders.

records, and political positions.[11] Media usage should also increase the likelihood that voters will be exposed to political information about the campaign.[12]

Accordingly, I hypothesize that information about candidates in the House and Senate is in part a product of individual levels of political attentiveness and informedness about politics. I include a summary measure of political interest,[13] the respondent's level of education, and strength and direction of partisanship. Education and partisan strength are additional realizations of informedness and attentiveness to politics (i.e., more educated respondents are more likely to recall political figures and stronger partisans are more likely to attend to political information). I include partisan direction in order to test whether the incumbent's partisans are more likely to recall the incumbent's name and less likely to recall the challenger's name.

The campaign environment also provides information to the voter. Higher levels of spending by a candidate should be positively associated with information about that candidate. For the incumbent, I need to control for the amount of time that the incumbent has been in office, under the assumption that more years means more campaigns and more chances to employ the tools of incumbency to place his or her name before the voters.[14] For the challenger, I need to allow for an independent contribution of candidate quality. Finally, I add campaign intensity, under the assumption that intensity provides an additional boost to voter information levels above and beyond that caused by campaign spending, candidate quality, and voter interest.[15]

---

11. Political sophistication plays a central role in individuals' evaluations of political candidates (Aldrich, Gronke, and Grynaviski 1999; Rahn, Aldrich, Borgida, and Sullivan 1990); in the susceptibility of individuals to "priming" (Iyengar and Kinder 1987); and, more broadly, in the way individuals respond to political stimuli (Zaller 1992).

12. Frequency of exposure to political information also affects the likelihood of exposure (Zaller 1992) and acceptance (Zaller 1992; Iyengar and Kinder 1987).

13. The summary measure is a combination of self-expressed political interest, how often the respondent reported reading a newspaper, and how often the respondent reported watching the network news. Weights were obtained via principal components analysis. Details are contained in appendix C.

14. I log the number years in office. The log reflects diminishing gains in recognition and recall as tenure increases.

15. Campaign learning also depends on the interaction between the credibility of the source, the direction of the message, and the individual's prior beliefs (Franklin 1993; Zaller 1992). Zaller presents a compelling argument for a complex non-linear specification of the effect of the campaign on the likelihood of defecting from the incumbent's party. I replicate the defection models in appendix C but do not use the non-linear specification. Zaller focuses on House elections, where he can assume that the bulk of information is incumbent-oriented, enabling him to use a simpler "one-way" message model (1992, chap. 10). The majority of Senate races, however, are high-intensity contests that require me to use the dual-flow model, which is substantially more complex.

The dependent variable in this model is the ability to recall a candidate's name. Recalling the candidate's name is a more difficult test of respondent information about candidates than is recognition, and it yields the most interesting empirical results.[16] The dependent variable is dichotomous, so the coefficient estimates are obtained via maximum likelihood probit. The model is shown below.[17]

$$
\begin{aligned}
Pr(Recall) \quad = \quad & \beta_0 + \beta_1 (Political\ Interest) \\
& + \beta_2 (Education) + \beta_3 (Strength\ of\ Partisanship) \\
& + \beta_4 (Partisanship) + \beta_5 (Challenger\ Quality) \\
& + \beta_6 (Incumbent\ Spending) + \beta_7 (Challenger\ Spending) \\
& + \beta_8 (Intensity) + \beta_9 (Institution) \\
& + \beta_{10,11,12} (Instit) * (ChallQual + Inc\$ + Chall\$) \\
& + \beta_{13} [\log(Tenure)] + \varepsilon.
\end{aligned}
$$

The equation can be read thus: the probability that a respondent is able to recall the name of the candidate is a function of a series of variables meant to represent interest in and attentiveness to politics and the media, including political interest;[18] education; strength and direction of partisanship;[19] campaign activity;[20] the intensity of the campaign; and remaining institutional effects. Because the strength of the relationship between recall and campaign activity might vary between the House and the Senate, I include interaction terms (Institution*Campaign).[21]

---

16. Recognition rates for incumbents in both institutions are so high that there is very little variance to explain. I did estimate these models using recognition and likes/dislikes as dependent variables. In the interests of brevity, I only present the recall model here. The results in the recognition models were substantially the same, except that the partisanship measure is statistically significant while it is statistically insignificant in the recall models. The likes/dislikes models yielded mixed results that are more difficult to summarize. Likes/dislikes can be thought of as both an information and an evaluation measure (i.e., Zaller 1992), so it might not be appropriate to force them into a learning model. The result was a confusing set of estimates.

17. In the results, I test for model stability across the House and Senate by interacting the institution dummy variable with each of the other variables.

18. Political interest is a scale consisting of interest in politics and attentiveness to the media. See the appendix C for details.

19. Partisanship is coded in a pro-incumbent direction.

20. The campaign measures include challenger quality and logged per capita spending by the incumbent and the challenger.

21. Unlike ordinary least squares coefficients, probit estimates cannot be interpreted as change in the dependent variable associated with a unit change in the independent variable. The magnitude of the effect changes with values of the independent variables (Aldrich and Nelson

Results

The results of these models, shown in table 6.3 lend support to most aspects of my model. Individuals who are more interested in politics and have more formal education are more likely to recall both the incumbent's and challenger's names. Partisanship (strength and direction) functions less well as an additional measure of political interest. Stronger partisans are more likely to recall the name both candidates, ceteris paribus, but the estimates are statistically indistinguishable from zero in the incumbent recall equation. The contextual side of the model operates as expected, with two surprises. Challenger spending, not surprisingly, is particularly influential in helping citizens learn about challengers. All campaign spending coefficients are correctly signed, but only the coefficient on challenger spending was statistically significant.[22] Respondents do not know more about quality challengers, contrary to my expectations.

Table 6.3 further shows that a respondent's ability to recall the name of the incumbent or the challenger is most strongly determined by that individual's general interest in politics and only secondarily (for challenger recall) by education and strength of partisanship. The relative strength of the other variables confirms my expectations about how challengers and incumbents gain recognition. For incumbents, tenure plays an important role in establishing name recognition (see also Zaller 1992 and Franklin 1991, 1993), as does the campaign. Ironically, however, only challenger spending and challenger quality

---

1984). The usual solution is to present predicted values of the dependent variable based on typical or interesting combinations of the independent variables. There are some complications in this case. It is unrealistic to increase campaign variables in isolation. For example, if challenger spending increases by one standard deviation, incumbent spending increases in response. Campaign "intensity" cannot be isolated from challenger spending, incumbent spending, and candidate quality. I employ a mixed strategy to explain the probit results. First, I interpret the coefficients based on their magnitude, signs, and statistical significance. I assess the contribution that the institutional block of variables makes to the goodness of fit of the model to the data. Finally, I interpret point estimates in two ways, first by the standard method (increase one variable, hold all others constant, report the change in probability), and second by selecting out particular illustrative cases and comparing relatively high- and low-intensity races in the House and Senate. This gives me a feel for the impact of campaign intensity on voter informedness with real combinations of intensity, spending, and candidate quality.

22. Challenger spending remained significant in the recognition and likes/dislikes models, while the estimated coefficient on incumbent spending was statistically insignificant in all models. One might suspect that multicollinearity is the culprit, but the coefficient remained statistically insignificant even when challenger spending and intensity were removed from the model.

have a statistically significant relationship with incumbent recall.[23] Respondents are much more likely to recall *both* candidate names in the presence of high-spending *challengers*.

Finally, note that institutional effects are evident in this model. Challenger spending is less productive in Senate than in House races, while incumbent spending is more productive. And there are institutional differences in recall that are not captured by other variables. Still, institution and the interaction terms improve the fit of the model less than any other block of variables.[24] Institutional differences have not been eliminated, but they do less to explain the patterns in the data than any of the other factors considered.[25]

Another way to illustrate the impact these variables have on citizen recall is to vary just one measure, holding all other measures constant, and examine changes in the predicted probability of recall. This exercise only reinforces the central role of individual interests in learning about political campaigns. Moving from the average level of political interest to one standard deviation above average causes a 15 percent increase in the predicted probability that a respondent will recall the incumbent's name and an 11 percent increase in the probability that a respondent will recall the challenger's name. Compare this to the impact of institution (an 8 percent increase, ceteris paribus) and intensity (a 7 percent increase, ceteris paribus). Even the impact of challenger and incumbent spending, the main focus of most studies of House voting, have

---

23. This is another indication of potential multicollinearity between the campaign variables. See also Erikson and Palfrey 1998 and Palfrey and Erikson 1993.

24. By sequentially restricting the coefficients to zero on blocks of variables and then comparing the log likelihood, I can see how much a set of variables adds to the goodness of fit (King 1989). In the incumbent recall model, the institutional variables only increase the goodness of fit by 15 points (two times the log likelihood ratio, where the log likelihoods are taken from the full model reported here, and the model with the institutional variables removed) out of a total reduction in log-likelihood of 704.4; in the challenger recall model, the institutional variables increase the goodness by 20.6 points out of 2,461.4.

25. I estimated these models under a variety of specifications: separately for the House and Senate, separately for high- and low-intensity races, and crossing the two categories (high/low ∗ Senate/House). I chose to report the full model because it tested all of the hypotheses made in the chapter, produced the highest correlation between actual and predicted probabilities, and produced the closest match between actual and predicted probabilities for various subsamples (low-intensity House, high-intensity Senate, etc). The most noteworthy result from these disaggregated models is the stability of these findings. Not only is the relative strength of the variables similar, but the estimated coefficients, particularly for the individual-level variables, are surprisingly close across various specifications. The estimated impact of political interest, for example, varies from .83 to 1.03 across 10 different estimations (for *both* challenger and incumbent recall). The coefficient on education is between .2 and .3 for nine of 10 estimates. While the estimated impact of spending, intensity, and institution obviously vary more as I select out House or Senate and high- and low-intensity contests, the direction and magnitude of their effects on recall are very stable, with some (challenger quality in particular) changing only in the second decimal point.

Table 6.3. Ability to Recall Candidate Names

Variable	1988: Recall Incumbent	1988: Recall Challenger	1990: Recall Incumbent	1990: Recall Challenger
Political interest	1.059 (.079)**	.893 (.103)**	1.561 (.067)**	1.236 (.295)**
Education	.154 (.076)*	.217 (.102)*	.242 (.058)**	.369 (.090)**
Strength Party ID	.233 (.140)	.369 (.175)*	.303 (.161)*	.327 (.182)
Partisanship	.023 (.037)	−.072 (.047)	.100 (.068)	.021 (.062)
Challenger spending	.098 (.027)**	.279 (.043)**	.134 (.045)**	.410 (.093)**
Incumbent spending	.028 (.057)	−.120 (.076)	.040 (.036)	−.073 (.057)
Challenger quality	.063 (.027)	.074 (.033)*	.000 (.032)	.101 (.043)**
Intensity	.186 (.083)*	.371 (.097)**	.201 (.092)**	.389 (.088)**
Instit*Chall$	−.118 (.056)*	−.199 (.070)*	−.097 (.076)	−.187 (.091)*
Instit*Inc$	.121 (.095)	.312 (.116)*	.038 (.089)	.290 (.094)**
Instit*ChallQual	−.089 (.046)	−.038 (.056)	−.104 (.087)	.001 (.060)
Institution	.238 (.168)	−.008 (.204)	.109 (.126)	.021 (.156)
Tenure (log)	.079 (.037)*	—	.092 (.033)**	—
Constant	−1.520 (.146)**	−2.073 (.192)**	−.903 (.123)**	−1.689 (.309)**
$-2\ln(L_0/L_1)$	704	2,461	691	1,916
N of cases	3,696	3,696	3,225	3,225
Percentage predicted	68	85	72	91

Source: 1988–90 NES/SES.

Note: Variable coding information is in appendix C. Entries are maximum likelihood probit coefficients. Standard errors are in parentheses. Coefficients with two asterisks are three or more times their standard errors; coefficients with one asterisk are between two and three times their standard errors.

less influence than individual characteristics. A one standard deviation increase in challenger spending is associated with a 6 percent increase in the probability of recalling the House challenger, and a 1.2 percent drop in the probability of recalling the Senate challenger; a one standard deviation increase in incumbent spending is associated with a 1 percent increase in House incumbent recall and a 4 percent increase in Senate incumbent recall, ceteris paribus.[26] Institution matters, but campaigns, and especially individual motivation to become informed, matter far more.

Citizen Recall and Campaign Environments

Finally, what do I make of the improved predictive power of our models when they are estimated in the challenger recall models and the off-year election? I know that candidate recall is lower in 1990 (as in most off-years contests) and that respondents are less likely to be able to recall a challenger's name than they are the name of an incumbent. Ironically, from the perspective of a survey analyst lower knowledge levels in the aggregate improve our ability to discriminate between the more and less informed and thus increase the statistical fit of our model. For example, note that the log likelihood is lower and the proportion correctly predicted is higher for both estimates of challenger recall. In similar fashion, the statistical model performs better in 1990 compared to 1988. While the log likelihoods cannot be directly compared, since these models are estimated with different samples, the coefficients in 1990 have higher t-statistics and the proportion predicted correctly is noticeably higher. Statistical jargon aside, this pattern comports with our intuition. It is easier to predict who will be informed or uninformed in a case of low information flow in which citizen knowledge levels are much more likely to be determined by the citizen's own interest in politics.

A final way to look at these results is to compare across years, across incumbents and challengers, and in high-intensity contests. These examples provide benchmarks with which to assess the impact of citizen information levels over widely varied informational environments. High intensity contests should be particularly instructive since here I can gauge the marginal contribution of individual variables when campaign information flow is at its peak.

I selected a subset of House and Senate races in 1988 in which the ratio of incumbent to challenger spending was less than 1.5 and compared the forecasted recall with levels in the "average" race and a low-intensity race. I chose 1.5 as a cutpoint using my own understanding of what makes for a competitive

---

26. The negative effect of challenger spending in the Senate is striking. This are another indication of how closely challenger and incumbent spending are linked, so closely that there is probably multicollinearity problems. If I increase both challenger and incumbent spending in the Senate, I produce the expected increase in recall rates for both candidates.

TABLE 6.4. High-Intensity Campaigns and Candidate Recall

Recall	Low-intensity Probability	Average Probability	High-intensity Probability	Increase (low to high)
House incumbent	.276	.293	.395	.119
Senate incumbent	.239	.408	.448	.209
House challenger	.075	.113	.288	.213
Senate challenger	.097	.216	.362	.265

Source: 1988 NES/SES.
Note: Entries are for the predicted proportion correctly identifying the name of the candidate. The entries in the low-intensity column were produced by setting the intensity variable to zero. High-intensity races are defined as races in which the ratio of incumbent to challenger spending is less than 1.5. The estimates were caculated by substituting the mean values for challenger spending, incumbent spending, and challenger quality from the subset of high-intensity race.

race (see appendix C for a more elaborate empirical justification). Under 1.5 qualifies as a hard-fought race by almost anyone's criteria, particularly for the House.[27] For the "low-intensity" comparison, I set intensity to zero, left all other variables at their mean, and calculated the predicted probability of recall. For "average" races, I took the mean value of the predicted probabilities (this means that "intensity" and "institution" take on rather odd values, somewhere between zero and one). For the set of high intensity races, I substituted the average value of challenger spending, incumbent spending, and challenger quality for the chosen subset of races.

The relative levels of recall make clear the importance of campaign intensity, more so for challengers than incumbents and especially for high-quality challengers. Respondents are 15 percent more likely to recall the name of a challenger in races with high levels of campaign spending and challenger quality than they are in an average race. For incumbents, the predicted increases are smaller: 10 percent for House and 4 percent for Senate incumbents (compare columns 3 and 4 in table 6.4). Campaign intensity works disproportionately in favor of challengers.[28]

---

27. In the House, the selected contests are CA 19, Lagomarsino vs. Hart; HI 1, Sakai vs. Bitterman; MI 2, Purcell vs. Pollack; NY 32, DioGuardi vs. Lowey; NC 4, Price vs. Fetzer; NC 5, Neal vs. Gray; OH 11, Eckhart vs. Muller; SC 4, Patterson vs. White; TN 3, Lloyd vs. Cutler; and WA 1, Miller vs. Lindquist. In the Senate, the selected contests are DE, Roth vs. Woo; SD, Melcher vs. Burns; NE, Karnes vs. Kerry; ND, Burdick vs. Strinden; and RI, Chaffee vs. Licht. In appendix B I explain in more detail how I selected out high-intensity races.

28. This is also evident in the recall figures in table 6.1.

Discussion: Candidates, Campaigns, and Citizen Information

What aspects of the campaign most improve the prospects for a challenger? Candidate quality has by far the largest impact. Of the 21 percent increase in recall of House challengers (from low-intensity races to the sample races in table 6.4), 8 percent is accounted for by changes in the level of challenger quality and 5 percent by increases in challenger spending. For the Senate, 14 percent of the 18 percent increase is accounted for by changes in challenger quality, with only 3 percent being accounted for by changes in spending.[29] Obviously, challenger quality does not "increase" in a vacuum: quality challengers spend more money. Still, recall rates are determined in large part by the quality of the challenger and much less by how much that challenger spends. This reinforces Gary Jacobson's (1990b) credo: you can't beat somebody with nobody, regardless of the seat for which you are running and whether you have money.

There is remarkable similarity in the ways voters learn about candidates in both the House and Senate. Individuals who care more about politics learn more about politics—there is nothing earth-shattering about this finding. What is surprising is the stability of this relationship, regardless of whether the candidate in question is an incumbent, a challenger, a senator, or a member of the House. Second, campaigns do matter but mainly for challengers. The most important feature that a challenger can bring to the table is himself—his or her previous political experience, previous time in office, or celebrity status. The "growing impact of the challenger" (Jacobson 1990b) is confirmed once more in these data. Finally, I found that institutional differences are exceedingly slight. Challenger spending appears to be somewhat more productive in the Senate and challenger quality hurt Senate incumbents somewhat more than House incumbents, but these effects pale in substantive significance compared to the impact of political interest, challenger spending, and challenger quality.

Does any of this really help us better understand House and Senate elections? After all, we saw in previous chapters that Senate candidates are generally of higher quality and spend more money. Now we discover that higher levels of challenger quality and challenger spending are associated with higher rates of challenger recall. Have I just confirmed the existence of a tremendous House/Senate difference via a roundabout path? In one respect, the answer is

---

29. I obtained these comparisons by setting intensity to zero, leaving all the other variables at their mean values, and calculating the predicted probability. Then, sequentially, I increased each variable from its mean value to the mean value for the selected set of races and examined the impact on the predicted probability. This is similar to the procedure followed earlier, except that I am not increasing variables by the standard deviation. Instead, I am increasing them to some number determined by the category "high-intensity race." On average, these increases are more than one standard deviation.

yes: when selecting out the most intensely fought contests, only 3 to 8 percent of House contests fall under scrutiny, compared to 18 to 26 percent of Senate contests. Even in these most similar races, Senate challenger quality ranks a good point above House challenger quality. The consequences for recall are made clear in table 6.4—Senate incumbents and challengers are better known than their House counterparts at all levels of campaign intensity. Whether this difference is attributable to the category "institution" rather than a consequence of different distributions of challengers and money is a topic that I will take up in the final chapter. Next, however, I would like to close the empirical analysis with a comparison of voting in the House and Senate.

Expectations and Evaluations of House and Senate Members

I began my study of House and Senate voting by examining the *amount* of information held by respondents. Now I turn to the *content* of that information. What are voter expectations about members of the House and senators? Are there differences in this realm that might cause me to expect different outcomes? Even if the overall level of information about, for example, a House incumbent and a Senate challenger is roughly the same, critical distinctions may appear in what voters want and therefore in what information they attend to, retain, and employ in the voting booth.

The intention here is to describe the basic outlines of voter expectations for House and Senate members. This should provide insights into differences that may emerge in the voting model. If, for example, I find no tendency to ascribe a "national" role to senators and a "district service" role to House members, it is unlikely that constituency service considerations will weigh more heavily when voters are choosing a House candidate. The results from this section challenge the proposition that House members are judged more on constituency service and senators on national policy stances. Respondents' descriptions of the jobs of a senator and House member are indistinguishable.

Potential Differences in Standards: Policy and Constituency Service

I often ask my students: what is the job of a member of Congress? I generally get answers that run the gamut from "writing legislation" to "being an ombudsman" to the inevitable "running for reelection." Eventually, however, some misguided soul provides the answer I am seeking—"representing their constituency"—and we proceed to discuss what this entails.[30] In the future, I

---

30. A good teacher can spend days deconstructing this phrase with students. What is meant by *represent* (delegate, trustee, something else)? Who makes up the *constituency* (geography, voters, supporters, contributors)? How does the representative know what the constituency wants?

will ask my students whether a senator's job is any different. The immediate response is likely to be: of course, the Senate is the forum for great debates, where issues such as tariffs, the national bank, slavery, a national income tax, and desegregation are argued. The House, in contrast, is where the nuts and bolts of local representation takes place, how much to spend here, how much to tax there.

These differences would be in line with our constitutional design, as Fenno (1983), Abramowitz (1988), and Baker (1995), among others, have noticed. The Founders hoped that institutional arrangements in the Constitution, combined with assumptions about human nature and political action, would have advantageous consequences. Regarding the Senate and House, the framers placed great emphasis on the salutary effects of bicameralism. The two chambers are different in almost every respect: term length, size of the chamber, and constitutionally assigned policy prerogatives.

Are these differences reflected in citizen evaluations of their Senate and House members? In this section, I present a series of tables showing how respondents view the jobs of their representatives and what they like and dislike about Senate and House candidates. These tables serve as an initial test of the proposition that respondents view the role of House members and senators differently and will help me anticipate whether these differences will carry over into voter decision making. They lead inexorably to the conclusion that actual differences in standards are hard to find. Voters view their legislative institutions through a single lens.

Actual Differences in Standards: Converging Institutions

What is the job of a senator or member of the House? One indication might be what is electorally beneficial. Mayhew (1974) pioneered an intellectual move to interpret congressional processes and politics as a product of the "electoral connection." The evidence that has accumulated since 1974 is compelling: the value for House members of constituency service and other varieties of constituency tending is well established.[31] The student who said "their job is to get

---

This makes students reflect upon big issues about representation and voting and also more practical issues such as what a member does with his or her time and how a member monitors constituency desires.

31. The literature on constituency service and "home style" activities is large and cannot be cited in full here. See, for examples, Fenno 1978; Cain, Ferejohn, and Fiorina 1987; and Fiorina and Rohde 1989. The *American Journal of Political Science*, volume 25, also contains a series of articles on the electoral benefit of casework.

reelected" was not that far off from the truth.[32] Much less attention has been paid to the electoral consequences of constituency service in the U.S. Senate.[33]

What happens when survey respondents are asked about the jobs of their representatives? The data indicate that respondent expectations of House and Senate members are virtually identical (see table 6.5). Respondents are no more likely to think a House member or senator will resolve a particular problem, vote the right way on bills, stay in touch with the district, or look out for local interests. The last three comparisons may be misleading because the National Election Study asked three questions about the senators and immediately followed with three questions about the House members. This may have been an attempt to get respondents to compare and contrast the roles. The result could have been the opposite—the close proximity of the survey items may have induced respondents to make sure their answers were consistent. Data from other surveys mirror these findings, however. Jacobson reports a table similar to this one, comparing respondent expectations for senators, from the NES/SES, with expectations about House members drawn from the 1990 and 1988 pre- and post-election NES. The response distributions are virtually identical (1997, 110–11).

The larger problem with these survey questions is that the socially acceptable response dominates: members should simultaneously stay in touch with the district, look out for citizens, and simultaneously attend to national issues. Respondents may say this to our interviewers, but this might not bear much of a relationship to the standards they apply when voting.

As an alternative, suppose respondents are provided with significantly more freedom than "yes/no" and closed-end responses allow. Such "open-ended" items allow respondents to freely supply answers, thus avoiding the problems associated with a closed response set. They let the respondent, not the survey analyst, determine what qualities are preferred in a senator or House member. The NES/SES has included an open-ended item, usually referred to as the "likes/dislikes" question, about presidential contenders and the two main political parties since the late 1950s, about House candidates since 1978, and about Senate and House candidates in 1988 and 1990.

---

32. While some observers of Congress mean this cynically, many political scientists do not and bemoan the low esteem in which Congress is held (Dodd 1993). The electoral connection was an attempt to see how far a strictly self-interested model could go toward explaining congressional structure. Members of Congress clearly have other interests besides reelection (e.g., Hibbing 1993; Fenno, 1978).

33. The analyses of Senate elections by Abramowitz (1988) and Abramowitz and Segal (1992, 1990) focus on national conditions, ideological extremism and moderation, and campaign activity, with little attention devoted to constituency service. Krasno (1994) finds that contacts and perceived helpfulness are beneficial to senators as well as House members.

TABLE 6.5. Job Evaluations of Senators and House Members

	1988		1990	
	House	Senate	House	Senate
Evaluations of performance				
1. If you had a problem that (senator/representative) could do something about, do you think s/he would be (VERY HELPFUL = 1)?	.634	.637	.592	.605
2. Do you happen to remember anything that (Senator/Representative) has done for the people in his/her (state/district) while s/he has been in Congress? (YES = 1)	.229	.220	.285	.234
3. Have you generally (AGREED = 1) with the way (Senator/Representative) has voted on bills?	.621	.622	.698	.692
4. How good a job would you say (senator/representative) does of keeping in touch ... in your (state/district)? (VERY GOOD = 1)	.728	.729	.685	.732
National versus local concerns				
5. How about helping people in the (state/district) who have personal problems with the government? (EXTREMELY IMPORTANT = 1)	.803	.822	—	—
6. Working in Congress on bills concerning national issues? (NOT AT ALL IMPORTANT = 1)	.095	.105	—	—
7. Making sure the (state/district) gets its fair share of government money and projects? (EXTREMELY IMPORTANT = 1)	.907	.901	—	—

Source: 1988–90 NES/SES.
Notes: Some questions were not asked in 1990. All variables have been recoded to the zero to one range.

The open-ended items surely will reveal some discernible differences in the things respondents like and dislike about Senate and House contenders. Yet, even when respondents are allowed to employ their own categories, there is little to distinguish Senate and House candidates.[34] I have already noted one difference: respondents are more likely to supply a like or dislike about Senate incumbents and challengers.[35] Even though nearly one-third of the states in the NES/SES did not hold a Senate election in 1988 and 1990 (and thus have no Senate likes/dislikes in table 6.6), there are still more total likes and dislikes about Senate than House challengers. The dropoff in the frequency of comments from likes to dislikes is also more dramatic in the House. Respondents simply had more to say about Senate candidates. This indicates that they were drawing upon a richer repository of information about Senate candidates and suggests that they might use this more elaborate set of concerns when voting.

The content of the comments, however, belies this hypothesis. The majority of respondent comments about incumbents and challengers, independent of institution, refer to personal qualities of the candidates, with somewhat greater frequency for challengers (see row 1 of table 6.6). The other categories, in order of frequency of mention, are party or ideology, domestic policy, government management and efficiency, group affiliations, and foreign policy.[36] The ordering of likes and dislikes is nearly identical across the columns, and the relative frequency of mentions are comparable for incumbents and challengers.[37] Partisan ties and ideological positions are mentioned somewhat more frequently as a reason to like or dislike challengers more than incumbents. Contrary to expectations, domestic policy is more often mentioned as a reason to like or dislike Senate than House candidates, whereas foreign policy is mentioned just as often. Total public policy mentions are greater for Senate candidates, but this is strictly a function of more domestic policy mentions.

---

34. I relied on the NES staff grouping of responses into various categories. It is possible that this induced comparability where it did not exist. A thorough reading of the actual interview protocols could reveal distinctions between House and Senate candidates, but I am doubtful that it would.

35. In table 6.1, I reported the average number of likes and dislikes. Respondents mentioned 80 percent more likes and dislikes, on average, for Senate challengers.

36. This is a rough ordering of the categories. There were more mentions of government management for House incumbents and fewer mentions of government management for House challengers.

37. The largest difference is in 1990 candidate mentions among House challenger dislikes (14 percent fewer mentions were made than for incumbents). Most differences are far smaller, on the order of 3 to 5 percent.

Table 6.6. Content of Likes and Dislikes in the Senate and House

| | 1988 | | | | 1990 | | | |
| | Incumbents | | Challengers | | Incumbents | | Challengers | |
	House	Senate	House	Senate	House	Senate	House	Senate
Likes								
Candidates	60.87	60.10	65.30	62.74	68.33	64.28	66.02	56.33
Party, ideology	11.12	12.29	18.55	17.75	9.03	10.75	15.63	19.34
Domestic policy	8.10	11.25	6.75	9.49	12.33	14.93	10.74	18.25
Gov't management	11.31	8.42	4.82	2.46	3.87	4.81	3.71	3.29
Groups	7.41	5.67	3.86	7.03	5.62	3.51	2.93	2.29
Foreign policy	1.19	1.46	0.72	0.52	0.83	1.75	0.98	0.5
N of likes	1,592	1,164	415	569	1,939	2,391	512	1,003
Dislikes								
Candidates	59.51	55.27	69.00	65.25	57.02	56.32	72.81	58.81
Party, ideology	17.48	16.5	18.67	18.68	15.45	14.66	17.60	21.75
Domestic policy	10.62	13.12	5.67	8.51	13.62	16.89	6.44	13.49
Gov't management	5.09	6.76	4.67	4.49	7.73	5.56	1.60	2.55
Groups	4.65	5.57	1.33	2.13	4.78	3.84	1.60	2.07
Foreign policy	2.66	2.78	0.67	0.95	2.67	2.73	0.00	1.34
N of dislikes	452	503	300	423	712	989	375	823

Source: 1988–90 NES/SES. Calculated by author.

TABLE 6.6. (continued)

| | 1988–90, Pooled | | | |
| | Incumbents | | Challengers | |
	House	Senate	House	Senate
Likes				
Candidates	64.97	63.82	65.7	58.28
Party, ideology	9.97	10.52	16.94	19.14
Domestic policy	10.42	13.17	8.95	14.81
Gov't management	7.22	6.06	4.12	3.22
Groups	6.43	4.91	3.34	4.12
Foreign policy	0.99	1.52	0.86	0.55
N of likes	3,531	4,934	927	2,174
Dislikes				
Candidates	57.55	56.14	71.11	63.41
Party, ideology	16.11	15.13	18.07	18.35
Domestic policy	12.36	14.99	6.07	11.89
Gov't management	6.65	6.27	2.96	3.04
Groups	4.69	4.89	1.48	2.28
Foreign policy	2.64	2.58	0.30	1.03
N of dislikes	1,173	2,168	675	1,842

Source: 1988–90 NES/SES. Calculated by author.

Once again, these data replicate tables that Gary Jacobson presents using House data from 1978, 1984, 1988, and 1994 and Senate data from the NES/SES (cf. tables 5.15 and 5.16 in Jacobson 1997). These are strong, consistent, and replicable results.[38]

Respondents know more about Senate candidates—this is evident here, as we saw earlier. The content of evaluations, however, differs only marginally. Voters apply one set of standards to the "jobs" of their elected representatives. While political cartoonists might draw the prototypical senator as a great debater in the tradition of John Calhoun and the prototypical House member as

---

38. My interpretation of these figures differs from that of Miller (1990). There are some differences in the way Miller and I categorized likes/dislikes. Although Miller claims that he used the NES staff coding scheme (532–33), the frequencies he reports differ from mine. According to his figures, more than 20 percent of challenger likes concerned issues, nearly double what I found. I was unable to reproduce the figures he presents on page 532. However, his figures do support my general claim that the ordering and relative frequency of mentions is remarkably similar across the institutions.

a ward heeler or pork-barreler in the tradition of Daniel Flood, respondents to this survey made no such clean distinctions. Of course, this may be due to the increasing number of "Senator Pothole" Al D'Amatos in the Senate, but this only reinforces my claim of converging institutions.

In the modern era, the Senate has become increasingly concerned with constituency service and reelection (Sinclair 1989; Ornstein, Peabody, and Rohde 1993). Others continue to claim that national issues and public policy concerns play a larger role in voter evaluations of senators (e.g., Fenno 1982; Abramowitz and Segal 1990, 1992). However, at least in the 1980s, the House was more able to respond and react to Reagan-era initiatives.[39] Perhaps these changes have been reflected in citizen evaluations of these two institutions. As their public policy roles have become increasingly indistinct, public perceptions have as well.

A single set of evaluative standards certainly fits the cognitive miser model. Experimental studies of political reasoning (Sniderman, Brody, and Tetlock 1993) as well as models of presidential voting (Rahn, Aldrich, Borgida, and Sullivan 1990; Alvarez 1999) demonstrate that citizens are apt to rely on simplifying devices, heuristics, and schematic assessments in order to make sense of a complicated political world. There is some evidence that the mass of the public holds a different set of expectations about the *institutions* of the House and Senate (Jacobson 1990b). Perhaps this reflects a distinction between Congress as a representative democratic institution and as a set of "members" (Hibbing and Theiss-Morse 1995). Regardless of the source of institutional distinctions, the data reported here show no evidence of different expectations of *candidates* for the House and Senate.

From Information to Choice

The information gap plays a large part in helping us to discriminate between these two institutions. Voters recognize Senate challengers more frequently and have more things to say about them, even when controlling for campaign intensity. At the same time, the content of those likes and dislikes are no different than in the House. This implies that the average Senate voter will employ a more information-rich decision rule, perhaps "turning on" more switches than the average House voter. In an information-rich House setting, however, there should be little difference between the Senate and House voter. These differences are easily testable with pooled House/Senate voting data. Now let us turn to this final test of House versus Senate.

---

39. The House, because of its more structured rules and ability to limit debate and amendments, was a more aggressive and effective policymaker in the Reagan years (Rohde 1991).

Toward a Unified Model of Voting

The final, and decisive, stage of the electoral process is the vote. My intent here is not to develop a comprehensive model of voter decision making in the House and Senate. Instead, I zero in on those considerations that could arguably make a difference in the ways voters evaluate House and Senate candidates. This analysis is one cut at pooling Senate and House voting models, but it is not intended to be the only one. My suspicion, however, is that other scholars will reach the same conclusions that I reach here: there really is little to distinguish the House and Senate voter.

As a point of departure, I rely on Gary Jacobson's well-developed model of House voting. Jacobson, along with many other authors, has developed these models over the past 15 years. The literature on congressional voting is too extensive to cite here. See the bibliographies in this book, Jacobson 1997, and Dodd and Oppenheimer 1997. The main determinants of choice in that model fall into four categories: individual characteristics, national forces, candidate likes and dislikes, and candidate contacts. I add to the basic model my measures of campaign intensity and institution. I perform a series of tests for institutional differences, relying on dummy variable interaction terms. Any difference in the coefficients that is larger than zero—not a difficult standard given the sample sizes—will be reported in the tables. I do not report the results from fully interactive models—in which all variables are interacted with an institution dummy variable—because the vast majority of the coefficients are statistically insignificant. In addition, I subject House/Senate differences to two more detailed tests, comparing the weight voters place on foreign policy considerations and national forces. The hypothesis is that Senate voters ought to place greater weight on these matters, ceteris paribus.

The results provide a strong endorsement of the pooled approach. As in the information model, the causal structure is comparable across institutions. The estimated probit coefficients are nearly identical. Almost every attempt to tease out institutional differences in the voting models failed. Most of the institutional differences that I did obtain are in the predicted direction: respondents who expressed foreign policy concerns penalized Senate but not House incumbents and national forces were mildly more important in Senate contests. None of the estimated coefficients passed conventional statistical significance tests.

The overriding considerations for voters in the House and Senate are much the same. First and foremost, most voters are loyal to their parties, loyal to their president, and loyal to their incumbents. The balance of voter evaluations of the incumbent and challenger (likes and dislikes) are the next most important consideration. Finally, candidate contacts are a way for both incumbents and challengers to improve the likelihood that a voter will select them. However, their relative influence on the probability model pales in comparison with partisanship, presidential approval, and candidate evaluations.

The Model

I consider three primary influences on the individual's vote: partisan leanings, evaluations of the two candidates, and the level of contact that an individual has had with the competing candidates. In order to test for institutional differences in the relative importance of constituency service, I add to this model the respondent's evaluations of whether the incumbent has "helped anyone with problems in the district/state." Second, I include a measure of presidential approval. This will account for the existence of presidential coattails as well as allowing me to test whether senators are more closely tied to the success or failure of the president. Finally, intensity and institutional variables are included in the model. As I did earlier, I interpret intensity as a summary measure of campaign activity. In an intensely fought campaign, voters will be exposed to more information about the challenger and will be comparatively less likely to vote for the incumbent. The institutional variable tests whether there are additional differences between House and Senate voting that are not accounted for by the other variables in the model. The equation shown here provides a mathematical representation of my model.

$$
\begin{aligned}
Pr(IncumbentVote) \quad = \quad & \beta_0 + \beta_1(PartyID) + \beta_2(PresApprove) \\
& + \beta_3(HelpDistrict?) + \beta_4(Intensity) \\
& + \beta_5(Institution) + \beta_{6,7,8,9}(Likes/Dislikes) \\
& + \beta_{10,11}(Contacts) + \varepsilon.
\end{aligned}
$$

Verbally, the model implies that the probability of voting for the incumbent is a function of partisan leanings,[40] whether one approves of Ronald Reagan's or George Bush's performance as president,[41] whether one thinks the incumbent is helpful to people in the district, whether one particularly "likes" or "dislikes" the candidates,[42] and the number of contacts (of seven possible

---

40. Partisanship is coded in a pro-incumbent direction

41. Presidential approval runs from -1 to 0 for Democratic incumbents and from 0 to 1 for Republican incumbents.

42. The four variables are simply the number of incumbent likes and dislikes and challenger likes and dislikes. I already showed that respondents cited more likes and dislikes, on average, for Senate candidates. This means that the variable cannot be included in the voting model because

total) that one has had with the two candidates. The model estimated is reported below.

My expectations are that partisanship, presidential approval, district help, incumbent likes and challenger dislikes, incumbent contacts, and incumbent tenure will all be positively related to the probability that a respondent will vote for the incumbent. Campaign intensity, incumbent dislikes and challenger likes, and challenger contacts should be negatively related to incumbent voting. I have no prior expectations about the institutional variable. Although House incumbents tend to receive higher proportions of the vote, they also are blessed with poorer quality challengers, low-intensity contests, and uneven partisan balance in the district. Institutional effects may wash out once other variables are controlled for.[43]

The Performance of the Basic Model

The results from this model from 1988 and 1990 are presented in table 6.7. In order to assuage any concern that House and Senate or high- and low-intensity elections look fundamentally different, I disaggregate the results by institution and intensity.

The estimates from the pooled model are reported in the first column of table 6.7. The overall performance of the model is quite good, correctly predicting more than 84 percent of vote choices. Partisanship, presidential approval, and perceptions of incumbent helpfulness are all positively and, in 1988, all statistically significantly, related to the probability of voting for the incumbent. This is not surprising: Republican identifiers and respondents who thought President Reagan had done a good job tended to vote for Republican incumbents. Democrats and voters who disapproved of Reagan's performance tended to vote Democratic. And voters who thought their incumbents helped people in the district tended to endorse the incumbent.

Campaign intensity also operates as anticipated: in 1988, voters were 12 percent less likely to vote for an incumbent in an intensely fought campaign, all other things being held equal. The candidate evaluation and contact variables are correctly signed and statistically significant. If a voter likes an incumbent (or a challenger), he or she is much more likely to vote for the incumbent; if a

---

it conflates "institution" and "candidate likes." I solve this by standardizing the variable within "institution". Now "likes" represents the degree to which a respondent liked a candidate more or less than the *average* candidate and so on for the other variables.

43. Previous versions of this model included tenure of the incumbent under the assumption that voters are more likely to endorse an incumbent they have known for many years. The estimated coefficient under multiple specifications was zero, so I dropped this variable.

Table 6.7. Incumbent Vote, Pooled and Disaggregated Models

	Pooled Model	By Institution		By Intensity	
		House	Senate	Low	High
1988 estimates					
Constant	−1.871 (0.262)***	−1.692***	−2.394***	−1.846***	−4.446***
Party identification	1.688 (0.185)***	1.527***	1.858***	1.912***	1.579***
Presidential approval	0.308 (0.164)*	0.991***	−0.049	0.408**	0.366
Help district	0.389 (0.223)*	0.305	0.521*	0.222	0.618**
Job approval	2.222 (0.251)***	1.708***	2.611***	2.157***	3.125***
Intensity	−0.361 (0.143)***	−1.795***	0.023	—	—
Institution	−0.162 (0.135)	—	—	−0.559***	1.638***
Incumbent likes	0.478 (0.084)***	0.425***	0.577***	0.451***	0.798***
Incumbent dislikes	−0.219 (0.112)**	−0.389*	−0.188	−0.245*	0.004***
Challenger likes	−0.777 (0.091)***	−1.019***	−0.752***	−1.028***	−0.628
Challenger dislikes	0.276 (0.168)*	0.713**	−0.011	0.269	0.080
Incumbent contacts	0.140 (0.041)***	0.161***	0.113*	0.182***	0.087***
Challenger contacts	−0.155 (0.039)***	−0.126*	−0.139***	−0.107*	−0.264***
N	1321	589	732	940	381
Percentage predicted	84.77	83.19	85.68	84.54	80.34

Table 6.7. (continued)

	Pooled Model	By Institution		By Intensity	
		House	Senate	Low	High
1990 Estimates					
Constant	-1.640 (0.230)***	-1.538***	-1.832***	-1.596***	-1.962***
Party identification	1.452 (0.164)***	1.099***	1.670***	1.247***	1.709***
Presidential approval	0.126 (0.141)	0.523**	-0.099	0.396**	-0.212
Help district	0.242 (0.193)	0.445	0.146	0.302	0.101
Job approval	2.171 (0.218)***	2.158***	2.262***	1.971***	2.549***
Intensity	-0.307 (0.121)***	-0.681***	-0.161*	—	—
Institution	-0.113 (0.115)	—	—	-0.226	0.138
Incumbent likes	0.266 (0.051)***	0.363***	0.226***	0.264***	0.274***
Incumbent dislikes	-0.244 (0.070)***	-0.340***	-0.156*	-0.296***	-0.212*
Challenger likes	-0.449 (0.058)***	-0.601***	-0.403***	-0.493***	-0.452***
Challenger dislikes	0.402 (0.100)***	0.403**	0.420***	0.597***	0.312**
Incumbent contacts	0.058 (0.034)*	0.074	0.045	0.068	0.049
Challenger contacts	-0.061 (0.032)*	-0.168***	0.000	-0.058	-0.064
N	1494	555	939	893	601
Percentage predicted	84.53	84.5	84.15	84.54	84.42

Source: 1988–90 NES/SES.

Note: Variable coding information is contained in appendix C.

*$p = .05$ **$p = .01$ ***$p = .001$

voter dislikes an incumbent, he or she is equally as likely to vote against the incumbent.[44] Voter contacts are beneficial, as expected. Contacts with the incumbent are positively related, and contacts with the challenger are negatively related, to the probability of voting for the incumbent.

Institutional effects disappear in both years. The estimated coefficient on the institution dummy variable is substantively small and statistically insignificant, although the sign is negative, as expected. I can push this argument even further. There is little to distinguish the pooled, House, and Senate estimates in columns 1, 2, and 3 of table 6.7. With a few minor exceptions, the same set of variables is statistically significant. The magnitude of the estimates is quite similar. Pooling not only provides greater statistical purchase on the choice process engaged in by the American legislative voter, but it solidifies the case for a "two-institutions, one-choice" conclusion, one that I argued for in chapter 2 and one to which I will return in chapter 7.

It is notable, however, that presidential approval benefits (and penalizes) House members, not senators, as I had expected. In contrast to the pooled model, this effect is discernible in 1988 and 1990. This might be indicative of greater personalization of Senate elections. Senators, who are more prominent in their own right (Hess 1986), might be individually more responsible for national policy but more immune from the negative consequences of presidential behavior.

Given the lower level of incumbency advantage in the Senate, how can I reasonably argue for "two-institutions, one-choice"? Incumbency "advantage" is not something that magically accrues to incumbent members of the legislature. Instead, incumbents build their advantages through multiple campaigns, frequent trips home, constituency service, and mass mailings. In an opinion survey, these activities show up as a positive balance in the "likes/dislikes" ledger. Jacobson illustrates this point in a simple yet powerful table (1997, table 5.12). By sequentially controlling for contacts and likes/dislikes in a model of the House vote, he is able to make the incumbency advantage disappear. Similarly, I have unpacked incumbency advantage in the Senate and

---

44. Including candidate likes and dislikes as independent variables might be viewed with suspicion. After all, how are likes and dislikes different from vote choice? These are distinct concepts. Theoretically, Alvarez (1999) and Kelley and Mirer (1974), among others, argue that likes and dislikes form only one portion, albeit a very important one, of the candidate choice process. Second, statistical diagnostics indicate that the measures are not collinear. First, none of the likes/dislikes measures correlates at greater than .3 with incumbent vote. Second, when these models are reestimated with likes/dislikes removed, the other coefficients in the model change only minimally. The estimated impact of campaign intensity increases, but that is not surprising. In more intense campaigns, voters cite more likes and dislikes. Institutional differences become *less* important. To reassure the skeptic, however, the results from a model excluding likes and dislikes are reported in appendix C.

House into its constituent parts. Candidate differences in recognition and evaluation are reflected via the likes/dislikes measure, regardless of the institution. If there is any remaining systematic tendency to vote for the incumbent, once I have controlled for these other effects, it ought to show up in the institution dummy variable. No such tendency is evident.

Another reason why institution fails to explain any variance in voter decision rules is that voters, unlike political scientists, opt for parsimony. As argued by Kelley and Mirer a quarter century ago (1974), and as shown in my discussion of voter expectations, voters generally choose simple decision rules. Prior beliefs (partisanship, presidential approval, and incumbent helpfulness) and reactions to the two candidates (likes/dislikes) are the most important determinants of the vote. A simple model containing only a constant term plus partisanship, presidential approval, and perceptions of incumbent helpfulness accounts for nearly half of the reduction in log likelihood relative to the null model. Likes and dislikes, when added to this simple model, reduce the log likelihood almost as much.[45] Put another way, if I know a voter's partisanship, attitude toward the president, and whether he or she has anything particularly positive or negative to say about the two candidates, I can make a very good prediction about that person's vote. Ninety percent of the explanatory power in this model is a function of attitudes that are largely exogenous to the campaign (partisanship, evaluations of Reagan or Bush, incumbent helpfulness) along with current reactions to the candidate. Adding contact and campaign intensity results in statistically significant probit coefficients, but provides comparatively little explanatory power. Institution adds *virtually nothing*.

Two other findings deserve comment: the lack of statistical significance of the presidential approval and "help district" variables in 1990. The presidential approval result can be explained, for 1990 was the first midterm election in the Bush administration. It was an election that the *Congressional Quarterly Weekly Report* described as being "like a series of hard-fought city council races [with] a pronounced absence of clear-cut national themes" (Alston 1990). Bush enjoyed high levels of popularity, yet many Republicans were unhappy with the broken "no new taxes" pledge. The savings and loan scandal and real and perceived ethical lapses resulted in a generally anti-incumbent mood, reducing incumbent margins but failing to translate into significant wins by challengers (only 15 of 406 House incumbents were defeated).

---

45. I obtained these figures by calculating the initial log likelihood and the final log likelihood from the full model. Then I calculated a model with *only* partisanship, presidential evaluation, and incumbent helpfulness. This accounted for 41 percent of the reduction in log-likelihood in 1988 and 39 percent in 1990. Adding likes/dislikes to this model accounted for another 49 percent (1988) and 44 percent (1990) of the reduction in log likelihood that occurred under the full model.

The insignificant result for "help district" is a cause for more concern. Member attentiveness to the district ought to operate in 1990 as in 1988 (as it does in most elections). The *Quarterly*, as we just learned, described 1990 as a year when local concerns predominated. Helpfulness to the district should be *more* important, not less. Most likely, the "help district" variable does not capture true voter perceptions of member helpfulness in the district beyond what is already reflected in the likes/dislikes term. Otherwise, it is just not credible to suggest that attentiveness to the district is unimportant in congressional elections.

Overall, these findings, while they confirm my expectations, deserve closer scrutiny. The null finding for institution flies in the face of many previous descriptions of congressional voting. The representation of institutional differences is sparse, to put it mildly. Also, campaign intensity has been left unexplored. Senate races are more likely to be intensely fought races. Is there more that I can say about the impact of campaign intensity on voter choice? I address each of these questions in the next two sections.

Searching for Institutional Differences

It is seldom the case that a scientific theory predicts a null finding. The first lesson in classical hypothesis testing is to "fail to reject" null hypotheses rather than accept alternative ones. There are numerous reasons why a statistical estimate might fail significance tests besides the obvious one of no effect, particularly when working with survey data. The sample might be too small, the model could be misspecified, or the operationalization of the theoretical construct could be flawed. I argue that institutional effects are minimal, based on statistically insignificant coefficient estimates and an eyeballing of the third and fourth columns of table 6.7. Does a closer look at institutional differences change this conclusion?

Not surprisingly, my answer is no. Across a wide variety of alternative specifications, the alternative hypothesis of institutional differences was rejected. Rather than just eyeballing the models estimates across institution, I tested model stability with a Chow statistic. None of the interaction variables (institution crossed with all other independent variables in the equation) was statistically significant. I estimated the model with partisanship, presidential approval, incumbent helpfulness, and institution only, to see whether any of the variation in likes/dislikes, contacts, intensity, or tenure might be taken up by institution. I then added to this previous model an interaction term (institution and presidential approval) to see whether Senate candidates are more closely tied to the president. In neither case were the institutional coefficients statistically significant. Finally, to see whether foreign policy matters more in

Senate voting, I created two special likes/dislikes variables, coded one if the respondent made any mention of foreign policy as a reason to like or dislike a candidate and zero otherwise. Here I found some hint of an institutional difference. If a respondent mentioned foreign policy in the likes/dislikes items, he or she was more likely to take this into consideration when voting for the Senate rather than the House. However, "more likely" only means that the estimated coefficients were larger than zero and correctly signed but still statistically insignificant.

It is difficult to find much support in these data for the claim that Senate and House voting models ought to be estimated separately. Institutional effects mean different things to different people, and this is unlikely to be the last word on the subject. I return to this issue in the conclusion.

The Effects of Campaign Intensity: Diversifying or Leveling?

Campaign intensity also merits a closer look. In previous sections, I theorized that intensely fought campaigns would result in a more elaborate and diverse set of decision rules. Voters would have access to more information and would presumably employ that information when choosing a candidate. The models here do not support this hypothesis. As shown in table 6.7, the *low-intensity* decision rule appears to be more elaborate. It is difficult to compare these two models directly because of different sample sizes. A larger N (1,232 in low-intensity contests vs. 564 in high-intensity contests) results in smaller standard errors and more statistically significant coefficients. Still I can compare the magnitude of the estimates. The impact of presidential approval and perceptions of incumbent helpfulness is smaller in high-intensity contests, and candidate contacts show only marginal effects. The model's forecasts are predominantly determined by individual partisanship and likes/dislikes.

How can these results be reconciled with claims that campaign intensity is a central variable in explaining electoral outcomes (e.g., chaps. 4 and 5; Kahn and Kenney 1997; Krasno 1994; Westlye 1983, 1991; Abramowitz 1988)? One possibility is that I have represented "information" far too sparsely. Perhaps policy opinions and ideological placements become activated in high-intensity contests. A more likely reason is that my model of individual perception and learning fails to properly describe voter behavior in low-information settings. In a low-information setting, voters may rely more on external cues such as partisanship but also on attitudes such as the "nature of the times" or perceptions of candidate helpfulness. While responses to these items are influenced by the campaign, there is an exogenous element. People generally know well before the fall campaign whether things are going well, the president has done a good job, and the incumbent has helped the district.[46] It is precisely in a low-information setting that I expect people to use general assessments of government and candidates.Similarly, candidate contacts are less crucial in the high-intensity contest because every voter has experienced a relatively high number of contacts. According to this explanation, presidential approval and district help are less relevant in a high-intensity contest because voters rely on candidate likes and dislikes.

I do not have direct evidence to support this hypothesis. However, if intensity acts to level rather than diversify voter decision rules, there are corollary indicators that might help us evaluate this hypothesis. First, the average number of contacts is higher in high-intensity contest and, more importantly, the variation among voters is smaller.[47] The number of respondents reporting one or fewer contacts with challengers drops from 28 percent of respondents to only 7 percent, whereas the number reporting five or more contacts doubles, from 13 to 26 percent of the sample.[48] More respondents in high-intensity races are exposed to information about the challenger and the incumbent, so contacts are less important, on average, in the final decision. Shaking a candidate's hand or seeing an advertisement on television does not distinguish one voter from another in high-intensity contests.[49]

Yet intense campaigns do diversify in a way that is missed in these analyses. The average number of likes and dislikes that respondents mention in high-intensity contests increases, as would be expected. But notice that the standard deviation in the number of likes and dislikes in high-intensity contests is also larger and the number of respondents who have nothing at all to say drops by roughly 25 percent (except for incumbent likes). In an intensely fought contest, fewer respondents have nothing at all to say, and thus fewer have to rely solely on prior beliefs such as partisanship or incumbent helpfulness. In an intensely fought contest, there is greater variability among respondents in the information they have about candidates and the responses they have to the campaign. Thus, as I argued earlier, intensity and information do

---

46. Kinder and Mebane 1983, for example, find that individual perceptions of economic conditions are a product of both "ordinary theories" about economics and political assessments of blame for economic conditions. They are neither determinative of nor completely determined by political information and opinions. Popkin (1991) also claims that voters rely on a variety of information, much of it based on apolitical everyday experiences, in order to generate political choices.

47. The average numbers of incumbent contacts in low- and high-intensity races are 3.26 (SD 1.92) and 3.57 (SD 1.48). The average numbers of challenger contacts are 2.66 (1.81) and 3.75 (1.55).

48. The comparison is made only for the 1,796 respondents who fell into the voting model.

49. This point is echoed by Zaller's (1992) exposure and acceptance model. An individual cannot react to information unless that individual is exposed to it. In high-intensity contests, one would expect that the exposure side of Zaller's model would become increasingly irrelevant.

TABLE 6.8. Likes and Dislikes in Low- and High-Intensity Contests

	Low Intensity	High Intensity
Number of likes/dislikes		
Incumbent likes	.870	.789
(SD)	1.037	.916
No mention	47%	46%
Incumbent dislikes	.248	.440
(SD)	.558	.709
No mention	81%	67%
Challenger likes	.236	.603
(SD)	.595	.883
No mention	83%	60%
Challenger dislikes	.209	.441
(SD)	.531	.729
No mention	84%	66%
Policy mentions (likes)		
House incumbent	10.53	10.85
Senate incumbent	13.41	12.97
House challenger	11.11	6.95
Senate challenger	9.73	11.56

Source: 1988–90 NES/SES.
Note: Entries under "Number of likes/dislikes" are the average number of likes or dislikes mentioned. Entries under "Policy mentions" are the percentage of likes or dislikes that are domestic or foreign policy mentions. Only respondents who fell into the voting model are included.

not level but instead function as a rising tide that lifts all boats. And, to extend the metaphor further, as the information tide rises, the detritus of past political experiences (partisanship, presidential approval, and incumbent reputation) is obscured.

I would be remiss not to mention one piece of evidence to the contrary. I expected that the *content* of likes/dislikes might change during intense campaigns. This turned out not to be the case. In table 6.8, I compare policy mentions in high- and low-intensity contests. No pattern is evident. Other major categories (candidate, party/ideology, government management) do not grow or shrink in a systematic way across campaign intensity. Nor is it the case that respondents agree more about the incumbent's helpfulness in intense contests (the standard deviation for "help district?" is .32 in low-intensity contests and .34 in high-intensity contests).

I theorized that high-intensity contests allow voters to employ a more elaborate decision rule. These results, however, indicate a more complex set of relationships between campaign activity, political information, and voter choice. In the intensely fought contest, partisanship and likes/dislikes are the only statistically significant predictors of the vote. Contrast this with the model estimated in low-intensity contests. Not only are the votes slightly better predicted, but all the variables in the model have a statistically discernible relationship with the dependent variable.

Conclusion

Voting is the final act in the electoral drama. It is the arena where previous studies have noticed the most differences between Senate and House: Senate challengers are more widely recognized and Senate incumbents are more likely to be defeated. Senate voters appear to employ a more elaborate decision rule. However, there are good reasons why voting behavior should show substantial similarity no matter what the setting or office. Voting is a repetitive act engaged in often (in some localities many times a year) in the same setting (the polling booth) and requiring similar kinds of actions (pull a lever, punch a hole, mark a ballot). It would be surprising if voters used different rules to make this kind of repetitive decision, especially since theory predicts that it is just this kind of situation that leads to standardized, routinized rules.

Voting begins with information. I have stressed throughout this chapter the distinction between information *levels* and information *content*. While voters know more about Senate than House candidates, the content of that information is basically the same. Abstract evaluations of the job of the representative are indistinguishable. The categories of likes and dislikes also bear a strong resemblance across the two institutions. It is as if the respondents to this survey perceive the same thing that many political observers have speculated on: a converging of the House and Senate.

Has voting converged as well? I believe that it has. The evidence here indicates that voters employ a standardized rule, or at least use the same set of considerations, when choosing their federal legislators. In a low-intensity election, voters look to their partisanship, impressions of the nature of the times, and the incumbent's reputation for helpfulness. Candidate contacts explain more variance in a low-intensity election because contacts are a way to differentiate among voters. Finally, voters tend to choose the candidate they like the most (or dislike the least).[50] In a high intensity election, things are actually simpler. Contacts are no longer a significant way to distinguish voters, and

---

50. This simple rule bears a remarkable resemblance to Kelley and Mirer's quarter-century old model (1974).

they play a much smaller role in the final decision. Prior beliefs—partisanship, presidential approval, and incumbent helpfulness—also decline in impact. Instead, short-term, immediate reactions to the campaign, as reflected in the balance of likes and dislikes, determine electoral choice. These results all point in the same direction: voters learn about and choose their House members and senators in a similar fashion.

CHAPTER 7

Two Institutions, One Choice?

Electoral scholars have a curious tunnel vision—we fixate in large part on one institution at a time. This is the easier path to take, but it limits our theoretical vision and the generalizability of our findings. A prime example is the gallons of ink spilled after every U.S. presidential contest. The presidential election, while undoubtedly the most consequential for the country as a whole, is just one of thousands of contests decided on election day. Furthermore, in innumerable ways the presidential election is an outlier: the political setting is continental in scope, candidates are universally recognized, media coverage is intense, and voter information and interest are high. As a way to learn about the American *presidential* voter, focusing on presidential elections is appropriate. As a way to learn about the American voter in the abstract, it is fraught with danger. Without knowing the ways in which presidential context differs from other electoral contexts, we cannot generalize to elections for other institutions.

Nor is it enough to look intensively at another institutional setting. Political scientists have expanded their field of vision (particularly in the last two decades) to include House, Senate, and to a lesser degree gubernatorial and state legislative elections. These studies provide hints about differences among offices. However, by remaining locked within one institutional context, the result is not much different from focusing on the presidency: specialized knowledge about a single institution but only speculative knowledge about institutional differences. We cannot really learn how institutions affect elections unless we consider settings, institutions, campaigns, and voters *simultaneously.*

In one respect, this is no more than a methodological rule: in order to estimate the effects of a variable, such as institution, it must *vary.* There are deep theoretical and substantive consequences to this decision, however. The choice of methodology—and of variables—limits the theoretical claims that can be tested. In order to evaluate the impact of certain contextual features on candidates and voters, I may need to add additional contexts. Otherwise, I cannot really estimate the explanatory power of contextual variables (of which

151

institutional arrangements are just one type). Methodological choices can also limit the generalizability of the results. The way that candidates and voters behave may be unique to one electoral arena, or it may reveal more general rules about political behavior. To discover the latter, we are obligated to replicate our models in other arenas. My theory of legislative elections has often been couched in methodological terms, but my conclusions have substantive import. I have explicitly contrasted institutional with other explanations of House and Senate elections. The findings modify in important ways the conventional wisdom about settings, campaigns, and voting for the U.S. Congress.

To conclude, I will review the ideas and theories that underlie the three-stage model laid out in chapter 2. The two most important claims I made there were, first, that there are three main sets of variables that affect elections—political settings, candidates and campaigns, and voters—and, second, that there are specific causal relationships among these variables. Next, I will summarize the empirical results, highlighting the ways in which my results support or challenge the conventional wisdom about House and Senate elections. Third, I speculate about how this study might be improved, suggesting ways that the House/Senate comparison might be sharpened and proposing other contexts in which this approach may be valuable. Finally, I ask whether these results indicate that the U.S. House and Senate are converging or diverging and what the consequences are for the future of the American electoral system.

Comparing Elections across Institutions

Comparing elections across institutions is hard and complicated. But these difficulties yield significant returns. They help identify the impact of diverse institutional arrangements. They demarcate the limits of an institutional account of elections. *Institution* comprises many meanings, and there are certainly many ways in which institutions can modulate electoral outcomes. Institutions have different constitutional prerogatives, and it is quite possible that these percolate throughout the electoral process. The rules of the game change: the number of seats per district, the length of the term, and the seat allocation formula. The interest and attention paid by other political actors—parties, interest groups, and the mass media—wax and wane according to the importance they attach to various offices. Constituencies vary as well, since the boundaries of electoral districts are seldom contiguous over multiple institutions. Finally, voters are more or less interested in outcomes, apply different evaluative or prototypical standards, and are exposed to higher and lower levels of campaign information.

Any one of these could alter electoral outcomes, and any one might be lumped into the category "institutional effect." The aim here is not to make these differences go away but to model them in such a way that I identify and understand the contents of each category. The hope is that this exercise will lead us toward perhaps a more restricted, but also more complete, understanding of the effects of House and Senate institutional arrangements on electoral outcomes.

Comparing across institutions is complicated, but it forces us to think carefully about how elective institutions are structured and how they influence the behavior of candidates and voters. I identified three general areas to think about in chapter 2. First, I considered variations in the context or background of elections: the makeup of the district, lines of communication, and long-standing political patterns. Second, I identified variations in the pool of candidates who choose to run for an office and what kinds of campaigns are conducted. Third, I attended to voters: do they evaluate the institutions in different ways and do they employ a particular set of considerations for each institution? Finally, I allowed for institutional differences unaccounted for by these three sets of variables. These differences manifest themselves both as different levels of dependent variables and as differences in interactions among the independent variables.

Institutional comparisons cannot be made when contextual differences are too great. This is the cause of unending debate in comparative politics: to what degree can disparate systems be compared on a common metric, and to what degree are such comparisons so general as to be meaningless?[1] Thus, much can be gained in the comparative approach by using simple, descriptive analyses. Most of my conclusions in chapters 3 and 4 were a product of simply arrays of House and Senate districts, candidates, and campaigns on common dimensions. This descriptive exercise was designed to answer two core questions. First, are there *observable* differences across institutions? This helps us to identify possible variables that might *explain* institutional differences. If, for example, states are no more racially diverse than congressional districts, then it is unlikely that racial diversity can explain any observed differences in Senate and House elections. Once I establish baseline differences, the second question is: to what degree is there *similarity* and *overlap?* Essentially, I presented the joint distribution of these measures in the U.S. House and Senate. This comparison tells me whether a particular variable can be *disentangled* from institution by taking advantage of cases from one institution that in some respects look like cases from the other institution. If all states are heterogeneous and all congressional districts are homogeneous, to take on one aspect of conventional wisdom, then heterogeneity cannot be disentangled from institution. In statistical terms, the variables are completely collinear. We need to answer this question at the outset.

---

1. For insight into this debate, see the discussion between comparative politics scholars and area specialists in a special issue of *Africa Today* (44) [April-June 1997].

The second step in my analysis, presented in chapters 5 and 6, tests the relative power of institutional arrangements versus the other variables in the second and third stages of the model. The causal models that include both sets of explanatory variables—institutional variables as well as other independent influences (depending on the particular stage of the analysis)—allow me to parcel out the independent contribution of each. Ideally, of course, I would have had empirical representations of institutional arrangements. This raises a contentious issue: what counts as an *institution?* I cannot resolve this argument here, though I addressed this point briefly in the second chapter. Still, even if there is disagreement on the labels attached to the three sets of variables, I still have fleshed out the contents of institution rather than employing it as a convenient shorthand for a series of unspecified effects. I do not suggest that institutional differences between the U.S. House and Senate are unimportant to voters. Instead, I want to compare the power of institutional variables after I have controlled for other correlated variables.[2] The result allows me to make some inferences about the strength of institutional effects relative to other influences on candidates and voters.

The last stage in the analysis is interpretive: relating the differences and similarities to my theoretical expectations about elective institutions. After controlling for other ways in which electoral districts vary, are institutional differences attenuated? If they are, this tells us that the makeup of the district has more to do with electoral outcomes than do institutional arrangements. Much of this work was done in chapter 6. Do voter expectations about the candidates map into our theoretical understanding about the roles these institutions play in the political system? This tells us whether the public views these elective institutions in different ways (at least when voting) and whether our expectations are supported by the empirical evidence. It may mean that we will have to change the way political scientists think about these institutions. As Fenno showed long ago (1978), the view from the district is quite distinct from the view in the Capitol.

Furthermore, our examination of *changes* in the House and Senate must take into account how voters view these institutions. I indicated one such example in chapter 6. Survey respondents apparently have different expectations of the presidency and Congress (Jacobson 1990b). This has been used as an

---

2. The baseline for comparison is the explanatory power of institution without these other variables in the model. A way to estimate this baseline is to first include only institutional variables in the model, then add other sets of variables, and finally examine how the explanatory power of the institutional variables changes. In experimental terms, if I can randomly assign district diversity, candidate quality, and campaign spending levels to states and congressional districts and just vary the "treatment"—institution—I can accurately gauge the magnitude and direction of institutional differences. In the language of causal modeling, I want to control for all spurious and confounding causes of institutional differences.

explanation of the prevalence of divided government. My results show that no such distinction is made between House and Senate, at least when respondents answer survey questions or report on vote choice. The prediction, therefore, should be that the two chambers will be affected in similar ways by electoral forces.

Finally, if the structural relationships among variables is similar while the levels of variables differ, what I referred to as inputs and outputs, we can say that the underlying dynamics of elections are alike across the institutions. It is just that the starting and ending points are not. The result should be a more embellished, more careful description of what institutional differences are in the electoral arena, in what ways candidates and campaigns vary across institutional settings, and how voters change their behavior (if at all) in response to changes in contextual, campaign, and institutional environments.

Comparing the U.S. House and Senate

I selected the U.S. House and Senate as the cases with which to test this approach. They are particularly good institutions for this. There are already many theories of House and Senate elections that implicate institutional differences, but these differences, where possible, should be reexpressed in the language of variables. Thus, modeling and unpacking institution becomes a much easier task. The Senate and House are similar enough that I can array settings, candidate spending, candidate quality, and voter information and evaluations on a single scale. Last, but not least, data on congressional districts, states, House and Senate candidates, and House and Senate voters are readily available.

How do the results reported here change our view of House and Senate elections? In some ways, it is appropriate to talk about the Senate *and* the House. States are no more diverse than congressional districts and vice versa. Consequently, higher levels of diversity are not associated with higher quality challengers and higher candidate spending. The implication is that Senate campaigns are not more competitive because states are more heterogeneous. Neither the descriptive nor the causal analyses support this claim.

Voters apply similar standards to their legislators, contrary to claims that the House is service-oriented and the Senate policy-oriented. I found no difference in voter expectations about the two houses of Congress or in the reasons why voters liked or disliked Senate and House candidates. This suggests that voters apply a common set of standards when voting and that differences in observed voting rules are more a result of different levels of campaign intensity and political information flow than of different institutional expectations.

In other ways, the descriptive analyses support the conventional wisdom of Senate *versus* House. House members face inefficient media markets, yet they benefit from districts with uneven numbers of partisans. The situation in states is reversed: efficient media markets but balanced numbers of partisans. This does not change the archetypal description of congressional districts and states, but it does restrict quite substantially the range of ways in which they differ. House incumbents are advantaged in another way: they face less well-funded, less prominent challengers. Even after spending is adjusted to a per capita basis, Senate challengers spend far more than their House counterparts do.

The causal analyses in chapters 5 and 6 compare the House and Senate in a different and more powerful way. Even though the levels of variables might differ (i.e., campaign spending or candidate quality is higher in the Senate), the relationship among variables might be the same. My results indicate that candidates react to the constraints placed on them by the political environment, and to each other, in comparable ways regardless of the institutional setting. The observed differences between House and Senate campaigns is a result of different starting values (higher quality, higher spending Senate candidates), not differences in the ways candidates interact with each other. These results do not change conventional wisdom about campaign spending but extend the results to the Senate.

In a similar fashion, the level of information that voters have about Senate candidates is far greater than the level of information about House candidates (particularly when comparing challengers), but the relationship between information levels and campaign activity is comparable. What emerges from these models is the central role of individual interest and attentiveness regardless of the institutional setting. Campaign information is like a rising tide that lifts all boats yet leaves differences between voters unchanged. Individual characteristics outweigh campaign intensity, campaign activity, and institutional effects.

The voting models further undermine claims that voters choose differently for the House and Senate. The descriptive analyses suggested that voters apply a common set of standards to House and Senate candidates, and the causal models reinforce this conclusion. A "simple model of voting" (Kelley and Mirer 1974) underlies Senate and House voting. Evaluative information about the candidates, as expressed in likes and dislikes, is the strongest determinant of electoral choice. In the absence of any recent information about the two candidates, voters rely more on long-standing partisan ties and overall evaluations about political conditions in the country and their districts. New information tends to trump old information. In intensely fought contests, respondents rely somewhat more heavily on candidate evaluations.

Future Challenges

While I have established the utility of a unified approach to House and Senate electoral studies, this study can be improved upon in many ways. In the interest of the author's and reader's sanity, copious amounts of data were ignored. Some additional data collection efforts could resolve some remaining puzzles. Other puzzles are more intractable. There is a gap between theory and measurement in the diversity measures. The endogeneity problem in campaigns has bedeviled this and other studies and is not easily solved. Finally, there are other places where this analytical approach can be fruitfully employed. I suggest some possibilities here.

Puzzles with Solutions

There are some relatively easy ways to improve upon this study by means of additional data collection. One improvement would be to add campaign content measures. I constructed an elaborate argument about the flow and content of campaign information but only examined flow. Without a flow measure, I cannot tie campaign information to voter learning. The difficult task is to collect comparably rich information about the Senate (not difficult) and House (difficult). This might be possible within a single election year, but it would be problematic for many years.

Another puzzle was created by small numbers of Senate races in a single year. Robust comparisons across the Senate and House are tenuous due to the small number of Senate races. Statistical estimates of institutional differences in the campaign models (chap. 5) were often statistically insignificant, but I wonder whether this is more a function of sample size than the lack of a real difference. One solution would be to expand the analysis of settings and campaigns into additional decades.[3] In a similar spirit, the voter learning and choice models are less convincing than they might have been had I included additional years in the analysis.[4]

---

3. Palfrey and Erikson (1993) were able to put together a data set very similar to mine that spanned three decades. There is no reason why the census and media market measures could not be produced for additional years.

4. At a minimum, the election studies conducted during the 1980s could easily be added, although there is a significant absence of items asking about Senate candidates. Lack of comparable measures limited my voting analysis to the 1988 and 1990 waves of the NES/SES.

More Difficult Puzzles

Other puzzles are harder to solve. I focused on the relationship between diversity and campaign activity in the Senate and House. All I might have showed, however, is that diversity is not a way in which politicians think about electoral settings. There are other ways in which distributions might matter. And there are other ways in which congressional districts and states might differ that have political import but little to do with distributions as I have characterized them.

The *shape* of a distribution is as important as the mean and variance. Are there peaks and valleys? Is it unimodal or multimodal? An illustrative comparison is Illinois and Virginia, both of which have roughly the same proportion of African Americans (around 15 percent). In Illinois, African Americans are concentrated in two urban areas, Chicago and East St. Louis, whereas in Virginia African Americans are much more evenly dispersed across the state (with some concentrations in Richmond, Petersburg, Norfolk, and Alexandria). On my measure of racial diversity, Illinois and Virginia will have the same score. But the strategic situation for a politician who worries about the African American vote is quite different. A politician like the retired senator Paul Simon (D-IL) could appeal to urban blacks when he was in Chicago and still maintain his folksy rural image in southern Illinois. In Virginia, a politician has to be continually concerned with appeasing both black and white interests, no matter where he is traveling. Similar peaks and valleys occur in every state and probably more frequently in states (since they are larger) than in congressional districts. It is difficult to envision a way of gaining statistical purchase on this kind of observation, but it is obviously relevant.

I also remained ecumenical about the political impact of various demographic categories. A district that is split 90:10 white/black is treated the same as a district that is split 10:90. While it might not be necessary to lump all kinds of diversity together, as a summary index does, it is still possible to use our knowledge about political divisions in the United States to develop more discriminating measures of political cleavages. For example, I might want to consider overall diversity along with such specific types of homogeneity as high concentrations of Hispanic, black, rich, or poor populations. This would require a more extensive treatment of social cleavages in the United States than I have attempted here.

It is also possible that I have missed important ways in which the setting matters to politicians. Kingdon (1988) found that dominant economic interests were an important part of the complex constituency, yet I do not consider major industries or employers. Only one part of constituency tending is picked up by the NES battery of candidate contact measures. Fenno (1978) writes of a congressman establishing a "fit" between himself and the district; Bianco (1994) discusses the complexities underlying "trust" and freedom of action by members of the House. How might this differ between the House and Senate? How might the representational relationship vary according to the structure of a congressional district and a state and the dynamics of House and Senate campaigns? One can imagine the real impact of size being the ability of House members to know important decision makers in the district personally, while the senator is necessarily more aloof. This will not show up in partisanship or diversity of market efficiency measures, but it helps House members cement ties, both personal and financial, to their constituencies.

There are also significant obstacles standing in the way of discovering the real impact of spending on citizen recall and choice. Incumbents react to challengers, and challengers react to incumbents. This simultaneity effect forces analysts to use complex statistical techniques when estimating campaign spending models and makes causal inferences about the impact of campaign spending difficult (e.g., Palfrey and Erikson 1993; Bartels 1991; Green and Krasno 1988). I also encountered this problem: my measures of challenger and incumbent spending and campaign intensity were so collinear that it was impossible to include all three in a single equation.[5] If campaign intensity is really a product of campaign spending and challenger quality, then any equation including all three will be misspecified and coefficients will be biased due to multicollinearity. And, because the relative size of the coefficients is a key part of the institutional comparison, coefficient bias needs to be taken seriously.[6] In the end, I agree with Palfrey and Erikson, who noted that "further progress in this direction necessitates the use of models that can disentangle very severe simultaneity problems" (1993, 23).

Other Institutional Settings

I have made two sets of claims here. First, I have made a set of assertions about House and Senate elections and tested these using data from the 1980s. I have also proposed a framework for evaluating the impact of institutional arrangements on elections. That claim remains untested. There are at least two ways to extend this study. I could turn to other elections in the United States, or we might turn our attention to cross-national comparisons. One proviso

---

5. In intensely fought races, the correlation between incumbent and challenger spending is over .90. The auxiliary R^2 on intensity is over .95. It is relatively easy to get a large auxiliary R^2 for a dichotomous dependent variable, but the high value remains a point of concern.

6. Zaller is able to ignore multicollinearity problems because he is interested in "the entire set of coefficients to simulate the overall effects of certain types of races" (1992, 236).

remains in force: if the goal is to estimate institutional effects, the cases cannot be *too* different.[7]

In the United States, these analyses could be extended upward to the presidential election and downward to gubernatorial and state legislative elections. One obvious and simple addition to the analysis is gubernatorial elections (and other statewide contests). All of the political setting measures are identical to the Senate measures; I would only need to calculate candidate quality, campaign spending, and voter information measures.[8] Political setting measures for state legislative districts would be more difficult to obtain since the census does not release demographic profiles for these districts.[9] The main problem with extending the study downward will be the lack of survey data for gubernatorial, other statewide, and state legislative contests. The situation for the presidency is reversed. A wealth of survey data on presidential voting is available. It is more difficult to characterize the electoral district as a whole nation. In both these cases, a comparative study of voters is easier to envision than a comparative study of political settings and campaign activity. It is still possible to test a unified model of voter learning and information, even while ignoring the other parts of the model.

My analytical approach should also appeal to comparative scholars of elections. I was purposely vague about the kinds of settings, electoral systems, and institutional arrangements that enter into the model. Theoretically, I should be able to compare across a wide variety of electoral systems as long as the differences are not yawning. For example, candidate reactions to an opponent's activity should be observed in any system that places single candidates in competition for a single seat (e.g., single-member, plurality systems). I could study the impact of institutional arrangements on voter learning and choice wherever there are multiple offices in contention at a single time (e.g., the French presidency and Parliament, the Senate and Chamber of Deputies in Italy,[10] or the Japanese Upper and Lower Diet). Comparative analysis of electoral systems holds the greatest potential, and the greatest complications, as I test the limits of a truly general model of campaigns and elections.

---

7. I laid out a series of comparability tests in the opening section of chapter.

8. There is another good reason to compare the Senate and gubernatorial races: the setting is held constant. Only the institution varies. This should allow a more precise estimation of institutional differences.

9. It may be possible to obtain demographic profiles from the redistricting offices in the states.

10. Like the U.S. Senate/gubernatorial comparison, the Italian case is a particularly interesting one because the districts are highly contiguous.

Convergence and Divergence in the U.S. Congress

Richard Fenno, in *The United States Senate: A Bicameral Perspective* (1982), called for increased attention to the U.S. Senate. Far too often, "Congress" meant no more than "House of Representatives." In Fenno's judgment, political scientists needed to extend their field of vision to include the upper house of Congress. This was more complicated than just taking what we had learned about the House and blindly applying it to the Senate. A bicameral perspective is attentive to the ways in which the House and Senate differ and the consequences these differences have for elections, policy making, and the public profile of these two legislative bodies. Fenno's monograph stimulated a burst of activity among political scientists. The Senate became a hot commodity.

I was part of this movement, as a graduate student and an employee at the National Election Studies. My reaction to Fenno's monograph was different, though I still think in the same spirit. While there are innumerable ways in which the Senate and House in Washington differ, there are many ways in which Senate and House elections are similar. The bicameral perspective, in my mind, means specifying the ways in which the House and Senate differ as a consequence of the bicameral structure and also seeing what features they share. In the electoral arena, this means disentangling institutional accounts of elections from sociological and intracampaign accounts. *Institution* was being used far too casually: a laundry list of Senate/House differences (heterogeneous settings, more prominent challengers, more campaign funds, interested and informed voters) are often appealed to as an explanation of electoral variation. In this book, I unpacked *institution*. I tested many of these claims about Senate/House differences by contrasting institutional and other explanations directly and discovered that a number of our conclusions about congressional elections are wrong.

In the electoral arena, the indications are that the House and Senate are becoming more and more alike. With the passage of the Seventeenth Amendment, Senators as well as House members had to fear the wrath of the voter. Senate and House incumbents continually raise money, an average of $5,700 in the House and $10,773 in the Senate *weekly*.[11] Turnover is also roughly comparable in the two institutions (if you adjust the House figure to the six-year Senate electoral cycle). Candidate responsiveness to district features, opponents, and voter learning and choice show remarkable similarity in the two institutions. Thus, it appears that *both* institutions display "intimate sympathy with the people" (Madison et al. 1961, 337). Lack of responsiveness

---

11. These figures were produced by taking average expenditures in 1998 and dividing by the length of the term. Of course, members do not raise money every week, but these amounts do point to the continual hold that campaigning has on our elected officials.

to public opinion is not a concern. Instead, the Founders' greatest fear—overattentiveness to public moods—may have come to pass.

Yet there are indications that senators are able to maintain some distance from the currents of public opinion. The longer Senate term and the greater prominence of the Senate do have an impact on the way that senators behave. The Senate term is split into a "governing" and a "reelection" phase (Fenno 1982). Senators strategically moderate as elections approach (Franklin 1993; Segura and Kuklinski 1991). As was anticipated in the constitutional design, senators are able to occupy ideological positions that are farther from the average opinion in their states than House members can. The major change that direct election of senators has brought is movement toward the district among those senators who are up for reelection. The House and Senate may be converging in the electoral arena, but they still diverge in their relative prominence and position in the policy-making system.

Elections in the modern era, regardless of the particular cases looked at here, have a basic three-stage structure regardless of the office. For those who look toward a more general model of elections, the results reported here are encouraging. Voters do not have split personalities, bringing to bear one set of considerations when pulling lever 1, another set when pulling lever 2, and so on down the line. It is more likely that voters apply the same basic set of criteria across many choices. Their ability to draw upon a wider set of considerations is conditioned by the amount of information they have been exposed to, and remember, about a particular race.

I do not think it is useful to talk about presidential, Senate, House, or gubernatorial elections as distinct archetypes. The question is when and why they look alike and when they differ. A generic language of elections, rather than talking only about institutional differences, should speak about elections are that are of high or low intensity, are held in heterogeneous or homogeneous districts with more or less efficient media markets, and involve high- and low-quality and high- and low-spending candidates. A theory of this type asks whether politicians and voters behave in similar ways across disparate political settings. It helps isolate the electoral impact of institutional settings. It should help organize in a reasonable and intelligible fashion a fuller array of local, state, and national elections.

Appendixes

Appendixes

APPENDIX A

Media and Demographic Measures from Chapter 3

Media Market Measures

"Area of dominant influence" (ADI) is a concept developed by Arbitron, Inc., to categorize every county in the United States as a television market. An ADI is determined via viewership surveys and television broadcast ranges. County:ADI mapping is exhaustive and exclusive. *TV Households* refers to the Arbitron estimate of households in counties (and larger aggregates) that have televisions. *Population* refers to the census person counts for these same statistical units. Congressional districts are designated CD. *Political district* is meant to refer to both states and CDs.

Variable Construction

Television market structure is measured in three ways: contiguity or "news mix", market dominance, and cost. Each taps a different dimension of media market efficiency, which affects the strategic decisions of campaigners.

News mix (Stewart and Reynolds 1990; Stewart 1989b) or *congruence* (Campbell, Alford, and Henry 1984) refers to the degree of overlap between a political district and the various television markets that serve it. Three distinct patterns of overlap have to be accounted for: a small television market encompassed by a large political district, a small political district encompassed by a large television market, and a district that is contiguous with only part of a television market or is covered by two or more markets.

News mix is a product of the proportion of the television market that is in the political setting and the proportion that is in the media market, summed across all relevant media markets. Suppose that:

- $ADI_1 - ADI_n$ = areas of dominant influence in a district, expressed as population size,
- P_D = the population of the political district,
- $ADI_n \cap P_D$ = the intersection of ADI_n and district D

Using these assumptions, contiguity is:

$$NM_D = \sum_{i=1}^{n} \frac{ADI_n \cap P_D}{P_D} * \frac{ADI_n \cap P_D}{ADI_n}$$

The measure runs from 1.0 (perfect overlap) to nearly zero.

Why call this measure "contiguity"? Suppose the proportion of coverage a television station allocates to a political campaign is a function of 1) the proportion of the ADI that is in the political district and 2) the proportion of the political district that is in the ADI. The product of these is used as a rough measure of the proportion of news that will be devoted to a particular district's political campaigns.

California's Nineteenth Congressional District is an example of nearly perfect overlap. The boundaries of the Monterey ADI and the CD are nearly identical. Delaware and Wyoming are examples of very inefficient media markets (among states with Senate races, they have the least-contiguous media markets). Delaware is a small part of a large ADI (Philadelphia), while Wyoming is served by six separate ADIs. Nevada is a nice illustration of a state that has a congressional district (the Second) with efficient media markets and another district (the First) with an only moderately efficient media market. As a state, Nevada has relatively efficient media markets. The Las Vegas ADI is completely contained within the state's borders, and the Reno ADI serves only 61,343 citizens not residing in Nevada. The main drag on the efficiency measure is caused by the 25,436 citizens who are served by the Salt Lake City market. These citizens are a small proportion of the ADI (lowering the efficiency measure), but they are also a small proportion of the total state (thus lowering their weight in the overall calculation). Looking at the Second District, 17 percent of its population is in the Las Vegas ADI, and only 15 percent of the *ADI* population is in the Second District. This is counterbalanced by the close fit between the Reno ADI and the rest of the Second District: 76 percent of the district's population lives in the Reno ADI, and the Reno district makes up 82 percent of the total ADI. While I may not expect that a great deal of coverage was devoted to the Second District race by Las Vegas television stations, the other 76 percent of the district could be expected to have received a heavy dose of campaign news. The result is a moderately high score on contiguity for this CD relative to other CDs. Finally, Wyoming is an example of a highly inefficient media market. If a candidate were to be so unwise as to blanket the state (i.e., to buy media time such that he or she appeared in every possible media market), that candidate would have to buy in six different markets with a population total of 4,565,409 (only 457,380 of whom live in Wyoming!). This is not a cost effective way to reach potential voters.

News mix takes into account all the ADIs in a political district. *Dominance* focuses on one part of this calculation; it shows whether the political district is dominated by a few ADIs (Stewart and Reynolds 1989). Dominance for district D (DOM_D) squares the first part of the contiguity calculation (proportion of the district in the ADI), in order to give greater weight to large overlaps, and then the squares across ADIs. DOM_D also runs from 1.0 (identical political district and ADI boundaries) to near zero:

$$\text{DOM}_D = \sum_{i=1}^{n} \frac{\text{ADI}_n \cap P_D}{P_D}.$$

Nearly all CDs have low contiguity scores, as would be expected (congressional districts seldom make up the bulk of a television market, and in many cases [New York City, Los Angeles] they make up quite a small proportion). The obverse side of the coin is that almost all are dominated by a single market. *If* he or she has the money, it is easy for a congressional candidate to decide where to advertise. Delaware, among states, scores high on dominance (the Philadelphia ADI nearly covers the state). In contrast, no single ADI comes close to dominating Wyoming. It is easier to allocate advertising dollars when dominance is high, it is easier to target news-making events when dominance is high, and voters receive more uniform political information when dominance is high.

The final constraint media markets place on campaigners is cost. The more costly advertising is, the more a candidate has to spend in order to inform and influence voters. I will experiment with three measures of cost. *Total cost* is the amount required to swamp a political district. Its calculation is straightforward:[1]

$$\text{TC}_D = \sum_{i=1}^{n} \text{Cost}_{\text{ADI}_n}$$

Per capita cost is total cost divided by the district population; thus, it can be interpreted as the per citizen cost of swamping a district in advertising.[2]

---

1. Cost is the average cost of a one minute spot during the local news in each ADI. These figures were provided to my by Charles Stewart. He only has figures for the top 200 ADI's. I impute the final 13 by substituting the value from the next smallest ADI in the state.

2. My measure of "per capita cost" is mathematically equivalent to what Stewart and Reynolds call "total cost." They describe total cost as "the amount of money required to but a one-minute television spot during the local evening news to reach 1% of the TV Households in the state." (1989, 16) This conflates two things, the total cost of advertising in a state, and the cost adjusted to a per person figure. Total cost and per capita cost are not the same thing; the degree

Average cost takes into account contiguity values as well as cost. Not all advertising reaches potential voters—Las Vegas and Reno television is seen by some California, New Mexico, and Utah residents. This waste (from a political perspective) drives up the cost per Nevadan. Average cost weights per capita cost by the degree of overlap. Note that:

- Cost is the cost of a 30-second advertising spot on the six o'clock news.
- $ADI_n \cap P_D/ADI_n$ is the proportion of the ADI population that is in the district. The reciprocal is the weight applied to advertising cost. When there is a lot of waste, the proportion is low, the reciprocal is large, and the cost is inflated.
- $ADI_n \cap P_D$ is the number of individuals in the ADI—the political district intersection. Its reciprocal converts cost into a per capita figure.

Putting these three terms together results in the average cost measure:

$$AC_D = \sum_{i=1}^{n} \text{Cost}_{ADI_n} * \frac{1}{ADI_n \cap P_D/ADI_n} * \frac{1}{ADI_n \cap P_D}.$$

Data Sources

I rely on three sources for television market data. The *Television and Cable Factbook, 1989* has maps of each state with ADIs drawn in, along with TV household counts by county. I purchased an ADI County Information data set from Arbitron, Inc., which has a record for each county in the United States (except for independent cities in Virginia, which are collapsed into the surrounding counties). Each record contains the state and county Federal Information Processing System (FIPS) code, ADI (name and numerical code), TV household count, and total household count. With proper aggregation and file matching, this data set can be used to calculate state TV households, ADI TV households, and TV households in the state-ADI intersections. From the Bureau of the Census, I obtained person counts for counties and congressional districts. From the state-level tapes, I was able to construct a county-to-CD conversion scheme (more on this later). Once this was attached to the Arbitron data set, I could proceed in a similar fashion to compute CD population, ADI population, and the population of CD-ADI intersections.

---

of overlap between ADI's and districts varies dramatically. My "total cost" (as I use it) and "per capita cost" measures more clearly distinguish the two.

TABLE A.1. Arbitron TV Households and Census Person Counts

	TV Households
Census persons, county level	.994
Census households, county level	.996
Arbitron estimate of households	.999
Census persons, state level	.992
News mix (persons)	.999
Dominance (persons)	.998

Note: The first four entries are the correlation between the Arbitron TV household count and a variety of other person and household measures; the last two entries are correlations between TV market variables calculated for states using census person counts and Arbitron TV household counts.

TV Households versus Population

Stewart and Reynolds (1989) use Arbitron TV household counts to calculate contiguity, dominance, and their version of total and average costs. I rely on census population counts instead. The main reason is a practical one: TV household counts are only available at the county level, and aggregating from county level to CD is very complicated.

No information is lost if Census population estimates are used instead of Arbitron TV household estimates. Census and Arbitron estimates correlate at .99 and above. More importantly, contiguity and dominance, estimated for states using population or TV households, correlate nearly perfectly (see table A.1). The advantage of being able to compare CDs and states on identical measures far outweighs any additional errors introduced by using census population counts instead of Arbitron TV household counts.

The following are sample calculations for California's Sixteenth District (see table A.2 for data):

$$
\begin{aligned}
\text{Dominance} \quad &= \quad \sum_{i=1}^{n} \left(\frac{\text{ADI}_n \cap P_D}{P_D} \right)^2 \\
&= \quad \left(\frac{22,303}{525,893} \right)^2 + \left(\frac{503,590}{525,893} \right)^2 \\
&= \quad .9188
\end{aligned}
$$

$$\text{News mix} = \sum_{i=1}^{n} \frac{\text{ADI}_n \cap P_D}{P_D} * \frac{\text{ADI}_n \cap P_D}{\text{ADI}_n}$$

$$= \frac{22,303}{525,893} * \frac{22,303}{454,129} + \frac{503,590}{525,893} * \frac{503,590}{503,590}$$

$$= .9597.$$

Demographic Measures

All the demographic data were drawn from the 1970, 1980, and 1990 censuses of the population, congressional-district-level extract (state data are simply aggregated from the CD level). All demographic measures were recoded as follows (table references are to tables in the census documentation):

TABLE A.2. Sample Calculations for Media Market Measures

District/State	Pop_D	ADI Name	ADI_n	$\text{ADI}_n \cap \text{Pop}_D$
Sixteenth CA	525,893	Salinas -Monterey	503,590	503,950
		Santa Barbara	454,129	22,303
Maine	1,124,660	Portland/ Poland Spring	791,572	728,494
		Bangor	304,835	304,835
		Presque Isle	91,331	91,331
Nevada	800,493	Las Vegas	471,815	471,815
		Reno	364,585	303,242
		Salt Lake City	1,615,422	25,436
Wyoming	469,557	Casper- Riverton	124,917	124,917
		Denver, CO	2,293,099	108,964
		Salt Lake City	1,615,422	95,749
		Cheyenne/ Scottsbluff	106,993	68,649
		Rapid City, SD	216,166	37,462
		Billings/ Hardin	208,812	21,639

Source: 1980 census (population figures) and Arbitron, Inc.

- *Urban residence* proportion urban, table 1, category 2, divided by total person count (hereafter, *total person count* refers to the 100 percent count of persons, table 3, which the census uses as the base for most tables, unless specifically noted otherwise).
- *Race,* proportion black, table 12, category 2 (black), divided by total person count.
- *Foreign stock,* percentage foreign stock, table 33, category 4 (foreign born), divided by total person count.
- *Education,* percentage high school, table 50, categories 1–2 (elementary through high school, one to three years; high school, four years), divided by persons 18 years and over.
- *Occupation,* proportion blue collar, table 66, categories 6, 10–13 (private household occupations [6]; precision production, craft, and repair [10]; operator, fabricators, and laborers [11–13]), divided by employed persons 16 years and over.
- *Income,* median income, table 69.
- *Population Density,* total person count divided by square miles (coded by author).

Diversity Measures

Lieberson's (1969) A_w, often described as a measure of heterogeneity within a population, has been used by a number of political scientists (Sullivan 1973; Bond 1983; Bullock and Brady 1983). It can be used with polytomous variables.[3] The variable runs from zero to 1.0, where zero means that every individual is different and 1.0 means that there is no variation (on the characteristic under examination).[4] The advantage of this measure is that it can be used for polytomous nominal variables. Any other calculation would have required me to either make unsupportable assertions about ordinality or collapse categories into dichotomies (e.g., white/non-white).

To illustrate how these scores are calculated, suppose I am comparing religious diversity within a state. If I randomly pair all members of the state, one way to think about diversity is to see it as the proportion of pairs that differ in religious affiliation. Another way to express this is to suppose I randomly choose a pair of individuals. What is the probability that they will have different religions? For one (hypothetical) variable with three categories, this calculation is straightforward:

---

3. As noted in the text, variance is a good measure of diversity using continuous variables.

4. If, for example, I calculated diversity of social security numbers, A_w would take on a value of zero.

Catholic	=	.25	Catholic-Catholic pairs $= .25 * .25$
Protestant	=	.50	Agreeing pairs $= .25^2 + .5^2 + .25^2$
Other	=	.25	Different pairs $= 1 - (.25^2 + .5^2 + .25^2)$

The diversity score, A_w, is calculated thus: given a variable, X, with n categories, and each category expressed as its proportion in the population (X_n),

$$\sum_{i=1}^{n} X_i = 1.0$$
$$A_w = 1 - \sum_{i=1}^{n} (X_i)^2 .$$

When more than one variable is under consideration, the situation is less obvious. In particular, how do I evaluate partial matches? Suppose I have three variables, with values $X = 1, 2, 3$, $Y = 1, 2$, $Z = 1, 2$. The combination $(111)(111)$ is obviously a perfect match, but what about pairs such as $(111)(112)$ or $(111)(123)$? I need to adjust for partial matches by 1) summing up the probability of exact matches, and 2) summing up all the probabilities of all partial matches, but at the same time, however, 3) weighting partial matches by the proportion of specified characteristics shared by the pair. Thus,

- C_i is the proportion of the population in some combination (e.g., 111, 121, 223, etc.)
- n is the number of possible combinations
- C_{ij} is a pair of combinations expressed as the cross-product of their proportions in the population
- W_{ij} is the proportion of specified characteristics shared in C_{ij} (e.g., for $[111][112]$, $W_{ij} = 2/3$)

For this example, $n =$ (the number of categories in X) $*$ (the number of categories in Y) $*$ (the number of categories in Z) $= 12$. Notice that $\sum_{i=1}^{n} (C_i)^2$ is the proportion of perfect matches and $2 * \sum_{i=1}^{n} \sum_{j>1}^{n} C_{ij}$ is the proportion of partial matches. A 2 is required because each match can occur twice, that is, $(111)(122)$ and $(122)(111)$. The final measure is calculated thusly:

$$A_w = 1 - \left[\sum_{i=1}^{n} (C_i)^2 \right] + \left(2 * \sum_{i=1}^{n} \sum_{j>1}^{n} C_{ij} W_{ij} \right) .$$

This measure is: "nicely interpretable in probability terms, since it represents the proportion of characteristics upon which a randomly-selected pair of

TABLE A.3. Demographic Diversity in Election Districts: Updating Bond

Variable	States	CDs	K-S Statistic
Bond summary measure	.424 (.033)	.389 (.060)	2.469 (.001)
Summary measure 2	.590 (.031)	.586 (.038)	1.370 (.047)
N of cases	50	435	—

Source: 1980 census.
Note: The entries in columns 2 and 3 are means, with standard deviations (i.e., the variance of the variances) in parentheses. The Bond summary is a diversity measure that considers race, occupation, foreign stock, and urbanness together (replicating Bond 1983). Summary measure 2 is a summary measure that includes all the measures in this table and does not collapse across categories (as Bond does). Mathematically, including more categories results in a higher (more diverse) score.

individuals will differ, assuming sampling with replacement" (Sullivan 1973, 70). Still, the diversity measure could be deceiving. Although it represents the underlying construct—diversity of interests in a district—it is probably too catholic about the political impact of various categories. Using this measure, a district that is 90 percent white and 10 percent black receives an identical score as a one that is 90 percent black and 10 percent white. If heterogeneity and homogeneity were the *only* concern here, this result would be fine.

However, I selected the demographic categories I did precisely because I know certain cleavages are politically more potent than others. The reader should be aware of this limitation of the diversity measure. Bond (1983) and Bullock and Brady (1983) both used a summary diversity measure. For purposes of comparison, I report updated summary scores in table A.3.

APPENDIX B

Variable and Model Information for Chapter 5

Variable Names and Sources

Challenger and Incumbent Spending

- Source: Federal Election Commission tapes, released through the Interuniversity Consortium on Political and Social Research.
- Recode: Any spending below $5,000 by a candidate was set at $5,000, following Jacobson 1985. I transformed to a per capita variable by dividing by state or congressional district population. I then logged in order to account for extreme values.

Closeness

- Source: The *Congressional Quarterly Weekly Report* election reports.
- Recode: The original variable runs from zero (safe Democratic) to 7 (safe Republican). I folded the variable about its midpoint so that it ran from zero (safe seat) to 4 (too close to call).

Ideological Extremity

- Member score on the D-Nominate scale developed by Poole and Rosenthal (1985, 1997) folded about its midpoint.

Partisan Split

- Source: Election results from assorted sources.
- Recode: The variable is originally coded as a normal vote variable, or the average percentage Republican vote for the last three elections. For Senate races, I took the average value of the normal vote in all congressional districts in the state for three previous elections. This variable ran from zero to 1.0. I subtracted .5 from the variable, so that it ran from −.5

(perfect Democratic) to zero (even) to .5 (perfect Republican). For Republican incumbents, I left the scale as it stood. For Democratic incumbents, I multiplied the scale by -1. Now the scale runs from $-.5$ (perfectly favorable partisan balance for the challenger) to zero (even) to .5 (perfectly favorable partisan balance for the incumbent).

Media Contiguity, Media Dominance

- See appendix A.

Income and Education Variance

- See Appendix A.

Racial, Urban, and Foreign Stock Diversity

- See Appendix A.

Stability of Coefficients across Institutions

As mentioned in chapter 5, a "fully-dummied" specification is analogous to a Chow test for the stability of coefficients across the Senate and House. The test involves a straightforward difference in F-statistics, comparing the constrained to the unconstrained model.[1]

The results for tables 5.1, 5.2, and 5.3 are shown below. Please note that a *non-significant* p-value indicates that the unconstrained model (separate relationships for House and Senate) provides no statistically discernible improvement in fit and is thus rejected. For the final model (table 5.3), I report the F-statistic both for a "fully-dummied" specification and a specification with a single Senate dummy variable. Only the model with a separate slope provides a significantly improved fit.

Tested Model	F-statistic	(d.f. numerator/ denominator)
Table 5.1	.55	(10/2442)
Table 5.2	1.0813	(5/2452)
Table 5.3	.922	(14/ 2434)
Table 5.3 (separate constant)	3.45	(13/2435)

1. No difference in coefficients implicitly assumes that all the dummy variable coefficients are zero. The unconstrained model allows different coefficients across the Senate and House.

Problems of Two-Stage Estimation

Serious sample problems undermine any study of the causes and consequences of campaign spending in both the House and Senate. The first problem is well recognized: many cases are lost because the instrumental variables (lagged spending) are missing. This study is especially prone to this problem because I compare across the two institutions. The maximum number of Senate races in any election year is 34. In a two-stage setup, I rely on lagged values in order to solve the endogeneity problem (at least for incumbent spending). This raises a number of quandaries. First, what to do with first-term incumbents or incumbents who were unopposed last time? Gary Jacobson set up a number of screening criteria for inclusion in his campaign-spending analysis of the House (1985). The incumbent has to face opposition at time t and time $t - 1$. The incumbent at time t has to be the same incumbent as at time $t - 1$ (spending in an open-seat race does not reflect a "generalized propensity to spend"). This eliminates unopposed incumbents at time t and time $t - 1$, all open-seat races from $t - 1$, and all incumbent defeats from time $t - 1$. Furthermore, a scattering of cases drop out due to retirements and deaths during the term and House members who retire or are defeated in a primary at time t. One result of this filtering rule, ironically, is that just those seats in which we are most interested—the most competitive—are eliminated from the analysis.

The consequences of the screening rule for the House are perilous. In 1978, for example, the number of races involving incumbents was 377 and the number of incumbents facing opposition was 327. Various additional reasons to drop cases reduced the working sample size to 236, resulting in a 28 percent reduction in the sample (see Jacobson 1985, 1990a; and Green and Krasno 1988, 1990). The consequences of the screening rule for the Senate are far worse. The population of Senate cases is already small. More cases are lost through filtering than for the House because Senate incumbents are defeated more often in primaries, Senate incumbents are defeated more often in the general election, and senators retire at higher rates (due perhaps to the longer term, a desire to run for governor or president, and the age of politicians who finally make it to the Senate). Whereas around 30 percent of the House cases drop out during the 1980s and 1990s , nearly 50 percent of the Senate races drop out, and this figure would have been even higher were it not for the unusually high number of cases that met Jacobson's criteria in 1988.

Incidentally, the small number of Senate cases is not a problem unique to this study. Richard Fenno, when attempting to reproduce *Home Style* for the Senate, apparently found that senators were too idiosyncratic to allow much generalization about constituency representation, campaign strategies, and Washington behavior. Instead of a Senate *Home Style,* he has written a series of books about individual senators. Canon, in his study of amateurism, could not produce some measures for the Senate because of instability due to small ns (Canon 1990, chap. 3). Much of the reason for the Senate being the forgotten side of Congress is numerical: there are not enough Senate races in a single election, or even a whole decade, to allow for very sophisticated quantitative analyses.

A more serious problem, however, is less frequently recognized. The cases that are excluded from the analysis are not a random sample of districts. Since they are districts held by freshmen or those where an incumbent was defeated in a primary, they are also districts where, on average, challengers would be expected to spend more and receive more votes than average. This could bias the estimates for campaign spending in unknown ways, and not just in this study. Most studies of campaign spending and incumbent vote totals encounter this potential bias.[2]

Two-stage estimation places severe demands on the data and the specification than does ordinary least squares, demands that typical congressional campaign data sets may not meet. As Bartels (1991) has shown, parameter estimates are heavily affected by specification error. I have the advantage in this case of relying on a well-established causal framework, one that is given some support in Bartels's article. The potential biases and sample size problems remain. Pooled results will be dominated by the House sample (a pooled sample, with filtering, consists of 20 times as many House as Senate contests). The two-stage estimates, then, should be viewed with some caution.

---

2. I am grateful to an anonymous reviewer for pointing out this problem.

Variable Information for Chapter 6

Measures Added in This Chapter

Political Attentiveness

- Source: All measures in the chapter come from the National Election Study's Senate Election Study.
- Recode: This is a combination of self-expressed interest in politics, number of days spent watching the network news, and number of days spent reading a daily newspaper. Weights were obtained via a principal components analysis of these three variables and education. No rotation was applied to the eigenvectors, and I limited the number of factors to two. Education occupies a separate dimension.

Presidential Approval

- Recode: This is a recoded version of a four-point scale, where 1=strongly approve and 4=strongly disapprove. The variable was recoded to the zero to one range, and multiplied by -1 for Democratic incumbents.

Help District?

- Recode: This item asked respondents whether they thought the incumbent would be helpful if the respondent had a problem. It is a three-point scale, running from very helpful to not very helpful. It was recoded to the zero to one range, with 1 = very helpful.

Likes/Dislikes

- Recode: Respondents provided open-ended mentions of things they liked or disliked about candidates. The NES coded up to five mentions. I totaled all mentions across individuals. This variable thus runs from zero to five. For the comparisons across various types of likes/dislikes, I used the coding scheme suggested by the NES. I standardized these measures by institution when I included them in the voting models.

Contacts

- Recode: The NES asked respondents about seven types of candidate contacts. I summed the contacts across individuals.

Vote for Incumbent

- Recode: This is a combination of reported vote for the incumbent and, for those who did not vote, expressed preference.

Isolating High-Flow Campaign Environments

In chapter 6, I compared voter information and choice models for "high"- and "low"-intensity contests. In order to reassure the reader that the threshold I chose is not arbitrary, I illustrate in this appendix the impact of other selection schemes.

I selected out particular contests to look at according to two criteria: per capita spending by the challenger was greater than one (meaning that the challenger spent more than one dollar per capita) or the ratio of incumbent to challenger spending crossed a low threshold, 1.5 and 1.0. The first criteria sets too high a barrier: too many cases are screened out, and it ignores spending by the incumbent. Campaign intensity is a *combination* of spending by both candidates along with candidate quality. [1]

As an illustration of the impact of various filters, I present the number of races, the number of respondents, and incumbent and challenger recall under three screens. These are shown in table C.1. The first thing to note is that significant numbers of respondents are experiencing a hard-fought House contest, even in a single election year.[2] In the third column, for example, 19 percent of

---

1. I exclude from consideration races where the incumbent spent less than 20 cents per capita, or about $100,000 for the House (this additional criterion had no impact on the Senate). This eliminate those few races where the challenger and the incumbent spent the same amount, but the campaign was a low intensity contest overall. By doing so, I increased the proportion of cases that fell into Krasno's "high intensity" category from 52 percent to 80 percent. This lends some construct validity to the ratio measure.

2. This figure is higher than might be expected using the typical NES post-election study because the 1992 NES/SES, in order to produce satisfactory samples within each state, has more sample strata at the sub-national and sub-state level.

TABLE C.1. Isolating High-Flow Campaign Environments

	All Races	High Challenger Spending	Ratio < 1.5	Ratio < 1.0
Races				
House	317	10 (3%)	25 (8%)	8 (3%)
Senate	27	5 (18%)	7 (26%)	5 (18%)
Respondents				
House	1588	74 (5%)	305 (19%)	87 (6%)
Senate	2538	476 (19%)	433 (17%)	298 (12%)
Recall name				
House incumbent	.292	.270	.331	.356
Senate incumbent	.402	.457	.448	.460
House challenger	.108	.189	.203	.184
Senate challenger	.220	.363	.356	.409

Source: 1988 NES/SES.
Note: High challenger spending is defined as races in which challenger spending is higher than one dollar per capita. Entries for recall and recognition are the proportion correctly identifying the name of the candidate. If per capita incumbent spending is less than .2 (or 20 cents per citizen), the case is dropped. This only affected the House sample. See chapter 6.

the House respondents and 8 percent of races fell into the high-intensity category compared to 17 percent of the respondents and 26 percent of the races.[3] "Significant overlaps" in Senate and House races is more than just an empty phrase; there are hundreds of respondents in the 1988 NES/SES who experienced hard-fought House races. While sample sizes of contests become quite low, sample sizes of respondents may not.

The information measure, candidate recall, behaves as expected: recall rates increase as the filter becomes progressively finer. Challenger quality also increases; when the spending ratio is at 1.5 or less, average Senate challenger quality is 3.38 (out of 4.00) and House challenger quality is 2.59. Still, this duplicates the results of chapter 3: even in comparably intense contests with comparable levels of spending (per capita), Senate challengers are more prominent and have more political experience than their House counterparts do. Based on table C.1, as well as readings of campaign coverage and some additional analyses, I chose to label those cases in which the ratio of incumbent to challenger

3. I am fudging on the definition of "intensity" only for purposes of illustration. In previous chapters, I set this to be either a) Krasno's and Westlye's qualitative coding or b) a spending ratio less than 2.0. For purposes of illustration, a more restrictive ratio is more revealing.

TABLE C.2. Voter Choice: Defection toward and away from the Incumbent

	Defect Toward	Defect Away
Constant	−0.545 (.133)**	−1.337 (.190)**
Presidential approval	0.642 (.070)**	−0.355 (.104)**
Help district?	−0.093 (.125)	−0.562 (.185)**
Intensity	0.034 (.102)	0.219 (.146)
Institution	−0.103 (.087)	−0.007 (.135)
Incumbent likes	0.136 (.041)**	−0.327 (.093)**
Incumbent dislikes	−0.204 (.075)*	0.170 (.091)
Challenger likes	−0.233 (.071)**	0.213 (.080)*
Challenger dislikes	0.078 (.066)	−0.329 (.149)*
Incumbent contacts	−0.091 (.026)**	0.079 (.040)*
Challenger contacts	0.029 (.025)	−0.091 (.040)*
Tenure	−0.000 (.000)	0.000 (.000)
$-2\ln(L_0/L_1)$	594.66	1,420.63
N of cases	1,377	1,377
Percentage predicted	78.94	94.63

Source: 1988 NES/SES.
Note: Only partisans are included in the table. The entries in column 2 are maximum likelihood probit coefficients with standard errors in parentheses. Coefficients with one asterisk are more than two times their standard errors; coefficients with two asterisks are three or more times their standard errors.

spending was no greater that 1.5 as "high intensity." This leaves enough cases and a large enough proportion of contests that any statistical estimates should not be inefficient or biased.

Alternative Models of Voting

Zaller presents voter defection models for the House (1978) and the Senate (1988). For comparison, I present in in table C.2 pooled versions of the model in equation 6.1, using incumbent defection as the dependent variable and relying on the 1988 data in order to retain comparability with Zaller (1992, chap. 10).

There are two ways in which defection might occur. First, partisans of the opposite party might vote for the incumbent, such as a self-identified Republican voting for a Democratic incumbent. I call this "defection toward the

TABLE C.3. Incumbent Vote, No Likes and Dislikes

Constant	.934 (.137)**
Party identification	1.145 (.106)**
Presidential approval	.317 (.092)**
Help district?	.790 (.092)**
Intensity	−.720 (.071)**
Institution	.013 (.010)
Incumbent contacts	.041 (.019)*
Challenger contacts	−.121 (.018)**
Tenure	−.092 (.048)
$-2\ln(L_0/L_1)$	550.2
N of cases	2,364
Percentage predicted	78.22

Source: 1988 NES/SES.
Note: The entries are maximum likelihood probit coefficients with standard errors in parentheses.

incumbent." Twenty-nine percent of the respondents reported this kind of behavior. The second kind of defection is more unusual but still a logical possibility: incumbent partisans vote for the challenger. Nine percent of the sample reported that they voted for or preferred the opposing party's challenger.

The results reinforce in most ways the conclusions in this chapter. Presidential approval, perceptions of incumbent helpfulness, and the balance of likes and dislikes are all important predictors of the likelihood of defection.[4] The results are mirror images: variables that are positively related to defection toward the incumbent (such as incumbent likes) are negatively related to defection away.

The discrepancies between these results and the results reported in the text are instructive. There is no discernible difference between the likelihood of defection in high- and low-intensity races, although the direction of the effect is positive, as would be expected, and nearly statistically significant in the "defect away" model. Voters who defect toward incumbents are basically voters who have positive things to say about the incumbent and have not had many contacts with challengers. They are, as Zaller notes, mainly individuals exposed to one-way information flows (1992). Campaign intensity has little to do with the likelihood of defection. Similarly, those who defect away mainly do so because they dislike incumbents and like the challenger, regardless of the

4. Partisanship is not in this model since partisanship crossed with the incumbent's party makes up the dependent variable.

intensity of the race. Finally, I include candidate likes and dislikes as independent variables in my models predicting the vote. I examined whether this was a misspecification: placing the dependent variable on both sides of the equation. The number of likes and dislikes that a respondent cites correlates with vote choice at .30. There is quite a bit of unexplained variation left in the vote. Second, as is shown in table C.3, there is only a minimal change in the other coefficients in the model when likes and dislikes are removed. The goodness of fit declines substantially.

References

Abramowitz, Alan I. 1980. "A Comparison of Voting for U.S. Senator and Representative in 1978." *American Political Science Review* 74:633–40.

—. 1988. "Explaining Senate Election Outcomes." *American Political Science Review* 82:385–404.

Abramowitz, Alan I., and Kenneth J. Cribbs. 1989. "Don't Worry, Be Happy: Evaluations of Senate and House Incumbents in 1988." Paper presented at the annual meeting of the American Political Science Association, Washington, DC.

Abramowitz, Alan I., and Jeffrey A. Segal. 1990. "Beyond Willie Horton and the Pledge of Allegiance: National Issues in the 1988 Elections." *Legislative Studies Quarterly* 15:565–80.

—. 1992. *Senate Elections.* Ann Arbor: University of Michigan Press.

Adler, Scott, Chariti Gent, and Cary Overmeyer. 1998. "The Home Style Homepage: Legislator Use of the World Wide Web for Constituency Contact." *Legislative Studies Quarterly* 23:585–95.

Aldrich, John H. 1980. *Before the Convention: Strategies and Choices in Presidential Nominations Campaigns.* Chicago: University of Chicago Press.

—. 1999. "Political Parties in a Critical Era." *American Politics Quarterly* 27: 9–32.

Aldrich, John H., Paul Gronke, and Jeffrey Grynaviski. 1999. "Personality, Performance, and Presidential Assessments." Paper presented at the annual meeting of the Midwest Political Science Association, Chicago.

Aldrich, John H., and Forrest D. Nelson. 1984. *Linear Probability, Logit, and Probit Models.* Newbury Park, CA: Sage Publications.

Aldrich, John H., and Richard G. Niemi. 1996. "The Sixth American Party System: Electoral Change, 1952–1992." In Stephen Craig, ed., *Broken Contract: Changing Relationships between Americans and Their Government.* Boulder, CO: Westview Press.

Alford, John R., and David W. Brady. 1989. "Personal and Partisan Advantage in U.S. Congressional Elections, 1846–1986." In L. Dodd and B. Oppenheimer, eds., *Congress Reconsidered.* 4th ed. Washington, DC: Congressional Quarterly Press.

Alford, John R., and John R. Hibbing. 1989. "The Disparate Electoral Security of House and Senate Incumbents." Paper presented at the annual meeting of the American Political Science Association, Atlanta.

——. N.d. "The Demise of the Upper House and the Rise of the Senate: Electoral Responsiveness in the United States Congress." Mimeo.

Alston, Chuck. 1990. "Warning Shots First by Voters More Mood Than Mandate." *Congressional Quarterly Weekly Report* 48 (10 November): 3796–97.

Alvarez, R. Michael. 1996. "Studying Congressional and Gubernatorial Campaigns." Paper prepared for presentation at the National Election Studies Research and Development Conference on Congressional Elections, Ann Arbor, MI: Center for Political Studies.

——. 1999. *Information and Elections.* Rev. ed. Ann Arbor: University of Michigan Press.

Alvarez, R. Michael, and Jonathan Nagler. 1998. "Economics, Entitlements, and Social Issues: Voter Choice in the 1996 Presidential Election." *American Journal of Political Science* 42: 1349–63.

Ansolabehere, Steven, and Alan Gerber. 1994. "The Mismeasure of Campaign Spending: Evidence from the 1990 House Elections." *Journal of Politics* 56: 1106–18.

Ashford, Nicholas. 1983. "Elections for Sale: The Corrosive Role of Money in U.S. Politics." *World Press Review* 30: 32.

Atkeson, L. R., and R. Partin. 1995. "Economic Voting and Referendum Voting: A Comparison of Gubernatorial and Senatorial Elections." *American Political Science Review* 89: 99–107.

Baker, Ross K. 1995. *House and Senate.* 2d ed. New York: W.W. Norton.

Banks, Jeffrey S., and D. Roderick Kiewiet. 1989. "Explaining Patterns of Candidate Competition in Congressional Elections." *American Journal of Political Science* 33: 997–1015.

Barone, Michael, and Grant Ujifusa. 1983. *Almanac of American Politics, 1984.* Washington, DC: National Journal.

——. 1985. *Almanac of American Politics, 1986.* Washington, DC: National Journal.

Bartels, Larry M. 1988. *Presidential Primaries.* Princeton: Princeton University Press.

——. 1991. "Instrumental and Quasi-Instrumental Variables." *American Journal of Political Science* 35: 777–800.

Baum, Matthew A., and Samuel Kernell. 1999. "Has Cable Ended the Golden Age of Presidential Television?" *American Political Science Review* 93:99–114.

Beck, Paul Allen. 1997. *Party Politics in America.* 8th ed. New York: Longman.

Bernstein, Robert A. 1989. *Elections, Representation, and Congressional Voting Behavior.* Englewood Cliffs, NJ: Prentice-Hall.

Bianco, William T. 1984. "Strategic Decisions on Candidacy in U.S. Congressional Districts." *Legislative Studies Quarterly* 9: 351–64.

—. 1995. *Trust: Constituents and Legislators.* Ann Arbor: University of Michigan Press.

Blalock, Herbert. 1979. *Social Statistics.* 2d ed. New York: McGraw Hill.

Bond, Jon R. 1983. "The Influence of Constituency Diversity on Electoral Competition in Voting for Congress, 1974–78." *Legislative Studies Quarterly* 8:201–17.

Bond, Jon R., Cary Covington, and Richard Fleisher. 1985. "Explaining Challenger Quality in Congressional Elections." *Journal of Politics* 47:510–29.

Box-Steffensmeier, Janet M. 1996. "A Dynamic Analysis of the Role of War Chests in Campaign Strategy." *American Journal of Political Science* 40: 352–71.

Brunell, Thomas L. 1997. "Short-Term versus Long-Term Forces in U.S. Senate Elections." Ph.D. diss., Department of Political Science, University of California, Irvine.

Bullock, Charles S., III, and David W. Brady. 1983. "Party, Constituency, and Roll-Call Voting in the U.S. Senate." *Legislative Studies Quarterly* 8:29–43.

Cain, Bruce, John Ferejohn, and Morris Fiorina. 1987. *The Personal Vote.* Cambridge: Harvard University Press.

Campbell, James E., John R. Alford, and Keith Henry. 1984. "Television Markets and Congressional Elections." *Legislative Studies Quarterly* 9: 665–78.

Canon, David T. 1989. "Political Amateurism in the United States Congress." In L. Dodd and B. Oppenheimer, eds., *Congress Reconsidered.* 4th ed. Washington, DC: Congressional Quarterly Press.

—. 1990. *Actors, Athletes, and Astronauts: Political Amateurs in United States Congressional Elections.* Chicago: University of Chicago Press.

Canon, David T., Matthew Schousen, and Patrick Sellers. 1996. "The Supply Side of Congressional Redistricting: Race and Strategic Politicians." *Journal of Politics* 58: 837–53.

Carsey, Thomas L., and Gerald C. Wright. 1998. "State and National Forces in Gubernatorial and Senatorial Elections." *American Journal of Political Science* 42: 994–1002.

Collier, Kenneth, and Michael C. Munger. 1994. "Comparing Reelection Rates in the House and Senate" *Public Choice* 78:45–54.

Cooper, Joseph. 1977. "Congress in Organizational Perspective." In L. Dodd and B. Oppenheimer, eds., *Congress Reconsidered*. Washington, DC: Congressional Quarterly Press.

Cover, Albert D., and David R. Mayhew. 1977. "Congressional Dynamics and the Decline of Competitive Congressional Elections." In L. Dodd and B. Oppenheimer, eds., *Congress Reconsidered*. Washington, DC: Congressional Quarterly Press.

Cox, Gary W. 1997. *Making Votes Count*. New York: Cambridge University Press.

Dodd, Lawrence C. 1993. "Congress and the Politics of Renewal." In L. Dodd and B. Oppenheimer, eds., *Congress Reconsidered*. 5th ed. Washington, DC: Congressional Quarterly Press.

Dodd, Lawrence C., and Bruce I. Oppenheimer. 1989. *Congress Reconsidered*. 4th ed. Washington, DC: Congressional Quarterly Press.

—. 1997. *Congress Reconsidered*. 6th ed. Washington, DC: Congressional Quarterly Press.

Duncan, Phil, ed. 1987. *Politics in America, 1988*. Washington, DC: Congressional Quarterly Press.

—. 1989. *Politics in America, 1990*. Washington, DC: Congressional Quarterly Press.

Erikson, Robert S. 1978. "Constituency Opinion and Congressional Voting Behavior: A Causal Model." *American Journal of Political Science* 22: 511–35.

—. 1981. "Measuring Constituency Opinion: The 1978 Congressional Election Study." *Legislative Studies Quarterly* 6:235–45.

Erikson, Robert S., and Thomas Palfrey. 1998. "Campaign Spending and Incumbency: An Alternative Simultaneous Equations Approach." *Journal of Politics* 60:355–73.

Erikson, Robert S., and Gerald C. Wright. 1980. "Candidates' Policy Positions and Voting in U.S. House Elections." *Political Behavior* 1:91–106.

—. 1989. "Voters, Candidates, and Issues in Congressional Election." In L. Dodd and B. Oppenheimer, eds., *Congress Reconsidered*. 4th ed. Washington, DC: Congressional Quarterly Press.

Erikson, Robert S., Gerald C. Wright, and John P. McIver. 1993. *Statehouse Democracy: Public Opinion and Policy in the American States*. New York: Cambridge University Press.

Fenno, Richard F. 1978. *Home Style: House Members in Their Districts*. Boston: Little, Brown.

—. 1982. *The United States Senate: A Bicameral Perspective*. Washington, DC: American Enterprise Institute.

Fiorina, Morris P. 1974. *Representatives, Roll Calls, and Constituencies.* Lexington, MA: D. C. Heath.

——. 1975. "Constituency Influence: A Generalized Model and Its Implications for Statistical Studies of Roll Call Behavior." *Political Methodology* 2: 249–66.

——. 1977. "The Case of the Vanishing Marginals: The Bureaucracy Did It." *American Political Science Review* 71:177–81.

——. 1989. *Congress: Keystone of the Washington Establishment.* New Haven: Yale University Press.

——. 1996. *Divided Government.* 2d ed. New York: Allyn and Bacon.

Fiorina, Morris P., and David Rohde. 1989. *Home Style and Washington Work: Studies of Congressional Politics.* Ann Arbor: University of Michigan Press.

Foote, Joe S., and David J. Weber. 1984. "Network News Visibility of Congressmen and Senators." Paper presented at the convention of Journalism and Mass Communication, Gainesville, FL.

Fowler, Linda L. 1993. *Candidates, Congress, and the American Democracy.* Ann Arbor: University of Michigan Press.

Fowler, Linda L., and Robert D. McClure. 1989. *Political Ambition: Who Decides to Run for Congress.* New Haven: Yale University Press.

Franklin, Charles H. 1991. "Eschewing Obfuscation? Campaigns and the Perceptions of U.S. Senate Incumbents." *American Political Science Review* 85: 1193–1214.

——. 1993. "Senate Incumbent Visibility over the Election Cycle." *Legislative Studies Quarterly* 18: 271–90.

Goldenberg, Edie N., and Michael W. Traugott. 1984. *Campaigning for Congress.* Washington, DC: Congressional Quarterly Press.

Gove, Samuel K., and Louis Masotti, eds. 1982. *After Daley.* Urbana: University of Illinois Press.

Green, Donald P., and Jonathan S. Krasno. 1988. "Salvation for the Spendthrift Incumbent." *American Journal of Political Science* 32:844–907.

——. 1990. "Rebuttal to Jacobson's 'New Evidence for Old Arguments.'" *American Journal of Political Science* 34:363–72.

Greene, William H. 1993. *Econometric Analysis.* 2d ed. New York: Macmillan.

Grier, Kevin B. and Michael C. Munger. 1993. "Comparing Interest Group PAC Contributions to House and Senate Incumbents, 1980-1986" *Journal of Politics* 55(3): 615–43.

Grofman, Bernard, Thomas Brunell, and William Koetzle. 1998. "Why Gain in the Senate but Midterm Loss in the House? Evidence from a Natural Experiment." *Legislative Studies Quarterly* 23: 79–90.

Grofman, Bernard, and Chandler Davidson, eds. 1992. *Controversies in Minority Voting.* Washington, DC: Brookings Institution.

Grofman, Bernard, Robert Griffin, and Amihai Glazer. 1990. "Identical Geography, Different Party: A Natural Experiment on the Magnitude of Party Differences in the U.S. Senate, 1960–84." In Ronald J. Johnston, Frank M. Shelley, and Paul J. Taylor, eds., *Developments in Electoral Geography.* New York: Routledge.

Grofman, Bernard, Robert Griffin, and Gregory Berry. 1995. "House Members Who Become Senators: Learning from a 'Natural' Experiment in Representation." *Legislative Studies Quarterly* 20: 513–29.

Grofman, Bernard, William Koetzle, and Thomas Brunell. 1997. "Rethinking the Link Between District Diversity and Electoral Competitiveness." Paper presented at the annual meeting of the American Political Science Association, Washington.

Gronke, Paul, and J. Matthew Wilson. 1999. "Competing Redistricting Plans as Evidence of Political Motives: The North Carolina Case." *American Politics Quarterly* 27: 147–76.

Gross, Donald, and David Breaux. 1989. "Historical Trends in U.S. Senate Elections: 1912–1988." Paper presented at the Annual Meeting of the Midwest Political Science Association, Chicago.

Herrnson, Paul S. 1995. *Congressional Elections: Campaigning at Home and in Washington.* 2d ed. Washington, DC: Congressional Quarterly Press.

Hershey, Marjorie Randon. 1984. *Running for Office: The Political Education of Campaigners.* Chatham, NJ: Chatham House.

Hess, Stephen. 1986. *The Ultimate Insiders: U.S. Senators in the National Media.* Washington, DC: Brookings Institution.

Hibbing, John R. 1993. "Careerism in Congress: For Better or Worse?" In L. Dodd and B. Oppenheimer, eds., *Congress Reconsidered.* 5th ed. Washington, DC: Congressional Quarterly Press.

Hibbing, John R., and John R. Alford. 1981. "The Electoral Impact of Economic Conditions: Who Is Held Responsible?" *American Journal of Political Science* 25:423–39.

—. 1990. "Constituency Population and Representation in the U.S. Senate." *Legislative Studies Quarterly* 15: 581–98.

Hibbing, John R., and Sara L. Brandes. 1983. "State Population and the Electoral Success of U.S. Senators." *American Journal of Political Science* 27:808–19.

Hibbing, John R., and E. Theiss-Morse. 1995. *Congress as Public Enemy.* New York: Cambridge University Press.

Hibbs, Douglas A. 1987. *The American Political Economy.* Cambridge: Harvard University Press.

Hibbs, Douglas A., Douglas Rivers, and Nicholas Vasilatos. 1982a. "On the Demand for Economic Outcomes: Macroeconomic Performance and Mass Political Support in the United States, Great Britain, and Germany." *Journal of Politics* 44:426–62.

—. 1982b. "The Dynamics of Political Support for American Presidents among Occupational and Partisan Groups." *American Journal of Political Science* 26:312–32.

Hill, Kevin. 1995. "Does the Creation of Majority Black Districts Aid Republicans? An Analysis of the 1992 Congressional Elections in Eight Southern States." *Journal of Politics* 57:384–401.

Hinckley, Barbara. 1980a. "House Re-elections and Senate Defeats: The Role of the Challenger." *British Journal of Political Science* 10:441–60.

—. 1980b. "The American Voter in Congressional Elections." *American Political Science Review* 74:641–50.

—. 1981. *Congressional Elections.* Washington, DC: Congressional Quarterly Press.

Huckfeldt, Robert, and John Sprague. 1995. *Citizens, Politics, and Social Communication: Information and Influence in an Election Campaign.* New York: Cambridge University Press.

Interuniversity Consortium for Political and Social Research. 1988. "The National Election Study/Senate Election Study." Center for Political Studies, Institute for Social Research, University of Michigan. Machine-readable data file.

Iyengar, Shanto, and Donald Kinder. 1987. *News that Matters.* Chicago: University of Chicago Press.

Jackson, John E., and David C. King. 1989. "Public Goods, Private Interests, and Representation." *American Political Science Review* 83:1143–64.

Jacobson, Gary C. 1978. "The Effects of Campaign Spending in Congressional Elections." *American Political Science Review* 72:469–91.

—. 1981. "Incumbents' Advantages in the 1978 Congressional Elections." *Legislative Studies Quarterly* 6:183–200.

—. 1985. "Money and Votes Reconsidered: U.S. Congressional Elections, 1972–1982." *Public Choice* 7:7–62.

—. 1990a. "The Effects of Campaign Spending in House Elections: New Evidence for Old Arguments." *American Journal of Political Science* 34:334–62.

—. 1990b. *The Electoral Origins of Divided Government.* Boulder, CO: Westview Press.

—. 1993. "Congress: Unusual Year, Unusual Election." In Michael Nelson, ed., *The Election of 1992.* Washington, DC: Congressional Quarterly Press.

———. 1996. "The 1994 House Elections in Perspective." In Philip Klinkner, ed., *Midterm: The Elections of 1994 in Context.* Boulder, CO: Westview Press.

———. 1997. *The Politics of Congressional Elections.* 4th ed. New York: Longman.

Jacobson, Gary C., and Samuel Kernell. 1983. *Strategy and Choice in Congressional Elections.* New Haven: Yale University Press.

Johnston, J. 1984. *Econometric Methods.* 3d ed. New York: McGraw Hill.

Kahn, Kim Fridkin. 1990. "Senate Elections in the News: Characteristics of Campaign Coverage." Paper presented at the annual meeting of the Midwest Political Science Association, Chicago.

Kahn, Kim Fridkin, and P. J. Kenney. 1997. "A Model of Candidate Evaluations in Senate Elections: The Impact of Campaign Intensity." *Journal of Politics* 59: 1173–1205.

Kazee, Thomas A., ed. 1994. *Who Runs for Congress: Ambition, Context, and Candidate Emergence.* Washington, DC: Congressional Quarterly Press.

Kelley, S., and T. W. Mirer. 1974. "The Simple Act of Voting." *American Political Science Review* 68:572–91.

Kenny, Christopher, and M. McBurnette. 1994. "An Individual-Level Multiequation Model of Expenditure Effects in Contested Elections." *American Political Science Review* 88:699–707.

Kernell, Samuel. 1977. "Presidential Popularity and Negative Voting." *American Political Science Review* 71:44–66.

Kiewiet, D. Roderick. 1983. *Macroeconomics and Micropolitics.* Chicago: University of Chicago Press.

Kinder, Donald R., and D. Roderick Kiewiet. 1981. "Sociotropic Politics: The American Case." *British Journal of Political Science* 11:129–61.

Kinder, Donald R., and Walter R. Mebane, Jr. 1983. "Politics and Economics in Everyday Life." In K. Monroe, ed., *The Political Process and Economic Change.* New York: Agathon.

Kinder, Donald R., and David O. Sears. 1985. "Public Opinion and Political Action." In G. Lindzey and E. Aronson, eds., *Handbook of Social Psychology.* 3d ed. New York: Random House.

King, Gary. 1989. *Unifying Political Methodology.* New York: Cambridge University Press. Reprint, Ann Arbor: University of Michigan Press, 1998.

Kingdon, John W. 1968. *Candidates for Office: Beliefs and Strategies.* New York: Random House.

———. 1988. *Congressmen's Voting Decisions.* 3d ed. Ann Arbor: University of Michigan Press.

Klinkner, Philip A., ed. 1996. *Midterm: The Elections of 1994.* Boulder, CO: Westview Press.

Koetzle, William. 1998. "The Impact of Constituency Diversity upon the Competitiveness of U.S. House Elections, 1962–96." *Legislative Studies Quarterly* 23:561–73.

Kostroski, Warren. 1973. "Party and Incumbency in Postwar Senate Elections." *American Political Science Review* 67:1213–34.

Kramer, Gerald. 1971. "Short-Term Fluctuations in U.S. Voting Behavior." *American Political Science Review* 65:131–43.

—. 1983. "The Ecological Fallacy Revisited: Aggregate- Versus Individual-Level Findings on Economics and Elections." *American Political Science Review* 77:92–111.

Krasno, Jonathan S. 1989. "Campaign Effects on the Public's View of Senators." Paper presented at the annual meeting of the American Political Science Association, Atlanta.

—. 1994. *Challengers, Competition, and Reelection.* New Haven: Yale University Press.

Krasno, Jonathan, and Donald Green. 1988. "Preempting Quality Challengers in House Elections." *Journal of Politics* 50:920–36.

Lee, Frances, and Bruce Oppenheimer. 1999. *Sizing Up the Senate: The Unequal Consequences of Equal Representation.* Chicago: University of Chicago Press.

Lewis-Beck, Michael S. 1985. "Are Senate Election Outcomes Predictable?" *PS* 18:746–54.

—. 1988. *Economics and Elections: The Major Western European Democracies.* Ann Arbor: The University of Michigan Press.

Lewis-Beck, Michael S., and Tom W. Rice. 1992. *Forecasting Elections.* Washington, DC: Congressional Quarterly Press.

Lieberson, Stanley. 1969. "Measuring Population Diversity." *American Sociological Review* 34: 850–62.

Lipinski, Daniel. 1998. "Shaping Public Perceptions of Congress through Franked Mass Mailings : An Examination of the Communication Strategies Used by Members of the United States House of Representatives in the 1990s." Ph.D. diss., Department of Political Science, Duke University.

Lipset, S. M., and S. Rokkan. 1967. "Cleavage Structures, Party Systems, and Voter Alignments." In S. M. Lipset and S. Rokkan, eds., *Party Systems and Voter Alignments.* New York: Free Press.

Lublin, David. 1997. *The Paradox of Representation: Racial Gerrymandering and Minority Interests in Congress.* Princeton: Princeton University Press.

Madison, James, Alexander Hamilton, and John Jay. 1961. *The Federalist Papers.* Rpt. New York: New American Library.

Maisel, L. Sandy. 1982. *From Obscurity to Oblivion: Congressional Primary Elections in 1978.* Lexington: University of Kentucky Press.

Mann, Thomas E. 1978. *Unsafe at Any Margin: Interpreting Congressional Elections.* Washington, DC: American Enterprise Institute.

Mann, Thomas E., and Raymond E. Wolfinger. 1980. "Candidates and Parties in Congressional Elections." *American Political Science Review* 74:617–32.

March, James G., and Johan P. Olsen. 1989. *Rediscovering Institutions.* New York: The Free Press.

Mattei, Franco. 1996. "Eight More in '94: The Republican Takeover of the Senate." In Philip Klinkner, ed., *Midterm: The Elections of 1994 in Context.* Boulder, CO: Westview Press.

Mayhew, David R. 1974a. "Congressional Elections: The Case of the Vanishing Marginals." *Polity* 6:295–317.

—. 1974b. *Congress: The Electoral Connection.* New Haven: Yale University Press.

—. 1986. *Placing Parties in American Politics.* Princeton: Princeton University Press.

McCubbins, Mathew D., and Terry Sullivan. 1987. *Congress: Structure and Policy.* New York: Cambridge University Press.

Miller, Arthur H. 1990. "Public Judgements of Senate and House Candidates." *Legislative Studies Quarterly* 15 (4): 525–42.

Morgan, David R. and Laura Ann Wilson. 1990. "Diversity in the American States: Updating the Sullivan Index." *Publius* 20:71-81.

Niemi, Richard G., and Alan I. Abramowitz. 1994. "Partisan Redistricting and the 1992 Congressional Elections." *Journal of Politics* 56:811–17.

Niemi, Richard G., Lynda W. Powell, and Patricia L. Bicknell. 1986. "The Effects of Congruity between Community and District on Salience of U.S. House Candidates." *Legislative Studies Quarterly* 11:187–201.

Ornstein, Norman J., Thomas E. Mann, and Michael J. Malbin. 1998. *Vital Statistics on Congress, 1997–1998.* Washington, DC: Congressional Quarterly Press.

Ornstein, Norman J., Robert L. Peabody, and David W. Rohde. 1993. "The U.S. Senate in a Sea of Change." In L. Dodd and B. Oppenheimer, eds., *Congress Reconsidered.* 5th ed. Washington, DC: Congressional Quarterly Press.

Page, Benjamin I., Robert Y. Shapiro, Paul Gronke, and Robert M. Rosenberg. 1984. "Constituency, Party, and Representation in Congress." *Public Opinion Quarterly* 48:741-56.

Palfrey, Thomas, and Robert Erikson. 1993. "The Spending Game: Money, Votes, and Incumbency in Congressional Elections." Social Science Working Papers, no. 851. Pasadena: California Institute of Technology.

Parker, Glenn. 1989. "Members of Congress and Their Constituents: The Home–Style Connection." In L. Dodd and B. Oppenheimer, eds., *Congress Reconsidered.* 4th ed. Washington, DC: Congressional Quarterly Press.

Pinderhughes, Dianne M. 1987. *Race and Ethnicity in Chicago Politics.* Urbana: University of Illinois Press.

Poole, Keith, and Howard Rosenthal. 1985. "A Spatial Model for Legislative Roll Call Analysis." *American Journal of Political Science* 29: 357–84.

—. 1997. *Congress: A Political-Economic History of Roll Call Voting.* New York: Oxford University Press.

Popkin, Samuel L. 1991. *The Reasoning Voter.* Chicago: University of Chicago Press.

Powell, Linda W. 1991. "Explaining Senate Elections: The Basis of Split Delegations and Party Polarization." Paper presented at the Stanford/Hoover Conference on Senate Elections, November.

Prinz, Timothy S. 1991a. "Media Markets, House Campaigns, and Candidate Evaluations: Exploiting the Candidate Likes/Dislikes Data." Paper presented at the annual meeting of the American Political Science Association, Washington, DC.

—. 1991b. "Watching the Races: The Democratic Benefits of Media Markets in Congressional Elections." Ph.D. diss., Department of Political Science, Harvard University.

Ragsdale, Lynn. 1981. "Incumbent Popularity, Challenger Invisibility, and Congressional Voters." *Legislative Studies Quarterly* 6:201–18.

Rahn, Wendy, John Aldrich, Eugene Borgida, and John Sullivan. 1990. "A Social Cognitive Model of Candidate Appraisal." In John H. Ferejohn and James A. Kuklinski, eds., *Information and Democratic Processes.* Urbana: University of Illinois Press.

Rohde, David W. 1991. *Parties and Leaders in the Postreform House.* Chicago: University of Chicago Press.

Rosenstone, Steven J. 1983. *Forecasting Presidential Elections.* New Haven: Yale University Press.

Rosenstone, Steven J., and John M. Hansen. 1993. *Mobilization, Participation, and Democracy in America.* New York: Macmillan.

Schlesinger, Joseph A. 1966. *Ambition and Politics: Political Careers in the United States.* Chicago: Rand McNally.

Segura, Gary M., and James H. Kuklinski. 1991. "The Temporal Proximity of Elections and Policy Moderation: A Reexamination of Senate Voting

Behavior." Paper presented at the Stanford/Hoover Conference on Senate Elections, November.

Shepsle, Kenneth A. 1986. "Institutional Equilibrium and Equilibrium Institutions." In H. Weisberg, ed., *Political Science: The Science of Politics.* New York: Agathon Press.

Sinclair, Barbara. 1989. *The Transformation of the U.S. Senate.* Baltimore: Johns Hopkins University Press.

—. 1990. "Washington Behavior and Home-State Reputation: The Impact of National Prominence on Senators' Visibility and Likability." *Legislative Studies Quarterly* 15: 475–94.

Smith, Eric R. A. N., and Peverill Squire. 1991. "Voter Sophistication and Evaluation of Senate Challengers." Paper presented at the Stanford/Hoover Institution Conference on Senate Elections, November.

Sniderman, Paul M., R. A. Brody, and P. Tetlock. 1993. *Reasoning and Choice.* New York: Cambridge University Press.

Sniderman, Paul M. and Thomas Piazza. 1993. *The Scar of Race.* Cambridge: Harvard University Press.

Sorauf, Frank J., and Scott A. Wilson. 1992. "Campaigns and Money: A Changing Role for Political Parties?" In L. Sandy Maisel, ed., *The Parties Respond.* Boulder, CO: Westview Press.

Soss, Joe, and D. Canon. 1995. "Partisan Divisions and Voting Decisions: U.S. Senators, Governors, and the Rise of a Divided Federal Government." *Political Research Quarterly* 48:253–74.

Squire, Peverill. 1989. "Challengers in U.S. Senate Elections." *Legislative Studies Quarterly* 14:531–47.

—. 1992. "Challenger Quality and Voting Behavior in Senate Elections." *Legislative Studies Quarterly* 16:247–64.

Stein, Robert. 1990. "Economic Voting for Governor and U.S. Senator: The Electoral Consequences of Federalism." *Journal of Politics* 52:29–53.

Stewart, Charles, III. 1989a. "A Sequential Model of Senate Elections." *Legislative Studies Quarterly* 14:567–601.

—. 1989b. "What Do They Get for Their Money? The Puzzle of Spending in Senate Elections." Paper presented at the annual meeting of the American Political Science Association, Atlanta.

Stewart, Charles, III, and Mark Reynolds. 1990. "Television Markets and U.S. Senate Elections." *Legislative Studies Quarterly* 14:495–524.

Stone, Walter J. 1980. "Dynamics of Constituency: Electoral Control in the House." *American Politics Quarterly* 8:399–424.

Stone, Walter J., Ronald B. Rappoport, and Alan I. Abramowitz. 1990. "The Reagan Revolution and Party Polarization in the 1980s." In L. Sandy Maisel, ed., *The Parties Respond.* Boulder, CO: Westview Press.

Sullivan, John L. 1973. "Political Correlates of Social, Economic, and Religious Diversity in the American States." *Journal of Politics* 35:70–84.

Tocqueville, Alexis de. 1969. *Democracy in America.* Rpt., translated by George Lawrence. Garden City, NY: Doubleday.

Tolchin, Susan J. 1996. *The Angry American.* Boulder, CO: Westview Press.

Turner, Julius, and Edward V. Schneier, Jr. 1970. *Party and Constituency: Pressures on Congress.* Rev. ed. Baltimore, MD: Johns Hopkins University Press.

Verba, Sidney, K. L. Schlozman, and H. E. Brady. 1995. *Voice and Equality: Civic Voluntarism in American Politics.* Cambridge: Harvard University Press.

Westlye, Marc. 1983. "Competitiveness of Senate Seats and Voting Behavior in Senate Elections." *American Journal of Political Science* 27:253–83.

——. 1986. "The Dynamics of U.S. Senate Elections." Ph.D. diss., Department of Political Science, University of California, Berkeley.

——. 1991. *Senate Elections and Campaign Intensity.* Baltimore: Johns Hopkins University Press.

Wright, Gerald C., and Michael B. Berkman. 1986. "Candidates and Policy in the United States Senate." *American Political Science Review* 80:567–88.

Zaller, John R. 1991. "Information and Incumbency Advantage in Congressional Elections." Paper presented at the annual meeting of the American Political Science Association, Washington, DC.

——. 1992. *The Nature and Origins of Mass Opinion.* New York: Cambridge University Press.

Index

Printed and bound by CPI Group (UK) Ltd, Croydon, CR0 4YY

09/06/2025